# —A—
# SOLDIER'S DISGRACE

# —A— SOLDIER'S DISGRACE

Ronald Alley died trying to clear his name.
His widow continued the battle. Finally a
writer uncovered the truth.

## by Don J. Snyder

A division of Yankee Publishing Incorporated
Dublin, New Hampshire

Books by Don J. Snyder

*Veterans Park* (a novel)

*A Soldier's Disgrace*

---

Designed by Margo Letourneau

Yankee Publishing Incorporated
Dublin, New Hampshire 03444
First Edition
Copyright 1987 by Don J. Snyder
Printed in the United States of America.

*Library of Congress Cataloging-in-Publication Data*

Snyder, Don J.
    A soldier's disgrace.

    Includes index.
    1. Alley, Ronald E., d. 1978. 2. United States.
Army — Officers — Biography. 3. Prisoners of war —
United States — Biography. 4. Prisoners of war — Korea
(North) — Biography. 5. Korean War, 1950-1953 —
Prisoners and prisons. 6. Korean War, 1950-1953 —
Collaborationists. I. Title.
DS921.S6 1987      951.9'042      87-13307
ISBN 0-89909-139-3

# DEDICATION

For my father. And for all the veterans who were
soldiers when they had to be.

*Mine honor is my life; both grow in one;*
*Take honor from me, and my life is done.*

William Shakespeare

# CONTENTS

# ACKNOWLEDGMENTS

I am in considerable debt to many people. The soldiers who searched a painful part of their past to reveal the truth to me. The Fund for Investigative Journalism, for a grant that helped in the researching of this book, and Howard Bray, director of the Fund, for his guidance and support. Mel Allen at *Yankee* magazine, for first bringing this story to the public's attention, and Sandra Taylor, my editor at Yankee Books, who prepared this manuscript for publication. C. Michael Curtis at *The Atlantic,* for his help from start to finish. Sara Rimer, now of *The New York Times,* and David Molpus at National Public Radio, who believed in the importance of Major Alley's story. Jack Leggett, James A. McPherson, Ron Hansen, and others at The University of Iowa Writers Workshop, for a fellowship that helped me complete this work. Victoria Pryor, my literary agent. And most of all my wife, Colleen, who lived the worst part of this story with me and never let me give it up.

# AUTHOR'S NOTE

T he United States Army told its version of the story of Major Ronald E. Alley in 1955, when the 1,500-page transcript of his court-martial became a matter of public record. For the first two years of my research I relied upon this version. It was only after interviewing dozens of former POWs, soldiers who had fought in the Korean War and were held captive by the Chinese along with Major Alley, that I discovered a different version of his story. What these soldiers told me cast into doubt much of the Army's official documentation, and I began to see that, while the Army's facts were voluminous and persuasive, these facts did not add up to the whole truth. And so this book attempts to reveal honestly the current views of the soldiers who fought in the Korean War.

Most of the material in this book is derived from personal observations and interviews. In reporting these interviews and reconstructing both face-to-face and telephone conversations, I have relied upon extensive notes and in some cases tape recordings. Any material not derived from my own firsthand observations, such as chapters detailing combat operations and life inside the prisoner-of-war camps in Korea, is based upon the accounts of soldiers who were actually present.

During the eight years it took to research and write this book I agonized over the question of Major Alley's guilt or innocence. In 1981 I was searching for a certain POW who had testified against Major Alley in 1955. I had been told repeatedly in interviews with other soldiers that this man had been a coward in the prisoner-of-war camps and that he had lied at the court-martial in order to protect himself. When I finally found him I was determined to expose him. I explained my intentions to him over the telephone on December 14, 1981. He was silent. Two days later his wife called me and pleaded with me not to write about him. I remember her saying to me, "Whatever my husband did, whatever he said against another man, it has already destroyed his life. You have no idea how he has suffered and what we've been through." She was right. And I have taken the liberty in this book of changing the names of those who were bound to suffer from what I have written.

---

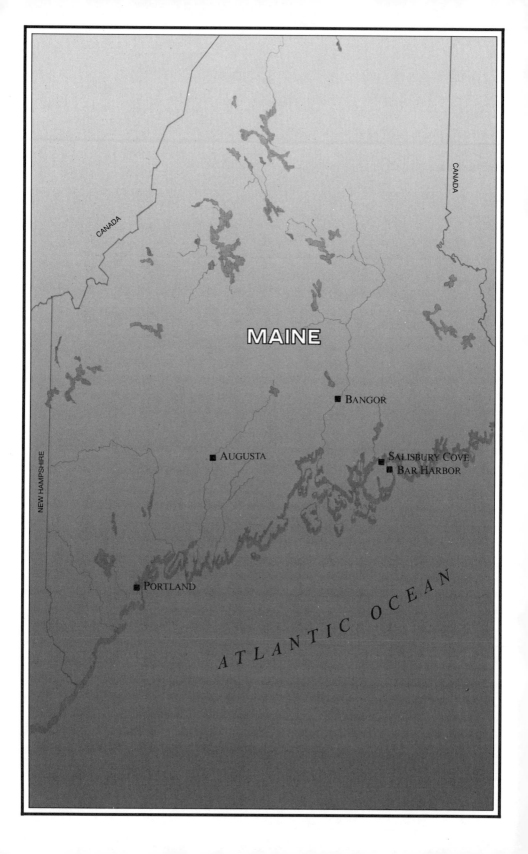

# PART · ONE

# PROLOGUE

I t was November of 1978 that first time I went to the cemetery where they had buried Major Ronald Alley. In the freezing rain someone from the American Legion hall had come to the cemetery, just outside Bar Harbor, to mark the veterans' graves with small American flags, the kind you see children waving at parades. The people who live on Mount Desert Island off the coast of northern Maine are proud, passionately independent, and patriotic without question. Their sense of duty is deeply rooted. They had placed a flag at the grave of Major Alley, even though the United States Army had once court-martialed him and sent him to prison as a traitor to his country.

Ever since his death, hundreds of people had come from all over Maine, traveling great distances to his grave because they had been struck by the way this one soldier had declared all his life that he loved the Army more than anything in the world and that he had committed no crime. They came because his widow had fulfilled her promise to him and buried him here in his uniform against the regulations of the United States Army.

Major Alley had grown up poor, in a house without plumbing just a few miles from the cemetery. He was the oldest of eight children and at age seventeen he left home to join the Army and to make something of himself. He fought in two wars and made the Army his life. And, after all of that, he ended up in a dishonored grave.

When I stood at the grave that first time, I had no way of knowing what an incredible story was buried along with this man. But four years later I would know him better than the people he had lived with on this island, than the soldiers he had fought with in France, in Belgium, and then in Korea. I would know him better than the Army lawyers who prosecuted him and the Pentagon intelligence officers and FBI informants who had watched him and opened his mail and searched the most private corners of his life. I would know him better than the newspaper reporters who had written stories about him and then forgotten him. Major Alley had died a mystery to those people.

He had died a mystery to his wife and son and daughter, too. He had sworn all his life that he was not guilty of the Army's charges, and then he died before he could prove this to anyone. They all were left with a hundred unanswered questions.

Eventually I would find the answers. I would discover something about him that no one had ever known: no FBI worker had ever recorded it in a report, no journalist had ever written about it. And even in 1979, twenty-four years after the Army had court-martialed him, officials at the Pentagon were reluctant to admit it. But it was part of the hidden truth about him.

On November 22, 1955, when Major Ronald E. Alley of Bar Harbor, Maine, was sent to prison for collaborating with the enemy while a prisoner of war in North Korea, he became the first and only officer in this century to receive such a sentence. Of the thousands of soldiers held captive by the enemy in World Wars I and II, Korea, and Vietnam, and of the hundreds known to have collaborated with the enemy and the dozens who were court-martialed for this offense, only this one officer was ever convicted and sent to prison. The case of Major Ronald Alley stood alone in military history and irrevocably altered the course of military justice in America.

After they court-martialed Major Alley and sent him to prison at Fort Leavenworth, Kansas, the Army closed a heavy door against his case. All the information pertaining to it was classified, sealed in crates, and locked away. Several times during his life Major Alley petitioned the Army to reopen his case. The Army always refused. From time to time a congressman or senator from Maine would appeal to the Army for the facts surrounding this case. The appeals went nowhere. Major Alley bore a singular disgrace in the history of his country and, now that he was dead, the Army wanted him forgotten.

But the disgrace had to be explained to the American people. It had to be explained to the men who had fought with Major Alley and had been held prisoner with him in North Korea, who wondered what had become of him. And it had to be explained to his children and his widow. His family had a right to know why this had happened, why the Army had called him a traitor.

"He made me promise to bury him in his uniform," Erna Alley, his widow, would say. "The uniform meant so much to him. I made my promise, and I kept it. I always stood with him, I believed him. But now that he is gone I need to know why they did this to him, why they ruined our life."

Erna Alley was fifty-nine years old when her husband died. The anguish of her years with Ronald had left her bitter and angry. It had worn her away on the inside so that she was far too weary to go searching for the truth.

The daughter, Evelyn, was twenty-nine years old. I would never meet her, and she would always refuse to talk about her father because, as far as she could see, the truth I was after would do her father no good now, and a struggle to find this truth would only end up killing her mother too.

Then there was the son, Gary. At the time of his father's death he was living in northern Maine, where he was a foreman in a paper mill. All his life he had wanted to believe in his father, but he had never been able to get close to him. Searching for the truth now would mean that his father's obsession had been passed on to *him,* an obsession that would take him away from his own son and wife who needed him. Gary wanted very much to be a good father and husband. I could see almost from the beginning that his way of surviving was to turn to his own little world. But I could also see that he would never be free, nor would his sister and mother, until the truth about Ronald Alley was known. All of them had lived so long half-believing, half-fighting what they could not bear to face — that Ronald Alley was the traitor the United States Army said he was.

That day in November, as I stared at the granite marker on his grave, I could picture Ronald Alley as a kid going off to join the Army. He believed the Army could do no wrong, and that there was only honor and dignity among soldiers. I wondered if maybe there had been something about this kid, something about the way he'd grown up, or the books he'd read, or the place he'd come from — something that had shaped his mind and his perceptions in such a way as to allow him to get caught in a web. Perhaps a web had started to form long before he left home that first time, and it was inevitable that *he,* out of a million others, would be the one to get caught in it. It was a tremendous web in which he became entangled, one with political and philosophical implications too vast and complex for a trusting and modest kid from Maine to understand. Perhaps he never had the faintest notion where the web began or how far it reached until the end of his life, when it was too late.

It seemed entirely possible that during his last days he had seen that the only way his family would ever be free of this dark web of disgrace and shame was if someone would find out the truth about his story and tell that story to the American people.

And so he came to me. I had recently been hired as editor of the *Bar Harbor Times,* when one day Ronald Alley called the office and said he had to talk with me about a story. We met briefly the next day and arranged to get together again a few days later. On the way to that next appointment, he dropped dead of a heart attack.

*　　*　　*　　*　　*

Over the next four years, I went often to Ronald Alley's grave. I went there frustrated after long, empty months of getting nowhere at the Pentagon and on Capitol Hill. I went there after traveling many thousands of miles back and forth across the country to find the soldiers who had known him. I went there angry after being torn up

18

inside because of this man. Once I stood there alone at the grave and shouted down at him.

The last time I went back it was July of 1982 and my search was over. I told him I didn't think I would be coming back again, but I wanted him to know that I had met the man at the Legion hall, the one who came here to put up the flags. He told me Major Alley had been a tough soldier and an honest man: "A leopard doesn't change his spots overnight," he'd said. "When you know a fellow over *here*, you know how he'd handle himself over *there*. Ronnie just rubbed someone the wrong way is all. That's why he got into trouble with the Army."

George Johnson, Major Alley's oldest friend, also taught me a lot about him. I learned about the day Ronald Alley went up to some young boys who were visiting the island for the first time and had never seen the ocean before. He told them that the towns on the island got their drinking water from the cove, and that if the boys were to come back in a few hours they'd see how much water the towns drank at the end of the day. He waited around just so he could see the expression on the boys' faces when the tide changed and the cove was turned to mud flats. George said Ronald Alley loved children, all children; that he had a childlike sense of humor. But a cloud would come over him from time to time and he would be lost then. That's how George described it. George always knew when Major Alley had started thinking again about the Army.

Sergeant Clyde Wilson remembered him fondly. Wilson was a private over in Korea, just another prisoner of war with mud on his face. The sergeant thought highly of Major Alley and swore to me that if it weren't for him he wouldn't have made it home alive.

There are quite a few soldiers on his side, some sergeants, some colonels. They are pretty old men now, but they remember Major Alley as a kid always talking about the future, about the way things were going to work out.

He has some enemies, too — people at the Pentagon who hate the sound of his name. They say he was a stubborn hick without any common sense.

I believe he *was* a stubborn man. I think he had a streak of independence running through him like a wick through a candle, and this prevented him from seeing what was happening. No matter how strongly he believed in what he was doing, he should have

---

known he couldn't defy the Army and get away with it. It came down to a question of honor: Alley had this rock-hard sense of honor, but he should have seen that the Army's honor was at stake, too. Next to that, his own honor didn't mean much at all.

It makes sense that Ronald Alley became a surveyor and earned his living at that trade for twenty years. He liked to draw the lines and figure out the boundaries and say exactly where the stakes should go in the ground. But he should have known better than to draw his own lines in Korea, lines that strayed from those the Army had drawn. He should have been able to see that the Korean War wasn't another World War II. It was a different kind of war with different kinds of right and wrong. But to him there was only one kind. He couldn't see beyond his own ideas.

His wife knows this now. She once told me that he died from a broken heart because he loved the Army and the Army had turned against him. I can see that she was right. But I wanted her to know the rest of the story. All I've done is put together all the pieces that show who he was and why he was the only one to go to prison. The Army knows him better now. And the men at the Legion hall.

Most of all his son can know him now. He's the one who has to carry on his name, and he was worried about that. He used to lie awake at night thinking about that and wondering what it would mean to *his* son, his father's grandson. At least he doesn't have to wonder anymore.

That last time I stood at Major Alley's grave I tried to tell him what all this had meant to me and to my life. I recalled what Bob Woodward at the *Washington Post* had once said to me: "Doing this story about Alley, you must feel the way I felt during Watergate, that somehow you were born to do it."

I *had* felt that way. Almost from the moment I first saw Ronald Alley, I knew there was something about this man that would change my life. It was as if fate or providence had placed me there at the newspaper where he was going, one last time, for help.

I have always been skeptical about such things as fate and providence, and I dismissed their influence as long as I could. But then, time and again, just as I was about to give up this story, something came along — a new name, a telephone number scrawled on a scrap of paper, a missing page from an FBI file — and I would be off once more. I was never able to explain how these things happened, and after a while I just accepted them and went on.

I wanted Major Alley to know why I went on, and what it had cost. The price had been high. At age thirty-two, I was living alone again; my wife, Lee, and I had divorced, and much of my future seemed strangely behind me. But there had been no other way for me. And finally I knew why. Of all the people in the world who might have been sitting at the editor's desk that day Ronald Alley came in, I was the perfect person for him to find there, waiting for a story. I had already decided that the only thing I wanted to do with my life was to write books. I had taken my vow of poverty and had prayed only for the chance to write books that were important.

But it was more than that. It was the way he had looked at me when he told me he had a son. And it was the way Gary had spoken to me about his father, a man he had never really known at all. My own mother had died when I was born, and I knew what it was like to live with unanswered questions and to wonder how things might have been.

And then there was the Army. I had been raised in a conservative family. My father had gone off to war in 1944, and later, as a boy, I ran around the neighborhood with his canteen tied to my belt and his sergeant's hat on my head. I had always believed blindly in the Army. I went to college in the late 1960s, but I never adopted the defiance and cynicism of those times. I listened to the body counts each night on the news and somehow I figured America wouldn't be doing this unless it was for some good reason. Ronald Alley's story threatened all I had ever believed to be true about the Army, about America. I couldn't turn my back on this threat.

I couldn't turn my back on my own questions or on Major Alley's son and widow. I couldn't turn my back on a man who had died coming to me for help.

Ronald Alley had been obsessed with the mystery of his past, and before he died he passed that obsession on to me. It takes time for an obsession to establish itself; like a splinter, it works its way under your skin and becomes embedded there. But I took it on, and I followed his story to the end because I believed in my heart that I was the only person on earth who ever would.

Standing at his grave that last time, I wanted to explain all this to Major Alley. I wanted to tell him what the Army thought of him. I figured he would have wanted to know that the Army had placed him in a group with two other men: Private Eddie Slovik and Lieutenant William Calley. Private Slovik was executed before a firing squad for desertion during World War II. Lieutenant Calley was convicted of killing women and children in the My Lai massacre during the Vietnam War. The Army had claimed these men were guilty; they were not the only ones who were guilty, but they were found guilty in order to set an example. The Army made Major Alley the example for the Korean War. Not a scapegoat, they claimed, just an example.

But it was really for the American people that Ronald Alley and Eddie Slovik and William Calley were sent to war and later punished. The people will have to decide whether or not it was right for the Army to make examples of these men. Major Alley was always talking about his honor; as far as his honor, *their* honor, is concerned, it is up to the people to decide that, too.

# CHAPTER 1

Maine's slow, blue summer days were still a long way off
when they came out into the snow that night in January
1978. Many had never seen Ronald Alley in his uniform.
They had known him for many years, known his son and
daughter, known his wife, known of their endless troubles.
Again and again over the years they had seen him walking through
town with his big shoulders drawn back and his head up. They had
seen him taking his long, purposeful strides up and down the streets
of Bar Harbor, strides that seemed forceful and sturdy because he
was such a big man. His body was broad and thick, and he stood well
over six feet tall. In the company of friends his face often showed a

gentle smile that reached to the corners of his gray eyes, but sometimes, when he walked alone down the street, his face was seamed and heavy, his expression sad. So sad you wondered if you should keep away from him, and so distant. Always so distant. There was something about the way he looked, the way he took his measured steps, the way he always carried papers in one hand, the other hand swinging briskly at his side, that told you this wasn't the life Ronald Alley had planned for himself. As he walked by — his shoes striking the pavement in quick, precise steps, his shoulders drawn back, his jaw set, his eyes fixed — you could see that there was something wrong. You could see that a man like this belonged in uniform.

The night they went to see Ronald Alley in his uniform, a wind full of wet snow had backed around to the northeast and blew in fitful gusts. But still people came — from all over the island and from as far away as Bangor.

That evening his wife, Erna, made dinner for herself at five o'clock, but sitting alone at the kitchen table she couldn't eat, couldn't even pick up her fork. She drank some coffee and smoked several cigarettes, scarcely aware that they were burning, that she was lighting them and crushing them in the glass ashtray. The house was so quiet she could hear the snow begging at the storm windows and the wind flying across the roof. She listened for a while and then she got up, walked to the bedroom, and stood in front of the full-length mirror. Normally she wore very little makeup, but she had had to do something about her eyes tonight, about the dark circles that blunted the blue in her eyes and made them look empty and aimless. And it had taken great effort to paint color on her cheeks. Still, as she looked into the mirror her face was pale and gaunt, her lips a thinly drawn line.

She reached for the hairbrush and had raised it into the air when she saw in the mirror that the door to Ronald's closet had swung open. She moved closer to the mirror and studied the framed reflection of the closet. As she looked she felt her breathing pick up and her palms begin to sweat and she knew, knew instinctively, that something was wrong. The uniform that had hung there for more than twenty years was gone. She turned and hurried across the room to the closet door, calling out to her husband. And then, in the very next instant, she remembered that Ronald was wearing the uniform, and that he was not in the house.

24

Of course — just two days ago she had taken the green Army major's uniform to have it cleaned and pressed for him. She had taken it from the closet herself. She wanted it to look just right. Of all the people going out into the storm tonight to see Major Ronald Alley in his uniform, only she — because she was his wife, because she had watched him wear it so many times, because she had seen him wearing it when he left her and when he returned to her at train stations and crowded wharves and airports through two wars — only she would know what the uniform meant to him. And only she would know that tonight he wore his uniform against the orders of the United States Army.

She knew this as she took her place beside him. She had promised him that she would always stand beside him. So many times when things were turning against them he had asked her if she would stay with him:

"You still believe in me?" he would ask.

"Yes, I believe in you, Ronald."

"And you won't ever stop believing?"

"No, never."

"And no matter what happens, no matter what they say, you'll see that I am buried in my uniform?"

Erna left the house early to be with him and to make certain everything was right. She stood next to him in the carefully lighted room waiting for the people to arrive. Very soon they would begin coming in. There would be women who would stay near her as if they expected her to fall over and to need someone to catch her before she hit the floor. There were men who would look down at Ronald and who would have to restrain the reflex to salute him. Many of them would be thinking the same thing and would even tell Erna what they were thinking — that her husband looked very handsome in his uniform.

She would never forget how he looked this night, the rows of bright ribbons like a tiny artist's palette of colors on his chest. There were so many ribbons and medals from World War II and Korea. The Army Commendation Medal with its white and green stripes and gold eagle; the United Nations Service Medal with a gold shield hanging from a blue and white ribbon. Many ribbons. At one time he had told her the meaning of each of them and as an officer's wife she had wanted to know. He had planned to tell his children what each of them represented, once they were old enough to understand. And tonight as she stood there with his children, who were grown now and had families of their own, it was unbelievable to her, and also unbearable, that they had almost no memory of their father in his uniform.

In a letter Ronald had written her in December of 1957 from the Army prison at Fort Leavenworth he spoke about his uniform:

> That's the thing that hurts me, Mommy. When they took my uniform away. In your last letter you said you were going to save the money to get a new one made by a tailor, but I know there isn't any money anymore. You and the children need every penny. But maybe someday when this is over I'll go talk to that tailor myself . . . .

Erna Alley had picked apples and sold cosmetics door-to-door in Bar Harbor, and she had managed to get the uniform for him. The children were small then. Now, standing here, watching her son and daughter, she knew that they had no idea what the uniform had meant to their father.

"They were just babies when their father went away," she would say to someone tonight. "Gary was just a few months old. His father was gone so long. Three years a prisoner of war, and then two years in the hospitals. He came home to Maine for a few days in 1955, and we picked him up at the bus station. But he did not look the same anymore in his uniform. Not ever the same."

Ronald's high school friends were here tonight. Long ago Ronald had told them about his plans to join the Army and get a uniform. One friend remembered:

"There was a bunch of us boys anxious as hell to enlist. That's practically all we ever talked about. Getting into the war and killing Germans. But Ronnie was the first to go. He lied about his age so he could get over there first. That was Ronnie all the way. He got a thing in his mind and he didn't do a lot of talking about it one way or another, he just went right ahead and did it his own way. He was a loner. But we were pretty close then, we were both from the same background, both poor. I remember him telling me he was tired of wearing pants that didn't fit. He had this one pair of corduroy pants that got shorter and shorter each year. He used to curse about his pants. He was a good-looking kid and he never had any trouble with the girls, but he seemed to think there were two strikes against him, you know, because he was poor. He was going to change that by getting a uniform."

As a young boy Ronald Alley had stood on Cottage Street watching the Fourth of July parades go by. He stood there, and all around him were the summer people who came to his town each year with their big sailing boats and their fine cars. He had watched them from summer to summer, and at an early age he had become aware of the great distance between them and him. It was a distance defined by a certain privilege they carried with them, a privilege that made them unapproachable. If he was envious of them it was not because of what they owned — their boats and cars — but because they seemed to have a confidence about them, almost a reckless confidence, and because the world they knew, as he imagined it, was much bigger than his own.

And he wanted a big world, certainly bigger than the one his father belonged to. Bigger than one small, weathered house on the side of a back road that led only to more roads and more houses just like his. As he watched the parades go by, he saw that even the summer people — those people of unimaginable wealth and advantage, people whose world reached far beyond Bar Harbor — were watching the soldiers march by in their uniforms. And it seemed remarkable to young Ronald Alley that these summer people, men his father's age, but looking nothing like his father, bothered to reach down and hoist their sons up onto their shoulders so they could see the soldiers march by in their uniforms. That was something Ronald Alley would never forget. It was one of those moments that began to give him an idea of how the world worked. He wanted, even as a young boy, to understand how the world worked and then to tell his father.

Howard Alley had worked hard all his life as a carpenter. He was a good, honest man without pretensions or affectations, but the home he provided his family still had no plumbing and it was not big enough for eight children. And there was always a struggle with bills. Looking carefully and critically at his father's life and listening to the man say how good it was going to be to have his eldest son join him in the business, shingling roofs and taking care of the summer people's property, Ronald panicked. To him, the world his father occupied was narrow and barren. He tried to make the old man see that he had an idea of how the world worked, an idea that was at odds with his father's. That he had a vision of a bigger world, a better world, a world where there would be more respect for him. And when his father failed or refused to understand this, Ronald Alley began to make plans to leave his father's home. He was ambitious and energetic — he had the energy of someone fleeing something dreadful. The rest of the poor kids on the island could spend their time hanging around street corners waiting for an event that never seemed to happen, but he had a plan of his own.

He explained this to his mother, how he planned to join the Army. To work his way up, straight up to the top, so that it would never matter again that he had not been able to attend college and that he had grown up poor. His plan was to go away and make something of himself and then come back to Bar Harbor in his uniform so that the people who knew him would be able to see for themselves that Ronald Alley had been right all along, that he *did* know how the world worked.

Right from the start he loved being a soldier. He was bright, and the Army had schools where they could teach bright kids to do whatever needed to be done. He learned quickly because he was so serious. They couldn't believe how serious he was — always reading, always studying, always volunteering, always the first in line. Very soon he began to stick out — this tall, brawny kid from Maine with that crazy, Down East accent of his was forever snapping to attention, forever drilling himself, forever taking orders. He had no trouble taking orders, because he believed that soon enough the day would come when he would be an officer *giving* them. And *that,* Ronald Alley figured out, was how the *Army* worked. Unlike the civilian world, the world of summer people, where so much was left to chance and the arbitrary accumulation of privilege, in the Army it was possible to see how one got to the top. Everything was spelled out and written down and perfectly straightforward. And that was the way he wanted to go — straightforward.

World War II gave him the chance to fight with an artillery unit in Belgium and France and to earn the respect of those who fought alongside him. It pleased him to find out, and to have others find out, that he was someone you could count on when push came to shove. By the end of the war he was a captain, and when the Army

28

appointed military governors to enforce the occupation of Germany, he was picked.

In those days things went very well for him. World War II had gone on and on, but he had lived through it. It seemed to him that for a few years the whole world had gone haywire, but then, finally, the soldiers from America had come across the ocean to change things around and get the world working again. It seemed to make such obvious sense.

As a young captain in occupied Germany he had a chance to put the world back together. In Esslingen the black stumps of bombed-out buildings were leveled and cleared away to make room for something better. Windows were opened again, gardens were put in, and the air hummed with the engines of American jeeps and the laughter of GIs. In hotel ballrooms the orchestras started up again, doing their best to learn the latest numbers from the States. The Yanks in their handsome uniforms were up and down the streets passing out chocolate bars and fresh cigarettes. There were heroes everywhere; you could tell who they were by their uniforms.

Not far from where Ronald Alley went to work every day, walking in his sharp, quick steps, Erna Laulies had grown up and lived through the war. Because she spoke English so well, she had been able to find a job as an interpreter in the Army's Central Intelligence Department. Her boss took a personal interest in her; she was a pretty girl, and he seemed to think she should be getting out more. So he persuaded her to attend a party one evening where she could meet some young Army officers.

The Army brought Ronald and Erna together that spring of 1947. They met in a sprawling hillside mansion, built by a rich German industrialist and known as Villa Heller. It was a baronial place, with rows of tall, shuttered windows and many chimneys and verandas and turrets that reached up into the sky. The American Army, in the habit now of requisitioning only the best buildings for their official purposes, had found Villa Heller to their liking. With a half dozen other officers, Ronald Alley lived there as comfortably and as grandly as any of the rich boys back home at Groton or Harvard.

Inside the front doors, doors as big and heavy as church doors, a staircase spun down to a broad room with a marble floor. He was coming down that staircase, and Erna was waiting below: "He used to tell me that it was like the whole room had become very still and then someone had snapped his fingers, when he first saw me. Many times he talked about it that way. And I always told him he was the most handsome soldier I had ever seen. It was true. I had seen many soldiers, American soldiers in their uniforms, but none like him."

Erna loved the way he looked, and at a dinner party that evening when he talked with the other officers, she loved the way he expressed himself. In a letter to her in October 1950, soon after he was sent to Korea, Ronald wrote about this first night together:

We came a long way in a short time, didn't we? When you think back to that first night, how we talked about what we wanted. We have two children now and there will be more. And as soon as this war is over and things get straightened out we will start building our house, Mommy. We have to have a house for the children. Maybe a few chickens and pigs would be nice. And someday we'll build another house near the ocean. You remember how I told you that that first night?

They talked about everything under the sun. They walked out into a garden and once, when he looked as if he might reach for her hand, she demurely pulled back. She had heard a great deal about the American soldiers and what they expected in exchange for their chocolate bars and cigarettes. But she felt she could trust this soldier. "Even when he tried to kiss me in the music room, I wasn't afraid. And then at the door, when he tried to kiss me again. And on the way home, when he pulled his jeep off to the side of the road and reached for me, I said, 'No, Captain,' and he just apologized and drove on."

Erna Laulies had grown up in a fine home where she had learned to dance and play the piano. She had a certain grace and sophistication that Ronald had not known before in a girl. He was impressed by this and he was also shy around it because he didn't know exactly how to behave. "I knew from the start that he had come from a different background. He was bashful and quiet about some things, things he didn't understand. But he was always determined to go on to a better life. He talked about America, how it was so free and wonderful and how you could get ahead in the Army. He found it easy to talk about the way things were going to turn out, and he said he knew it would take hard work. I knew it too. And I think one of the things he saw in me right away was that, even though I had been raised in a nice home, nice surroundings, I was strong. Oh, I was very determined myself. I was determined to make a good life for myself and to have a family. I wanted to make a good life out of the terrible world all around us then. And he always told me we could have everything and that an officer in America could go very far. He was devoted to this idea. He was devoted to the Army."

His devotion was so earnest that sometimes it was comical. One night in the big mansion he surprised Erna with a cake for her birthday. Some of the other officers were there, and one of the Army cooks had baked an enormous cake for her. At the end of the evening when much of the cake was left, one of the men went to the kitchen to put it in a box so she could take it home. No, they didn't understand, Ronald told them. She couldn't take the cake because it had been made with government ingredients and so it was technically government property and could not be taken off the premises. He was perfectly serious about this. And so they all had to sit back down at the table with Captain Alley and eat the rest of the cake.

He had this powerful sense about what was right and what was wrong, and Erna would learn very quickly that he would not shy away from what he believed was right, not for anyone — not even for the Army he was devoted to. In the city of Crailsheim, a city within his authority as military governor, a farmer had been arrested for possessing a German military rifle. The American military court found him guilty and sentenced him to three years in jail. Several weeks later, another farmer, this one with money and some influence, on trial for the same offense received a sentence of only six months in jail. This did not sit well at all with Ronald. The arbitrary nature of the ruling did not fit his idea of how the world should work, and he proceeded to file a formal complaint with the military government. When nothing was done about his complaint, he pursued the matter relentlessly, until finally the military government had no choice but to transfer him away from the case and to another city in Germany.

Erna complained to him about this: "I told him the Army had been wrong, wrong in its decision and wrong in transferring him. But Ronald managed to find a way to defend himself *and* the Army. He said he had the right to speak his own way and so did the Army. He said that was the kind of freedom there was for an officer in America. But I always wondered if it could be that way."

It took the Army three months to approve their plans to be married. There were countless forms to be filed and a seemingly endless set of documents to be assembled. There were interviews and questionnaires and interrogators for the Army who wanted to know again and again how Erna felt about the Nazi party. She told them repeatedly that she had never held any sympathies for the Nazis; she and her father had hated what they were doing to Germany. She would turn to Ronald, and he would tell her that the Army just had a job to do and she should not take it personally.

The Army was finally satisfied, and on September 7, 1947, Erna and Ronald were granted permission to marry. "We were married first before a justice of the peace, but I wanted a big wedding, and on September 20 we were married in an old stone church in Esslingen. It was a Lutheran wedding. There were many bridesmaids and ring bearers. The bright flowered dresses. All my relatives came. Even my aunt, who had to get through the Berlin zones. That was the best day. The best day we ever had."

There wasn't time for a honeymoon. Ronald had to report to his desk the next morning. Six weeks later Erna said good-bye to her father and brother, visited her mother's grave in their hometown of Gaggenau, then sailed with Ronald for America on an old Army transport that had been tied up at its dock in Bremerhaven until enough German girls had married American soldiers and the Army's requirement for the minimum number of passengers had been reached.

They sailed into New York City and then rode the train to Schenectady, New York, where Captain Alley had been assigned as an instructor to a reserve unit.

"The war was very far away then," Erna recalled. "Riding the train together, seeing America for the first time, it was magical for me. We were so young and there was so much to look forward to."

# CHAPTER 2

The Army had chosen Schenectady, and so they went there to live. They bought a used stove and moved into a four-room flat with peeling walls and linoleum that had seen its better days. The cockroaches soon appeared, and they had to move again. At the supermarket and the Laundromat Erna was reminded that she was a war bride, an outsider living in someone else's country. American women had heard stories about the German girls who had corrupted the GIs at the end of the war. But Erna loved Ronald, and she had married him and come to this country with her eyes open. They had both decided at the outset that the drawbacks of military life — the transfers and rootlessness, the shabby apartments, the need to acquiesce to the wives of other men higher in rank — would not impair their life together.

There were other wives in Schenectady, soldiers' wives, who told Erna that Ronald's promotions would not come quickly. He was not from an Army family. He was a reserve officer, not a West Point man. This would make a difference.

Someone took the time one evening at the Officers Club to explain to Erna and Ronald how the Army worked: "You'll learn that the United States Army is a big corporation, and West Point owns most of the stock."

For a young woman who had had no experience with household chores and who had been urged by her wealthy aunts to marry a man who could pay someone else to do them, Erna did her best around the apartment. She was up early in the morning brewing coffee. She learned how important curtains could be. She went without other things in order to afford to have some music in their world, and when Ronald came home in the evening she had candles lit and Brahms or Wagner on the scratchy record player.

"Those were our days for dreaming," she remembered. "Ronald never liked going out very much. He didn't like the Officers Club at all. We just enjoyed our little apartment, and we spent lots of time rearranging the secondhand furniture to make it feel like a home. We had very little money, but it seemed like enough."

They loved to dance, particularly Erna. They loved to push the living room furniture up against the walls and dance, just the two of them, to records they knew by heart. One night in January of 1948 they danced until the sun came up to celebrate the news that Erna was pregnant.

Soon after their daughter Evelyn was born in September 1948, the three of them took the trip to Maine that Ronald had been avoiding since they had returned from Germany. Whenever Erna had asked to meet Ronald's family he had changed the subject. Now the first grandchild had been born and they prepared to go to Bar Harbor.

It was late fall when they drove to Maine in their old Dodge. "The island was just as Ronald had described it to me a dozen times. It was beautiful everywhere. The ocean was so near. Ronald loved this place so much, but he didn't seem happy to be back. We drove around and around the island and finally I said, 'Will you take me to meet your family?' "

Erna and the baby were made to feel at home in the plain clapboard house Ronald had been so anxious to leave eight years earlier. Ronald's younger brothers hounded him with questions about his life in the Army. They still wanted to talk about the war and the killing. They talked and passed plates that first night, and after dessert Erna excused herself to go to the bathroom. Ronald got up from the table with her and led her out through the kitchen to a path that curved away from the back door through the woods to an outhouse. He handed her a flashlight and waited at the door. "I didn't want him to think I was shocked, and I told him to go on back, that I would be all right by myself. I *was* shocked though.

"When I walked back to the house I stopped at the screen door and I heard them talking about me. Ronald's mother said I was very pretty. Then his father said, 'You know how I feel, Ron. If the Army had fought in Russia, you'd all be married to Russian girls.' I turned and ran."

During this first visit to the island Ronald and Erna walked along the beach at Seal Harbor talking about their future. "Ronald always wanted to tell me about the future we would have together, about how things were going to turn out for us. We talked about a house we would build near the ocean. A cottage. He wanted to come back here to settle; I knew that. But he didn't want to come back until he had made something bigger of his life."

They returned to Schenectady, but soon the simple, contented life they had built there began to change. A new commanding officer had been assigned to the reserve unit, a major one rank higher than Ronald. Ronald came to dislike this man: "It got so that Ronald was very unhappy," Erna remembered. "This man came in and took over and took credit for all the work Ronald had done. Ronald had worked day and night, and then he felt that it had all been for nothing. We always used to spend Sundays in the park with Evelyn. That was our special time away from the Army. We had wonderful times there. But soon even our Sundays were ruined."

The atmosphere at the reserve unit was influenced not only by the new commanding officer, but by larger, global events. In 1949, the Soviet Union had exploded its first atomic bomb. The US-backed Nationalist forces under Chiang Kai-shek had been driven to Formosa as China fell to Communism. Alger Hiss had been convicted of spying and politicians had begun declaring that the threat to democracy had never been greater. It soon became apparent that the Army would be called upon to head off this threat.

In the spring of 1950, when the weather had improved enough for them to resume their Sunday afternoon excursions to the park, Ronald began telling Erna that there could be another war.

"I remember him saying something about Korea one afternoon. That was the first time I'd ever heard him talk about that place. He seemed to think the Army would be sent there to fight."

By this time Gary, their second child, was six months old, and as parents Erna and Ronald were consoled by unofficial word around the reserve unit that men with children would not be ordered to fight in a war in Korea.

But seven weeks after South Korea was invaded by the North, Erna drove her husband to a small airport outside Schenectady for the first leg of his journey to Korea.

"That last night in our apartment I made a nice dinner for us. Ronald was still packing his things. I kept going in from the kitchen. I just wanted to be in the same room with him. I didn't want to be apart. I couldn't believe he was going away.

"I didn't sleep much that night. I would doze off and then wake myself so I could hold him. Asleep I would forget, but then awake I saw again that this was our last night.

"When we got to the airport it was early. Ronald held each of the children and then he kissed me good-bye. We watched him walk to the plane. He turned back three times to look at us. The plane went up, and I stayed there until it was out of sight. I always remember thinking, Why does this happen to us?

"It wasn't like the other war. It seemed to be just us who were suffering. I always remember that Ronald was the only one in uniform that morning at the airport, the only soldier."

He promised to write her letters. He often wrote three letters a day. As he traveled farther and farther away it took longer for the letters to arrive. The following excerpts from his letters, written in 1950, depict the concerns and apprehensions of a young soldier leaving for war, and also serve as a chronicle of the fighting in Korea.

---

30 Aug.

Darling, arrived at Anchorage Alaska this morning at 6:00. We thought we were flying by way of Hawaii but it was changed at the last minute. Will be in Japan tomorrow morning.

4 Sept.

I am finally located and am assigned to the 57th FABN, a part of the 7th INF. Div. My duties are counter-mortar liaison officer and I will spend most of my time with the infantry commander of the 31st Infantry Regiment. It is not a bad assignment, nor is it a good one as I'll be very close to the front lines.

5 Sept.

Dear Mommy, before your receipt of this letter I will probably be in combat. This is not a good thought but as I said before, the good Lord knows what the outcome will be. We anticipate very heavy losses during the first days of the invasion.

7 Sept.

I don't imagine you have received the jackets and table clothes [sic] yet but you should very soon. I am presently lying beneath the stars and sleeping on the ground just south of mountain Fugi [sic].

7 Sept.

I have a very funny feeling about the whole operation to come, Erna. But I will do my duty and have a prayer for you and the children daily. I love you and the children with all my heart and soul. I long for the day when we are together again.

8 Sept.

We are combat loaded in ships and have been sitting here in Yokohoma [sic] Harbor for the past three days. We are in a large convoy which will include at least two divisions and supply units. We are in on the invasion of Korea which you will hear about within the next week or ten days.

9 Sept.

We expect at least ten days on this ship. We will get off this ship near land and get into small boats to make a beach landing. This operation will really be large and we hope to make history. However, the organization so far could be one of the greatest disasters in American military history. These units are manned by men just over from the states such as me. A few of the officers have become temporarily insane and two have tried to commit suicide so far.

10 Sept.

Mommy, I realize now how you must have felt when I was working so many nights and paid little attention to you and our children. If I get through this conflict I will put the family first from now on.

15 Sept.

Mommy, I really miss you and the children. Looks as if this war should be over by Thanksgiving though.

28 Sept.

My dearest Erna, our first battle ended last night. We suffered heavy losses for the amount of prisoners we captured. About half of the casualties were officers. I haven't got a scratch yet. With the good Lord willing I'll get through.

29 Sept.

The enemy can hardly be seen. He dresses in civilian clothes and shoots at you from behind. Hope I get some word from you soon. Did you get the suitcase as yet?

30 Sept.

I'll be glad when this so called police action is over. Maybe in a few months I can get back to you and the children or bring you over here, to Japan I mean. That is, if Uncle Joe doesn't send the Chinese Communists to Korea.

30 Sept.

I sure got to combat sooner than I had expected, but I'm in the army and there is nothing we can do about it. Honey, I hate to be away from you and the children but I chose the army as a profession and had to leave.

5 Oct.

We had a hell of a battle for the past three days and lost considerable men and officers. I will say that the dead North Koreans were a little more than ours.

7 Oct.

No letter from you today. I have information which you should know. Our units are being relieved from our present positions and we are to be outfitted with extra winter equipment, and within a week we will probably be on another boat going north for another landing, far north of the 38th parallel. Rumors are that it will be very close to the Russian boarder [sic]. This could be the beginning of a long and bitter struggle but let's hope not.

8 Oct.

Mommy, I have already been recommended for the Bronze star medal for duty performed over and above that called for in my assignment. If my interest in my job makes an impression I'll be glad to accept any and all awards they wish to give me.

13 Oct. Pusan, Korea

If we were still going to be home by Thanksgiving I don't think we would have been issued this heavy winter clothing.

14 Oct.

Please Erna take care of your health, and get plenty of food and rest. I would like to see you as stout as you were when I met you. How about it? Say hello to Evelyn and Gary. I miss you three very much. Say hello to Al and Edith, Sylvia and Earl, Erika and John. Love and kisses, Daddy.

16 Oct. Pusan, Korea aboard the USNS Marine Lynx

I have been thinking much on what to do about building a house for us when I get to the USA. I believe that we should build a small home at the first duty station I have in the USA. I believe with the insurance money I can borrow I can in sixty days build a four or five room house. At least it will be home. I hope that I'll be able to retire as an officer. That way I'll get over $250 per month.

19 Oct.

I look back on the past ten years of my military life as a period of relative easy life. I believe it would be wishful thinking if we let ourselves believe that the next ten years will be. We can hope and pray that the world will someday be peaceful and let us live in peace and raise our children. Is Evelyn talking yet?

---

20 Oct.

Darling, I have been faithful and will for always. I hope and pray that you will not fail me and most of all be true. I love you very much, it hurts me to think that someone may someday take my place.

Erna had been seriously ill the first week in October and she had been unable to answer Ronald's letters for several days. Finally she wrote him and told him what had happened:

I woke up in the middle of the night, Sunday night. I had such pains in my stomach. Terrible, terrible. I was on fire. I crawled down on the floor and out down the hallway to the kitchen. I called Sylvia. I could only say a few words to her. They operated and the doctor found it was a pregnancy in the tube. He told me I was lucky to be alive. Another hour and it might have been too late. There couldn't be any more children he told me. I asked and he is sure. I asked the Red Cross lady if you could come home. I said I needed help with the children. She said you are a German girl, why don't you go home to Germany. She told me I should take the children and go to Germany. I won't leave here without you Honey, don't worry.

Erna kept this letter around several days and then decided not to send it as it was. She didn't want to worry or upset her husband, so later she wrote and said she had had an operation but that everything was fine.

21 Oct.

I hope and pray you are making a speedy recovery. Please, Mommy, please get well. I love you. I'd like to know the answer to one question based on that operation. Can you or are you able to have more children, Mommy?

22 Oct.

Honey, I'd sure like to be with you tonight. You know what I mean. I pray that you'll never let another man touch you so long as I live. Think of the wonderful moments we can have when I return.

———

25 Oct.

The weather here is becoming cold. We expect to see snow soon. I feel better today, at least I am not running to the toilet every other minute and don't have a headache. I think about the house I will build for you and the children when I get back. I love you darling. Please don't ever fail me.

26 Oct.

Mommy, don't worry about the hospital bills. You have to get your rest and not worry. I should be home with you to help. Did the Red Cross tell you anything yet?

28 Oct.

You'll need some money for Christmas to buy the children some things. Evelyn should enjoy Christmas. I wish I could be with you and the family, but it doesn't look possible. Let's pray that next Christmas will be different.

1 Nov.

My dearest Erna, this is my second letter today. We just got bad news about the war. We were handed a radio intercept message which read as follows: The big allied held port of Hamhung was threatened by a twin pronged enemy counter attack led by thousands of Chinese troops. We were always told the Chinese were just laundrymen who would run from the Americans. I guess they were wrong.

2 Nov.

You said you had to go back to the doctor but you didn't tell me why.

3 Nov.

We are waiting to go ashore. Looks as if we will be going north to the boarder [sic] next week. They expect many will die from frost bite. The Chinese Communists are in the fight definitely now. It has been confirmed.

9 Nov.

We are in the mountains now. The mountains are beautiful for a scenic view but are hell on fighting a war. We lost many men last night in an attack. We haven't seen any Chinese Communists yet.

10 Nov.

Erna, I think it is best not to plan on any more children although I'd like to have a third. Your health and happiness count more than a third child. We can spoil Evelyn and Gary even more.

10 Nov.

The prospects of getting back home look very doubtful. No one seems to know how far the Chinese Communists are going into this Korean war. There's only one sure way of getting back to the States and that is by losing an arm or leg or being blinded. God knows I would rather take my chances fighting it out here for four or five years if I have to.

14 Nov.

It was 15 below zero this morning and has stayed 5 below all day. Three men were found froze to death this morning in our unit.

15 Nov.

I know you want me home with you and so do I. Someday I'll make it up to you, Mommy. I'll build us a home by the ocean like we planned and you'll see that the army has been good to us. We will not be fighting the Communists forever.

16 Nov.

I'm glad to hear that you don't want any company for a week after I get home. I read between the lines that you must be as anxious as I to show one another our love for each other.

17 Nov.

We hope the wind will die down soon. You can stand the cold but not the wind so good. I don't know how the enemy puts up with it. We don't see the enemy except when he shoots at us from behind at night.

18 Nov.

I am worried about you and the children with winter coming on. I want you to be warm and well fed, Mommy. I don't believe

I've ever been as cold as it is here. A few more men were sent to the hospital this morning from the cold. Frozen ears, feet and hands. About 2,000 of our men do not even have sleeping bags. We are in pretty bad shape now. We expect to lose about 50 percent of all officers and men during this clean up of Korea.

19 Nov.

Dear Mommy, a few lines to let you know I am alive and that I love you and the children with all my heart. I don't know how much longer we will be here, or why we have to go so far north since we came here to free the south.

22 Nov.

I hope now that Evelyn is talking she won't learn many bad words. How about teaching her a small prayer to say before she goes to bed each night. I hope I will be there soon.

22 Nov.

We never know what day of the week it is until the chaplain conducts service. I miss our Sundays in the park. Do you remember how much fun we had Mommy?

23 Nov.

It is 2:30 Thanksgiving day. We have our turkey and will have dinner at 3:30 this afternoon. We have shrimp, turkey and pumpkin pie. I wish we could be together for just one hour today.

25 Nov.

It is no good to be separated from you and miss the children growing up. Sometimes I wonder if we were not born at the wrong time. It looks as if our lifetime will be spent fighting.

25 Nov.

We will be moving out tomorrow but I will write again as soon as I can.

Later that day Captain Alley's unit began moving again, higher into the mountains, farther north, toward the Yalu River. Their objective was to join the Eighth Army and eventually link up with the 1st Marine Division, moving through the snow and ice around the western shores of the Chosin Reservoir. The bloodiest battle of the war and one of the costliest in modern military history would take place on the ice-covered hills and the frozen ridges surrounding Chosin. The Chinese sent several hundred thousand troops down over the mountain ranges, swarming in hordes that crushed American positions. Never before had American generals seen an enemy advance in such numbers or attack so relentlessly. The attacks continued constantly throughout the day and night for more than sixty hours. Many Army and Marine units were completely surrounded, pinned down until their ammunition was depleted and then slaughtered in hand-to-hand combat.

Temperatures were below zero throughout the battle. Men remained in their positions so long their limbs froze and they could not retreat when the enemy pushed over them. The wounded died because plasma was frozen solid and could not be administered in time. Others froze to death when their clothes were cut away by medics desperately trying to treat their wounds. Men walked around completely dazed and disoriented, their faces white as snow. The winds screamed down through the mountain passes. In most places the ground was frozen and there was no way to dig in for cover. Automatic weapons froze and jammed as the enemy advanced. The battle raged through the long nights in dozens of isolated areas, and at dawn the snow-covered hills were strewn with piles of corpses.

Many of the Marine positions were overrun by Chinese suicide assaults. The word had gone out that it was far better to be killed by this enemy than taken prisoner, and so the wounded GIs tried to escape, crawling on their stomachs across the frozen reservoir. The Chinese dispatched killing parties to hunt down the wounded and summarily execute them with a shot to the back of the head. Eventually the Chinese would admit to having suffered more than thirty-seven thousand casualties in the battle for Chosin. Casualties for the Army, Marine, and United Nations forces were extremely high, with more than seven thousand killed, three times that many wounded, and more than three thousand troops missing in action or captured by the enemy.

About the time Ronald's letters stopped, Erna began hearing more and more about this fighting at Chosin Reservoir. "I was reading the newspapers, and I had a map of Korea spread out on the kitchen table. I knew this was bad. They said we had been trapped by the Chinese. It was called a bloodbath. I kept going back over Ronald's letters trying to figure out if he was there.

"Finally there were no more letters. Nothing. The Army could tell me nothing. I went to the minister and the Red Cross for help. Finally I went to a fortune-teller. We believe in these things in Germany. Many Europeans believe in fortune-tellers. The woman told me that my husband was alive and would be coming home, but not for a long time. She told me there were hard days ahead. I asked, 'For the children too?' And she said, 'Yes, for all of you.' "

Just before Christmas, Erna left Schenectady with the children and traveled to Bar Harbor to move in for a while with Ronald's parents. On February 15, more than two months after his last letter, Erna received a telephone call from a friend in Schenectady who had seen Ronald's name on a list of prisoners of war published in the *New York Times.* Two days later the Pentagon confirmed that he was being held by the Chinese and North Koreans somewhere in North Korea. They could not say where.

"I had never thought before of him being taken prisoner. You think black and white, dead or alive. Not prisoner. I remembered then that when I was a girl during the war, I was visiting a friend in Munich and I saw two British pilots shot from the sky and then paraded through the city streets with guns pointed at them. Now I couldn't stop thinking about those two men, wondering what had ever happened to them after they were captured. I thought about them day and night. They became so important to me.

"At least my husband was alive. He was not dead. The Army told me that negotiations had started and that he might be released soon. When I looked at the children I had to believe that."

# CHAPTER 3

Soon it became obvious to Erna that her husband might be gone for a long time, and that she would have to try on her own to make a life for herself and the children. She had moved to Maine with the idea that she would get some sort of life started *there,* so that when the day came for her husband to return home he would have a place to come to.

She found a small house for sale just off the main road that led to Bar Harbor, and with two thousand dollars borrowed against a life-insurance policy, plus a mortgage from a local bank, she was able to buy the place. She took part-time work waiting on tables in order to cover the monthly expenses, but she was confident that making ends meet would not always be so difficult. Out behind the small house, on the piece of land that came with it, there were a half dozen old bungalows that could one day be refurbished and rented to summer tourists.

"I always believed that Ronald would come home and that this would be our place together. He was good with his hands, and we could fix the place up someday. But a year went by, and then two years. After so much time you begin to think of yourself as being alone, on your own, forever. I was alone. I had to look out for myself. And for the children. What was so sad was that the children were growing up in this little world of ours, and it was the only world they knew; they didn't know their father, and so they didn't miss him. And for their sake I had to hide my loneliness. I was always torn about telling them about their daddy, because then they would miss him too, like I did. . . . It was like there was just the three of us, and it would always be this way."

There were people on the island who wanted to help her, and Erna was always glad for their help. By the end of August 1953, three years after Ronald had left for Korea, she had two of the bungalows ready to rent. She hung a sign out in front of the house just a few yards from the road: ERNA'S GERMAN MOTEL. Soon she had her first overnight guests.

In the last week of that month in Panmunjom, Korea, Operation Big Switch took place, and prisoners from both sides were exchanged at a location the newspapers called Freedom Village. Erna read that over twelve thousand prisoners were being released by the Chinese and North Koreans at Freedom Village. Among them were nearly four thousand American soldiers. "I was never far from the radio that day. And the telephone. Gary was sick in bed with a cold, and I brought him downstairs and made up the couch for him in the living room so I could stay near the telephone. Finally the call did come through. I stood there with tears running down my face. It was Ronald's voice, very weak, very far away. But he was alive! I said to the children, 'It's your daddy! It's your daddy!' They looked at me. I just cried and cried. . . .

"Ronald said he could not come home right away. He said there was something wrong with one of his lungs. My heart stopped. I asked how long he would be, and when would he come home. He said it would be soon. He told me to put the children on the telephone for him. He wanted to hear their voices. He had not heard their voices before. I tried to get them both to say something, but they were too shy. I remember Ronald said to me, 'We're almost there, Mommy. We're almost there.' "

Instinctively she cleaned the house, cleaned it again and again and waited for the phone call that would tell her he was on his way to Maine. Five days after she had spoken with him an Army doctor called her from a hospital in Tokyo to tell her that her husband was being flown to the States, to St. Albans Naval Hospital on Long Island. "He sounded very serious, very grave. I had read that the prisoners were coming home by ship, so when he said Ronald was being flown home, I knew it was bad. He said it was either TB or a lung tumor. He said Ronald was coughing up blood and was very weak. He said they would tell me when it was all right to go visit him."

Two months passed, and it was late November of 1953 when she was finally told to come to the hospital. Friends from Bar Harbor helped her get ready for the trip and volunteered to take care of Gary and Evelyn. By now she had enough money from her overnight guests to pay for the train ticket.

"This hospital was full of sick soldiers. Rows and rows of beds. Some of these men had been here since the Second World War, but many were from Korea. Just rows of them.

"A nurse walked with me to one of the tuberculosis wards where there were more beds. She took me to a private room, and right away I knew how sick my husband must be. She wanted me to wear a mask. She asked me how long it had been since I'd seen my husband. I told her thirty-nine months. She said I could take off the mask to kiss him.

"I saw him there, lying there, not moving, and I thought to myself, Oh God, he's dead. I leaned over and kissed him on the lips and he was so cold. He looked at me like he didn't know who I was. I put the children's pictures on the bed and I talked to him, kept talking to him. He would close his eyes, and I kept talking, telling him everything I'd planned to tell him. He was not the same man I had said good-bye to three years ago. I was sad, but then not sad, just angry. I was mad at the Army for sending my husband home to me like this. He had lost almost a hundred pounds. He was just skin and bones. You could see his bones poking through the skin. And he was a terrible color. Terrible."

Erna stayed for four days that first trip. Then she returned home. She was counting on him coming home for Christmas, but the doctors were planning surgery to remove part of one lung. They told her it would be summer before he could be moved.

She visited St. Albans a half dozen times in the next year. She wrote him every day, and gradually his condition improved.

"I could tell near the end of the first year that he was getting stronger and more like himself. Once when I got to the hospital he was arguing with one of the Army doctors who wanted him to take a medical discharge from the service. Ronald was so angry with the doctor. They wanted him to sign papers.

"When we were alone he asked me to help him. He asked me to tell the doctors he had thirty good years left in him to give his country; that was how he said it, those were exactly his words: 'I have thirty good years left to give my country. Don't let them take away my uniform,' he said to me."

Eventually the doctors stopped bringing up the subject of a medical discharge, and Ronald grew stronger, more determined to restore himself to active duty. It was decided that he could take a thirty-day leave to spend Christmas in Maine.

"We picked him up in Bangor, our first Christmas together. He hadn't seen the children since they were infants. They didn't know him. I cried so hard on the ride back from Bangor when Gary said to me, 'Is this man my daddy?' It was so horrible for me to think that four years were gone, and things had happened that would never happen again in the children's lives. Their first steps and their first little sentences.

"Ronald was good with them. He was supposed to rest, but he went all over the place buying toys for Christmas. He put these toys together up in the attic at night after the children went to sleep. I could hear him coughing, going up the attic steps.

"We had just two weeks together and then he had a relapse. I went back to the hospital with him."

By March the doctors decided he was well enough to report for duty. He telephoned Erna with the good news. "He was in such good spirits. He had his uniform back and he had been promoted to major by then. He was going to Washington, D.C., to pick up his new orders, and then he was coming home on leave to spend a month with us. I remember how high his hopes were. He said to me, 'Mommy, Ike is in the White House and the sky is the limit for a major!' "

Major Alley rode a train to Union Station in Washington, D.C., and then caught a bus for Fort Meade, Maryland, north of the city, where he was to pick up his orders, a paycheck, and the final approval for his thirty-day leave.

The trip to Fort Meade took just over an hour by bus, and it was early evening when he presented himself at headquarters, a one-story brick building at the southwest corner of the 400-acre fort. A sergeant met him at the door and told him to have a seat. He offered him a cup of coffee, then left the room. When the sergeant returned he was accompanied by two officers. Ronald rose to his feet and saluted. One of the officers asked him if he was Major Ronald E. Alley. He said he was. He was asked for his service number, and he repeated it from memory. The second officer then began reading from an official memo. He read quickly through a list of charges brought against him by the United States Army. There would have to be a general court-martial convened at Fort Meade. The orders for this court-martial had already been approved, he was told. He would be confined to his quarters. Major Alley said that there must be some mistake. He wanted them to check his record. He told them he'd been a prisoner of war for three years and then confined to a hospital for two more. They said they knew about his record, that there was no mistake. He was taken to his quarters, and two military policemen were posted outside his door.

"He called me that night," Erna remembered. "I was so excited about him coming home I just talked about the children and all the things we could do now. I talked, and then he told me there was some problem. He told me what had happened. He said it was all a mistake, and that the Army would straighten it out. 'Don't worry, don't worry,' he told me. 'This will all be straightened out in a few days, and I will be on my way home.' "

Three days later Erna drove to Fort Meade with the children. "He was not coming home. I knew that. And he had been told we could come to be with him. He had been told he would not be under house arrest. But when we got there and were settled in a rented house near the fort, he *was* placed under house arrest. He argued, but it did no good. He wanted to take the children on picnics, but he couldn't leave the house.

"He kept telling me that he had done nothing wrong and that everything would be all right. He believed this. I wanted to believe it too, that it was just a mistake. I wanted to think that soon we could all go home, to Maine, together.

"They said he had done things wrong over in Korea. He was telling me every day that he was innocent. I believed him, and so did his lawyer, Colonel Logan. We spent many weeks with Colonel Logan. It always seemed that he was a good man and that he was trying hard. He knew how much the prisoners had suffered, and that this was the first time in history that the Army had turned against the POWs. I trusted him. But then one day he told me that we were not going to win. He said he had just come from a meeting of higher-ups, and that the decision was going to be bad for Ronald no matter what kind of defense he gave. He said Ronald would be found guilty. Ronald didn't believe this. But I did. I really knew then.

"Colonel Logan wanted Ronald to get a civilian lawyer. Ronald said, 'I will keep you as my lawyer. The Army will stand behind me and straighten this out.' "

On August 22, 1955, the general court-martial of Major Alley was convened at Fort Meade, Maryland. For two and a half months the Army, presenting more than fifty witnesses, argued its case: that Major Alley had behaved dishonorably in Korea during his period of confinement as a prisoner of war; that his communication with the enemy exceeded his duty to give the enemy his name, rank, service number, and date of birth; and that this communication resulted in collaboration with an enemy of the United States of America.

Defense witnesses took the stand to say that Major Alley had been a loyal officer, that he had done only what was necessary to support his men in a difficult position. They explained that all prisoners to some degree had been forced to cooperate with the enemy, and that often the prisoners created the illusion of cooperation just to get food and medicine from the enemy or to be spared harsh interrogation and punishment. In interviews with the press covering the trial, several defense witnesses called the court-martial a farce and accused Army prosecution witnesses of lying on the stand to protect their own careers and reputations.

---

Colonel William T. Logan, appointed by the Army to defend Ronald, believed his best chance was to attempt to show that Major Alley had been so abused by his captors in an atmosphere of constant fear and duress that he was mentally and emotionally incapable of responsible actions. He refused to allow Major Alley to take the stand in his own defense, fearing that cross-examination would reveal a man with unimpaired judgment, thus detracting from the image he was trying to convey to the jury. He was also afraid Ronald's temper might get him into deeper trouble.

"Day after day Ronald just sat there in the courtroom," Erna said. "Every day would be the same. Ronald would shine his shoes and polish his brass. Gary used to help him. And then the guards would come and take him to the courtroom. I was always there. He sat next to Colonel Logan and said nothing. I told him to tell them how he had been beaten, and how they had buried him in a hole in the ground. But Ronald said to me that this was just in the line of duty and he wasn't going to brag about it. He wasn't a martyr, he said. But he was wrong. He should have spoken up. And the way he looked was so good in his uniform; they couldn't see how he had looked when he first came back from Korea, how he had looked when I first saw him in the hospital."

On November 3, 1955, a jury of ten officers deliberated for five hours before finding Major Alley guilty of the following charges:

**1.** One offense of communicating with the enemy in violation of Article of War 81.

**2.** Four offenses of communicating with the enemy in violation of Article of War 96.

**3.** Four offenses of communicating with the enemy in violation of Article 104, Uniform Code of Military Justice, 10 USC 904.

**4.** One offense of communicating with the enemy in violation of Article 134, Uniform Code of Military Justice, 10 USC 934.

Four days later he was sentenced to dismissal from the service, forfeiture of all pay and allowances, and ten years at hard labor.

"They took him away in handcuffs. I followed them to the stockade. The door closed behind him, in his cell. He yelled to me to help him. 'Won't somebody help me?' That was the last thing he said that day. 'Help me!' What could I do? I was told by Colonel Logan that if I went to the press it would only make things harder on Ronald when he got to Leavenworth Prison.

"I took the children back to Maine. I cried myself to sleep every night for months. I had a nervous breakdown. There was no money. My father died, and I didn't have enough money to go to Germany for his funeral.

"I wrote Ronald every day. He was angry, so bitter and angry. He said, 'Ten years, ten years. What will be left to us after ten more years?' I didn't tell him about the hate letters that came to our house, and the newspaper articles calling him a traitor, and a Red. The children were made fun of at school. Gary would come home crying, having been in fights with the boys who said his daddy was a traitor."

On June 13, 1959, three years and seven months after the Army sent him to prison, he was released without explanation and put on a bus for Maine. Just before he arrived home Erna told a newspaper reporter in Boston that she was sure the Army would someday correct this injustice done to her husband. "He did only what he thought was right to protect himself and his men. They all did. My husband and I will fight and we will get justice. This is America. There is justice here, I am told."

Erna assumed that they would begin fighting right away, but when she saw her husband get off the bus she knew that he was in no condition to fight anything.

"He came home and lay on the couch looking up at the ceiling. Staring and staring. He didn't want to go outside. He didn't want to play with the children. He was thirty-six years old. Lying there day after day, he was just like a man already dead."

After many more months things began slowly to change. John F. Kennedy was in the White House, and the whole country began feeling better after the crises in Berlin and Cuba were over. Eventually Ronald took a job selling Fuller brushes door-to-door in Bar Harbor. Then he began his own surveying business, using a skill the Army had taught him when he was a teenage boy. Life began to seem normal for Ronald and Erna and the children — normal but for the fact that Korea and the court-martial had changed them all. There was always someone else to write to, someone who might help persuade the Army to change what had happened to Ronald. They would get excited at each new prospect.

In 1975, twenty years after the court-martial, Ronald was offered the chance to apply for a presidential pardon. A congressman was willing to support his application and use his contacts in the White House, but Ronald said no. He said that pardons were for guilty men, and he was not guilty.

"The uniform I had had tailored for him we just hung in his closet. Every once in a while someone would want to do a newspaper story and the paper would send someone to take pictures of Ronald in his uniform. This was always very hard for him, putting on the uniform but not being allowed to wear it.

"It was one of those times after NBC sent John Cochran to our home in 1976 to do his television story that Ronald made me promise to have him buried in his uniform. I said, 'Nothing is going to happen to you, Ronald.' But I made my promise anyway."

# CHAPTER 4

T he newspaper office in Bar Harbor sits right on the sidewalk a few hundred feet from the harbor, at the center of town where the two main streets run into each other. It has wide glass windows in front and, just inside, the editor sits behind a desk.

On New Year's Day in 1978 my wife, Lee, and I were packing up our belongings to move from Bar Harbor after having lived there ten months. I had hoped to make ends meet as a writer, but couldn't, and so we were going to Portland, Maine, where things might be easier. On January 2 the owner of the *Bar Harbor Times* telephoned and offered me a job as editor of the paper.

I had occupied the desk in the front windows less than three weeks when I received a telephone call from Ronald Alley, whose name I had never heard before. He told me he had to talk with me about a story. I was always looking for stories then, so we set an appointment for one o'clock the next day, January 20, 1978.

The wind was blowing hard and the snow was slanting through town as I walked to work that Friday morning. I was out in the back room when one of the boys from the print shop approached me from his press. "You seeing Alley today?" he asked.

I said I was.

"You know the major?" he asked.

"No."

"He did some time, d'you know that?"

"Time?"

"He was a traitor in Korea. Spent some time in the slammer for helping the enemy. The Commies."

On Friday afternoon Ronald Alley made his way to my office, walking the length of Cottage Street. For some reason I looked up from my typewriter and spotted him as he passed the post office. By now the storm had turned into a blizzard, and he was the only person out on the street. He was a big man and he wore no hat.

Inside the front door he stomped the snow from his boots and we shook hands. "Looks as if it could snow forever," he said in a clipped-off baritone that sagged under a heavy Down East accent. He was wearing a tan khaki shirt and matching trousers, a uniform of sorts. And the shine on his boots had been worked at.

We talked about the storm and looked out at the drifting snow. Once, by accident, I called him "Major." His eyes darkened and he looked hard at my face. Then he asked me suddenly if I had any children. I thought this was an odd question and I said no, that I had just been married. He wanted to know how old I was. I told him I would be twenty-eight that summer. He nodded then and said with a half-smile that he had a son the same age.

That's about all he had a chance to tell me. We were interrupted by a telephone call from a fisherman at the dock who said that one of the summer restaurants was being torn from its cedar posts and carried out to sea on the tide. I had to go take some photographs. I asked Ronald Alley if he would come back Monday morning. He was disappointed, but he shook my hand again and said he would.

I spent most of Saturday and Sunday working on my first front-page story. I had photographs of the island buried under three feet of snow and of the restaurant at the town dock drifting out to sea.

Monday morning, I left the house early; Lee was still sleeping upstairs. The dog watched me fill the woodstove and followed me to the door when I went out. It was a beautiful cold day, and the snow was piled so high along the streets that it was like walking through a tunnel in the center of town.

Our house, only five blocks from the *Bar Harbor Times* office, was a two-story box covered with cedar shingles. We had bought it for five thousand dollars in June of 1977. It was uninhabitable then — the floors heaved and pitched at odd angles and the roof sagged in the middle as though someone had thrown a saddle over it. We spent the next year gutting the inside and rebuilding it ourselves from bottom to top and falling in love with it.

At the drugstore I stopped to buy a *New York Times,* but the papers from New York and Boston had not made it through the storm. The island was still sealed off from the rest of the world.

When I opened the front door of the office I saw the note I'd left on my desk Friday night: "Major Alley. 8:30 A.M." I spent an hour in the darkroom enlarging photographs, then I put on a pot of coffee and walked around the print shop waiting for it to brew. I liked walking around the old Linotype presses — great, iron monstrosities that racketed like freight trains when they were running and still seemed to give off an eerie sound when they were silent. These machines and the scent of ink and newsprint were a part of my past I remembered only in fragments. Both my grandfathers had spent their entire working lives standing behind Linotype presses. And then my father had apprenticed in a print shop after the war. He was working the night shift in 1949 when a man yelled to him over the clatter of the machines that he had a daughter my father might want to take on a date. They ended up getting married a short time later. This job at the newspaper had made me begin to feel connected to my past.

I wrote headlines and typed copy most of the morning. It was early afternoon when a woman called to say she had an obituary for this week's paper. I asked her to please hold and then I gave the call to the secretary sitting at a desk a few feet from mine. I heard her spell the name out loud and I turned around and waited for her to hang up the telephone.

"Someone named Alley was supposed to come in this morning," I said.

She read her note, then said, "This is Ronald Alley. Major Ronald Alley."

Monday morning, leaving his house to come meet with me again, Ronald Alley died of a heart attack. His wife, Erna, found him lying face down in the snow. He was fifty-five years old.

I typed the obituary that afternoon, a few modest paragraphs that seemed to describe the average man living and dying in anonymity in a small rural town in America. Father, grandfather, active in the church, a member of the Masons, a veteran. He left behind a widow and two children.

*     *     *     *     *

Lee and I had friends over for dinner that night, and I did the best I could to be hospitable. But I was distracted by what had happened earlier in the day, and finally, when I had an excuse to be alone in the kitchen, I closed the door behind me and made a call to Mrs. Alley. I identified myself to a male voice and I heard him call "Ma," and a moment later she came to the phone. I was solicitous, and apologized for bothering her. When I told her I was the town's newspaper editor I half expected her to chide me for calling her on the day her husband had died. But she kept her voice very low and level, and said she appreciated my concern.

"I saw your husband on Friday," I said. "He came into the office for a few minutes."

"Yes, I know."

"I wanted to talk with him but we didn't get a chance."

There was a long pause and then she went on. "He was on his way back there this morning."

That was all she said. I stumbled on for a minute or two, finally managing to ask why he had come in the first place. "That's why I'm calling," I said. "I was hoping you might know what he wanted to talk about."

She didn't answer. Instead she said, "You can write this in your newspaper. The Army killed my husband, the United States Army." Her voice rose. She repeated this and added, "The Army broke his heart."

Later that evening I told Lee about the call I had made to Erna Alley.

"She probably wants you to do a story," Lee said. "There would be some consolation for her in a story."

First I wondered what kind of consolation. Then I realized Lee was right. I'd seen a kind of consolation descend upon people I knew at college once the media began standing on their side, vilifying the Army for the war in Vietnam.

"It's an easy thing to print," I said to Lee, "but not so easy to prove."

"That doesn't mean it isn't true," she said.

I was skeptical. But there was something that prevented me from dismissing the idea completely. It was Erna Alley's voice on this, the night of her husband's death. An informed and perfectly seamless voice — not at all the voice of a woman whose reasoning had been overpowered by emotion.

Lee and I talked a while longer that night about Major Alley. I recalled how he had mentioned his son. "I have the feeling there was something on his mind and it had to do with his son. I mean, anyone who walks through a blizzard to keep an appointment has something on his mind. He mentioned that he was thinking about running for Congress in the spring primary. I told him I'd be glad to interview him with the rest of the candidates. He was going to run as an Independent. I'm not sure he knew there isn't a primary for Independent candidates."

I said to Lee, "I'd like to know what he did wrong for the Army to send him to prison."

"You'll have to find out," she said. "You'll have to find out everything about him."

She was completely matter-of-fact about this, but I was still reluctant. All through college I'd been reluctant to reach conclusions about political issues that were beyond my full understanding. I'd decried the war protests and argued with friends who would listen to me, saying we didn't have the right to criticize until we had the facts. *Both sides* — that was my battle cry.

I had always criticized journalists who neglected to present both sides of a story. Now that I was a newspaper editor, I could hold the line for caution, thoroughness, balance. A journalist's duty is what I called it.

Lee asked if it wasn't just ambivalence.

*     *     *     *     *

On Thursday morning Ronald Alley's obituary appeared in the *Bar Harbor Times.* That afternoon I had some newspapers to deliver to the back side of the island. I took the pickup truck and, after making the delivery, I drove to the beach at Seal Harbor.

The sun was high and strong, and even with all the snow banked along the road you could imagine spring coming. I parked the truck and went down to the beach. I was going to walk from one end to the other, but I went only a little way before turning back and driving to the Alleys' house.

I parked in the driveway and found Erna sitting out back in a lawn chair, facing the sun. She wore a heavy quilted coat that was wrapped around her legs. Her blond hair and bright blue eyes were luminous in the sunlight.

I apologized for coming unannounced.

"Sit down," she said. "I had a feeling you would come by."

She was a striking woman to look at. I could tell by looking at her eyes that she was tired, but if she was in her mid-fifties like her husband, I thought, she looked ten years younger. The sun had colored her cheeks, and she looked fit and athletic.

"Do you sit out like this all winter?" I asked.

"When it's not too cold," she said. And then she turned and gestured to the stairs. "I found Ronald right there — he was lying face down in the snow. I thought he'd fallen down the steps."

Then she looked away and told me he couldn't be buried until spring for they had to wait for the ground to thaw.

"He's in his uniform," she said, and went on to explain that the Army had prohibited him from wearing his uniform. "It was taken from him after the trial," she said. She looked past me to the place where her husband had died. "But I don't care about the Army. They killed my husband. They can do whatever they wish to me."

I didn't know what to say, and she seemed to sense my uneasiness. "I can tell you everything," she said. "Do you have time to come inside?"

The house was dark, and Erna walked ahead of me, opening the curtains as she went. There were flowers in vases on the kitchen table and lined up on the stairs. There were letters and cards piled everywhere, many of them unopened. In the living room she stopped and gestured to a low, round table at one end of the room. The table was heaped with loose pages, newspaper clippings, old magazine articles, and photographs. I glanced down at one picture of Erna and Ronald at their wedding in Germany. When she saw me looking, she said, "Didn't he look fine in his uniform?"

It was all there on the table, she told me. All that they knew. "For twenty years this is where we worked on Ronald's case." She shuffled through pages and handed them to me. I read about his service in the Army: He finished high school at age seventeen and joined the National Guard on February 1, 1939, attaining the rank of master sergeant before he was called into active duty on February 24, 1941. He was sent to Fort Sill, Oklahoma, where he was given an IQ test and graded "130 Superior." He was trained as a survey officer at Fort Sill and promoted to the rank of second lieutenant. On November 19, 1944, he was promoted to the rank of first lieutenant and stationed at Fort Jackson, South Carolina, as a first survey officer. He left for overseas duty in January 1945 and joined the battle of the Ruhr Valley Pocket. He saw combat in France and Belgium, and in September of 1946 was promoted to captain. He served in occupied Germany as a military governor after the end of World War II. In 1947 he was assigned as an instructor on active duty to the 142nd Army Service Unit Organized Reserve Corps, located at 1092 Catalyn Street in Schenectady, New York. He was ordered to Korea on August 1, 1950, to join the 57th Field Artillery Battalion of the 7th Infantry Division as a liaison officer. He was captured in North Korea on or about December 1, 1950. He was promoted to the rank of major while a prisoner of war, on September 17, 1952. He was released by the Chinese on August 29, 1953, and was evacuated by air to St. Albans Naval Hospital on Long Island, New York, by way of Tripler Army Medical Center in Hawaii, Travis Air Force Hospital in California, and Andrews Air Force Base outside Washington, D.C. On December 16, 1953, he was operated on at St. Albans. He was transferred to Valley Forge Army Hospital in Phoenixville, Pennsylvania, on March 2, 1954. In September of 1954 he underwent more surgery to remove a portion of one lung. In March 1955 he was returned to limited duty for a two-year tour with the 2101st Service Unit at Fort George G. Meade, Maryland. The day he reported for duty at Fort Meade he was charged with collaborating with the enemy and placed under house arrest. In November 1955 he was found guilty of the collaboration charges, dismissed dishonorably from the service, and sent to Fort

Leavenworth Prison with a forfeiture of all pay and benefits from the Army. While incarcerated he was put to work as a typewriter repairman, a layout man in the decal department, and an instructor of science in the education department. On June 13, 1959, he was released from prison and given a brown prison-issue suit and twenty-five dollars.

During the years he served in the Army he received the European-African-Middle Eastern Campaign Medal, the American Campaign Medal, the American Defense Service Medal, the World War II Victory Medal, the Good Conduct Medal, the Army of Occupation Medal (Germany), the Korean Service Medal, the United Nations Service Medal, and the Armed Forces Reserve Medal.

In his high school yearbook below his picture was a quote by Thoreau: "If one advances confidently in the direction of his dreams, and endeavors to live the life which he has imagined, he will meet with a success unexpected in common hours."

I read newspaper clippings about his court-martial in 1955.

An article from the *Washington Post:* ALLEY'S WORK FOR REDS TOLD — "An Air Force officer testified today Major Ronald E. Alley took a leading part in the enemy's propaganda campaign while he was a Korean prisoner of war. . . ."

*Baltimore Sun:* ALLEY CALLED RED MONITOR — "Major Ronald E. Alley insisted fellow prisoners in his squad participate and pay attention during communist-sponsored discussion groups which he led in a Korean Prison Camp."

*Washington Post:* ALLEY CALLED RED WRITER — "A witness said today that Major Ronald E. Alley received a 'chit' for five hundred Chinese dollars for an article he wrote for an enemy prison camp newspaper in Korea."

*Washington Star:* ALLEY'S KEEN INTEREST IN SOCIALISM IS CITED — "Major Ronald E. Alley, who is accused of misconduct while a prisoner of war in Korea, was described yesterday at his Ft. Meade trial as a person interested in Socialistic political beliefs even before he became a prisoner."

*Washington Post:* 'ADVISED,' ALLEY TRIAL WITNESS SAYS — "A defense witness said today that a prosecution witness had told him he believed it would help his own case if he made a statement against Major Ronald E. Alley, who is being tried on charges of misconduct while a prisoner of war in Korea."

*Washington Post:* EX-POW SAYS ALLEY WAS TORTURED — "A fellow prisoner testified today he and Major Ronald E. Alley were subjected to a form of torture at a communist prison camp in Korea."

*Washington Post:* ALLEY'S WIFE TAKES STAND — "The wife of Major Ronald E. Alley, Army officer accused of misconduct while a prisoner of war in Korea, took the stand in his defense today in a surprise move. She testified she knew something was mentally wrong with her husband after his release by the Communists . . . . 'I was shocked when I first saw him. He treated me like a stranger,' the German war bride testified."

*Washington Star:* ALLEY GETS TEN YEARS AT HARD LABOR FOR ACTIONS IN KOREA — "Major Ronald E. Alley of Bar Harbor, Maine, a 35-year old Field Artillery officer was sentenced today to ten years at hard labor for misconduct while a prisoner of war in North Korea. . . . Alley, a strapping, big, sandy-haired man showed no emotion as the sentence was pronounced. . . . Mrs. Alley, a German woman he married while on duty overseas, wept quietly after the sentence was announced."

In a *Boston Globe* article in 1958, Erna spoke about her life now that her husband was in prison:

And only thanks to my many wonderful American friends was I able to struggle on alone here. I have my little home, and my children. They don't know what happened to their father, they still believe he's away working. I felt it was better for them, for their health and welfare that they not brood on the injustice.

There were many dozens of these clippings. One said that, from Leavenworth Prison in 1956, Ronald told a reporter for the Associated Press that he was going to bring charges against 142 Army officers "more guilty than I was." And there was a picture in the *Bangor Daily News* in 1976 of the Alleys' car under the headline

BULLET-RIDDEN ALLEY CAR, DISHONORED VET'S CAR HIT.

"They never found who did this," Erna said. She handed me another clipping and went on. "But the people on the island were always on our side."

The next clipping was an editorial from the *Bar Harbor Times* on December 29, 1955:

Last week — just before Christmas — Ronald E. Alley, former Major in the US Army convicted by court-martial of misconduct while a prisoner in Korea, was transferred from Fort Meade to the Federal Military Prison at Leavenworth, Kansas. . . .There is no change in his status, he is just farther away from home. A few days ago Mrs. Alley wrote three letters in appeal for an early review of her husband's case. The letters were written to senators Margaret Chase Smith and Frederick G. Payne and to Congressman Clifford G. McIntire. I have written my three letters and my hope is that you will too.

I asked Erna what came of the review. She smiled an ironic half-smile. "That's what we've been working for all these years. There never was a review. The Army has always turned us down, no matter who tried. They always said we needed more evidence. More, more, always more."

I read letters, dozens of letters written to members of the US Congress since 1955. The Alleys had written to any senator or representative who happened to be in the news at the time. Senator Edward Kennedy. Senator Herman Talmadge. Senator Howard Baker. Senator Edmund Muskie. The replies were addressed to Erna.

I asked if she had written all the letters.

"Whenever Ronald got discouraged, I would write. He always believed the Army would clear his name, but after so many years he was very discouraged. *I* would not give up."

One of the last letters Erna had written was to Ronald Reagan after he had served as governor of California. He had replied: "While I appreciate your problem, I am just a private citizen and there is nothing I can do."

I sat there reading a 1958 letter from the Veterans Administration notifying Erna that Ronald's National Service Life Insurance had been cancelled. When I looked up, Gary Alley was standing there. He stood in the doorway, tall and broad-shouldered like his father, looking like many of the old photographs of Ronald spread out on the table in front of me. It was eerie, almost as if his father had stepped into the room.

Erna introduced us, and then she said, "Mr. Snyder is going to do a story."

I hadn't said anything about doing a story, and I was somewhat surprised. But I looked straight at Gary and stood to shake his hand. He nodded his head, said he was going out for a while, and then turned and walked into the kitchen.

After a few minutes I put the papers down on the table and said that I'd better get back to the office.

"You have to understand," she said. She swept her hand over the table. "All this, all these years we waited for someone to help us. And Gary still doesn't know what to believe. There were many men who testified for his father at the trial. The Army believed who they wanted to believe. Those men on the jury, they didn't know Ronald. You had to know him to know he wouldn't have done anything to hurt his country. He loved this country. But Gary never knew him well enough to be sure."

I went home empty-handed that day, but for the next month I thought about what I had read on that table and what Erna had told me. I thought about her son standing there in the doorway, looking so much like his father had when he was a young officer.

Erna called me many times, at the office and at home. She sent me things to read. Once she said to me, "The *Bar Harbor Times* stood behind Ronald when everyone else was against him. He came to you hoping you would help."

I asked what it was she thought I could do.

"A story," she said. "A story would make people remember. I told you that Ronald believed the Army would give him his honor back, no matter how long it took. But for this to happen people must not forget."

Eventually I wrote a story and published it on the front page of the newspaper under the headline PRISONER OF WAR. The story told of the Alleys' long suffering, their struggle to get someone to listen to their claim that Ronald was not guilty. The main point of the story was that Erna was still a prisoner of the war that had ended in 1953, that she would continue to be a prisoner until the Army restored her husband's honor, granting him the honorable discharge he had sworn he deserved.

It was not a good story. It was inconclusive and it relied upon emotional texture to compensate for a lack of facts. But it did make people remember. They called the newspaper office for weeks and wrote letters to the editor, all supporting Erna's claim that her husband had been wronged by the Army.

The story came out on a Thursday, on one of the first days of spring, and I took a copy to Lee in the hospital. It had been a long, difficult winter for her. This was the second time she had been hospitalized for a heart condition that resulted from open-heart surgery she had undergone when she was a child.

Lee was pleased with the story. As I watched her reading it in the hospital bed, I began to wonder if everything that had happened to her health over the years since she was a girl had left her feeling a greater urgency about life than I felt. Life in general and this story specifically. The story of a man running out of time, a man whose heart had given out before he could achieve his dream of honor.

"It's a wonderful story," she said. "He would have been very grateful."

I said it was sloppy journalism. "I gave only their side."

"What other side is there?" she asked.

"The Army. I'm sure the Army has a different side."

She put the newspaper down on the bed. "You worry about the Army? They told their side at the court-martial."

# CHAPTER 5

T here was only one side that mattered to Gerald F. Williamson, a lawyer from Brockton, Massachusetts, who'd met
Ronald Alley several years before his death. "Ron and I had
an agreement," Gerry told me. "I'd argue this damn-fool
case all the way to the Supreme Court if that's what it took to
get his honorable discharge."

It was the Fourth of July, 1978, and I had just taken photographs of the parade through Bar Harbor. Gerry was visiting Erna
for a few days, and she had sent him to talk with me. He met me on
Cottage Street and told me he'd read the story I'd done that spring.
"That's just the tip of the iceberg," he claimed. "This case is going to
make history before it's over."

---

I walked down the street with him while he went on. He talked in a buzz-saw style, gesturing grandly with his hands, straightening his glasses on the bridge of his nose. He was in his early forties, but he had a crew cut and a boyish earnestness about him. He spoke about the Alley case with dramatic statements that seemed to have been rehearsed and designed in preparation for some future trial he imagined would be the biggest in his career.

We stood under an oak tree across the street from the VFW hall. "You have to understand that the Army framed Ron. There's a condition in military law called command influence, when the conduct of the court-martial is affected or prejudiced by commanding officers. If there was ever a case for that, it was Ron's trial. If I can prove command influence I can get the court-martial declared null and void."

"*Can* you prove it?" I asked.

He seemed surprised. "Not yet," he said. "But we're getting close."

Gerry had secured statements from a few former prisoners of war who had been held captive with Ronald, but the more we talked, the clearer it became to me that there was no hard evidence that would prove anything. And as hard as Gerry had worked on this case with Ronald, they had never come up with the concrete evidence to persuade the Army to reopen the case.

Gerry's enthusiasm and his devotion were based upon his belief in Major Alley. "You had to know him like I did," he said. "If you were going to fight alongside anyone, it would be Ron. This country sends men like him off to fight stinking little wars, and then when those wars don't end the right way the Army turns on them." He threw his hands up in the air: "Korea was the first war we didn't win. The shit hit the fan in a big way in the Pentagon. But every other branch of the service — the Navy, Air Force, even the Marines — *everybody* but the Army refused to prosecute their own men. Those kids had been through hell over there in the prison camps, and then the damn-fool Army sticks a knife in their backs. It stinks."

I asked him if he believed Major Alley was innocent.

"Yes," he said. "I'm certain. Absolutely certain."

Gerry wanted me to come back to Erna's house with him. He said she had asked him to bring me back. I followed in my own car, and was surprised when we drove right by her house in Salisbury

Cove. We went another ten miles and pulled up on the wooded lawn of a cottage sitting by a bay. Erna came out onto the porch and waved. She had been sitting in the sun all morning, she told me. She and Ronald had bought this cottage in Oak Point just a year before his death. He'd had one summer to work on the place where they were planning to spend their years together after he retired and sold his surveying business.

"This was our dream world," she said, smiling.

"Why don't we go on inside?" Gerry said.

In the living room were several boxes on the floor, boxes that had been filled with papers from the table in the Alleys' house. We sat before wide windows looking out on the ocean, and I took notes for several hours while Erna spoke about her husband, pausing from time to time to allow Gerry to underscore or clarify certain things.

Again I was struck by her absolute certainty that Ronald had not been guilty. She had never once doubted his innocence, she said. "I want you to know that the truth will prove him innocent. My son has to know the truth."

Her son was the reason she gave me when she talked about needing to find the truth. It was as if by telling me this she could make me see that, even though *she* was already convinced, the truth still had to be found for her *son.* She also said that someone had to be willing to tell the truth to the people. The implication was that, because I was a writer, this could be left to me.

There was something quietly compelling about the way Erna spoke that afternoon. And also something very sad. She said it still did not seem that Ronald was dead, that this time he was truly gone — that there would be no letters from him and he would not be coming home again. He had been gone from her so much over the years. "It's like it always was," she said. "I write things down, things to ask him about when he comes through the door again."

She believed he may have had some notion of his death approaching when he went to my office. The day before, she had gone cross-country skiing along the beach, and when she returned to the house Ronald was waiting for her at the front door. "He said he was worried about me. I told him that was silly, and he said he didn't know what would become of him without me."

Later that afternoon they spoke again, but this time Erna mentioned that someday he ought to write down the combination to the safe upstairs, just in case anything ever happened to *him*. The day after he died Erna found that he had left the safe unlocked and he had put a large sum of cash in an envelope with her name and the combination written on it.

When she spoke today in Gerry's presence she was very critical of the Army. She made the Army out to be a feckless and immoral institution. She referred to the Army as "they." *They* ruined our life. *They* killed my husband. *They* covered up the truth about Korea. Her anger for the Army was limitless. It spread over a nameless, undefined group of people who had conspired to get her husband.

"At the court-martial," she explained again, "Colonel Logan told me he could not save my husband. He said higher-ups had told him Major Alley must be found guilty. And then, one afternoon near the end of the trial, a member of the jury, a man I remember as if it were yesterday, came to me and said, 'I wish I could do the right thing for your husband, but I have no choice.' "

She said that Ronald had never criticized the Army in front of Gary. During the Vietnam War, when even the conservative town of Bar Harbor had publicly voiced opposition to the war, Ronald tried to make Gary see that the Army was not all bad. "He said that the soldiers fighting there were not the ones to blame. He wanted Gary to respect those men who had been sent to fight for their country. And he tried to explain that there was not just one Army, but *two.* There is the Army that makes policy and the Army that follows the orders. The first Army was in the Pentagon, in Washington, and they were never to be trusted. Not ever, he said. But the other Army deserved to be honored. And Ronald always told Gary that the Korean War was the first Vietnam, the first war where the soldiers were sacrificed to the Army in the Pentagon."

Erna was describing her husband in a way I could readily understand. I got a clear picture of him as the archetype of the fiercely proud, independent man who can be found up and down the coast of Maine. He had a Mainer's mind, a mind full of dichotomies. He saw through these dichotomies with a clear, uncompromising vision, and he was puzzled when others interpreted his opposing points of view as contradictory. There were many men in Maine who would have eagerly subscribed to his theory about there being two armies in this country.

"He expected Gary to understand all this," Erna said sadly. "If

Gary had known his father the way a son is supposed to know his father, then he would be certain what Ronald stood for. But too much is missing. Too many years missing."

Of course, Erna had told me much of this before — her side of things.

Gerry interrupted finally. "I'm going to file a suit," he said.

"We plan to sue the Army," Erna said.

Their idea was to bring a three-million-dollar lawsuit against the Army for the premature and wrongful death of Major Alley. They wanted to know if I would write a story.

"I can," I told them. "But I don't think it's a good idea." I was tired of lawsuits against the government for prodigious sums of money. I turned to Erna. "I think this cheapens your cause," I said.

She responded by saying that the money meant absolutely nothing to her, but she was hoping Gerry's suit would help uncover the truth. "I only want to have the truth told," she said again.

I wrote the story the next week, and when Erna stopped by the office to thank me she brought a large envelope. "Letters," she said.

I took the envelope home and didn't open it. I had heard enough and read enough, and I felt a pressure building inside me over this story. People had begun to stop me on the street asking what I was going to do next.

I came home late from a meeting one night a few weeks later and Lee was sitting with the envelope in her lap. "You have to read these," she said.

I sat down and read them. They were letters Ronald had written Erna from Korea before he was captured. They were very personal. They made me see Erna and Ronald as just two people very much in love. I realized then, for the first time, that beyond the deep complexities of Major Alley's struggle with the Army and the Army's condemnation of him, there was the clear and simple story of two young people in love. In its simplicity the story was accessible. His letters were letters I might have written.

\*      \*      \*      \*      \*

It was cold and raining hard the day Erna took me to Ronald's grave. We parked on the side of the road and walked up the hill together. There were little flags at all the veterans' graves and they blew stiffly in the wind. When we stopped at Ronald's grave Erna got down on her knees and picked up twigs and small scraps of paper from the wet grass. The geraniums had died in the first frost of autumn.

"Winter's coming already," she said. She stood up next to me, and I wondered how I would bring myself to tell her that by the time winter arrived I would be gone. Lee and I had decided to put the house up for sale. We were planning to move to Portland. I had decided to take some time to work on a novel; anything to get away from this story, I thought to myself standing there with Erna. There had been scarcely one day in the last ten months when Ronald Alley's story hadn't been on my mind.

"I've been thinking about my daughter," Erna said thoughtfully. "She blames me for her father's death. She says if I had been willing to give up the fight, her daddy would have stopped. There *were* times when he wanted to give up and I wouldn't let him." She paused, lifted her eyes from the granite gravestone, and gazed across the cemetery. "Evelyn believes that this fight for Ronald's honor will kill me, too. She doesn't understand — I can't stop now. This is my life, this has been my life for so long." She turned to me and said, "If you write a book, Don, and I am gone, will you remember this?"

I smiled at her and told her she would be here for a long time. "Nothing's going to happen to you," I said.

"Oh, I don't know," she said. "I feel tired sometimes. And blue. I get the blues a lot, and I want to just put my head down." She watched a sea gull coast overhead. "A book would be so wonderful, though."

After a minute I said, "Erna, I'm going to be leaving." I was looking down at the grave, and when I looked up she was still staring out across the cemetery.

"A book would tell everything. I remember the day at the court-martial, there was a major called to testify, and Ronald was so . . . confident, because he had carried this man piggyback during a forced march. Ronald had saved this man's life, and he told me, 'He will tell the Army what I did.'

"He was on the witness stand, and Ronald's attorney asked him, 'Did Major Alley carry you piggyback when you collapsed?' He answered, 'No.' Ronald got tears in his eyes. It was the only time he cried. You could tell all this in a book."

"I'll be leaving in a month," I said.

She looked surprised and terribly hurt. Her expression seemed to say that she had believed *I* would not be just another of the many people who had been drawn into her life by a story, but were only passing through.

I had a list of reasons for leaving, and I told them all to her. I guess she believed them. I wasn't sure whether or not Lee really believed them, but I was relieved to be going to Portland.

*　　*　　*　　*　　*

My best friend, a friend from boyhood, John Bradford, was the only person to whom I told the truth that autumn. John had come to visit us with his wife, Marge. They were expecting their first child and were living in New York City, where John was an intern. In another year they would be moving to Washington, D.C., to begin his three-year residency in orthopedic surgery at George Washington University.

John and I had some time to ourselves, the first time in a long while, and we talked about many things. We had the kind of friendship that nourished dreams and pardoned failings. And John was to me the kind of friend to whom you would tell those things you could tell no one else.

In the evening we walked through town to my office. We had taken some pictures that afternoon, and we stood in the darkroom talking under the faint glow of the red light while the film was developing.

"You seemed happy here," John said. "I'm surprised you're leaving."

I told him it wasn't because of Lee's health or my novel or anything else I'd spoken of that day. I had sent him my story on Major Alley and I'd written him about Erna. "She wants me to write a book," I told him.

"You *want* to write books," he said.

"When Ronald Alley came to the office that day I had this strange feeling. It still doesn't make any sense, but I felt certain my life was about to change in some way. It's an important story, and I was the one who always said I wanted to write serious stories."

"You're not sure he's innocent," John interrupted.

"And I can't tell Erna that. She's absolutely certain. She's survived all these years because of her certainty. If her survival is at stake, how could I write a book?"

"You could do it," John said.

---

"And if I find he *is* guilty, then what happens? I'm sure that's why their son has stayed out of this; his father's obsession, his mother's too — she keeps telling me a book would clear his name, but Gary doesn't know that and neither do I."

I tried to explain that there was a part of me that couldn't let go, despite my uncertainty. "I feel very close to that man. Whenever I'm in this office I can almost feel his presence. A stranger is on his way to see you, coming to you for help, and he dies — I defy anyone to turn his back on that. But I need some distance from him, from his family. From his island."

I couldn't face Erna again. I wrote her a letter saying good-bye and thanking her for trusting me. When we drove out of town the last time I couldn't even look back at her house in the rearview mirror. She *had* trusted me and revealed many of her private memories to me, and I was leaving.

I did go back to Ronald's grave one last time before we left. I think I was hoping to feel more certain about things. From the beginning I had had conflicting thoughts — even on this day, standing at his grave. I began to wonder why he hadn't ended this story himself, why he had allowed Erna to go on fighting. Perhaps he believed *that* strongly in his innocence; surely a guilty man would have figured out some way to end it before his guilt was exposed.

But then I was torn again, and I wondered if *how* his story ended no longer mattered to him. Maybe his guilt or innocence no longer mattered. Maybe he knew that all the unanswered questions he and his wife had struggled to answer were killing him, and would kill his wife as well, unless someone could find the answers and end the story for her before it was too late.

# CHAPTER 6

I n Portland I found work at a weekly newspaper that was new and trying to get a foothold in the city. We wrote the tough, investigative pieces no other newspaper in the city had the courage to print. It was good work, but I was not content. All the writing I was doing for the paper and on my novel was, oddly enough, leading me back to Major Alley. It was like being caught in an undertow. The characters I had begun to create in my novel were emerging on their own as people who go through life planning, having faith in certain things, and doing what they believe is right. Then one day they wake up and find that nothing is the way they had always thought it was. They struggle to hold on, to keep believing.

---

The more my characters resembled Ronald Alley, the more guilty I felt about abandoning him for these characters who existed only in my imagination. Then one evening in the library where I had gone to write, I found myself reading about the Korean War. Over the next two months I read everything I could get my hands on. I read about a war full of contradictions, a war which must have sharpened the dichotomies that already existed in Ronald Alley's mind.

In the first place, no one was really sure it *was* a war. There were people killed and wounded, but the Pentagon was insisting it was only a "Police Action," not a war, and no one was quite certain what that meant.

If the story of the war was confusing, it became even more so when a cease-fire was declared, the prisoners of war were released, and the Pentagon began to say publicly that some of these men had misbehaved. Twenty-one GIs (described by *Time* magazine as marijuana smokers and homosexuals) were in the media spotlight after they declared they would not return to the United States, because they had discovered in Communist captivity that America was a land of capitalistic warmongers.

Every major publication in the United States seized the POW story. The articles covered broad philosophical issues, all boiling down to a series of questions: Were the POWs brainwashed and indoctrinated by the Communists? Did the POWs behave differently from those in previous wars? Did the POWs collaborate with their Communist captors? Should the POWs be punished?

In August 1955 *Time* magazine published an article entitled "A Line Must Be Drawn," which described the president's and the Defense Department's response to POW conduct in Korea:

"By virtue of the authority vested in me as President of the U.S., and as Commander in Chief of the Armed Forces of the U.S.," President Eisenhower last week enunciated the U.S.'s first formal code of conduct for prisoners of war. The code resulted from the bitter experience of the Korean War, in which 38% of 7,190 U.S. prisoners of war died of disease, malnutrition or maltreatment, (The highest death rate among U.S. prisoners since the Revolutionary War. During the Civil War, 14% of the Union's P.W.s died in Confederate captivity, including 26% of the 49,485 prisoners at Andersonville, Ga. During World War I, 4,120 U.S. soldiers were captured, but only 147 died in the German Kaiser's prison camps. During World War II, the toll was 14,090 out of 129,701 U.S. prisoners — a cruel 10.9%; 10,031 out of 26,943 U.S. Army and Air Force prisoners died in the hands of the Japanese — 37% — while only 1,238 out of 96,321 Army and Air Force prisoners died in the European and Mediterranean theaters.) and in which at least 192 P.W.s were found chargeable with collaborating with the enemy. It was a stern document, founded upon "the qualities which we associate with men of integrity and character," for it summoned U.S. fighting men to defy enemy interrogators, and to deny the enemy the advantages of luring Americans from their allegiance.

"A line of resistance must be drawn somewhere, and initially as far forward as possible," the Defense Department's Advisory Committee on Prisoners of War reported to the President. "The name, rank and service number provisions of the Geneva conventions is accepted as this line of resistance. However, in the face of experience, it is recognized that the P.W. may be subjected to an extreme of coercion beyond his ability to resist. If in his battle with the interrogator he is driven from his first line of resistance, he must be trained for resistance in successive positions. And, to stand on the final line to the end — no disclosure of vital military information, and above all no disloyalty in word or deed to his country, his service or his comrades." President Eisenhower appended his own soldierly footnote: "Every member of the armed forces of the U.S. is expected to measure up. . . ."

The *Time* article contained the official Defense Department response to a lengthy POW study, a formal Code of Conduct that President Eisenhower promulgated on August 17, 1955, one week before Ronald Alley's court-martial thirty miles north of Washington, D.C.:

**1.** I am an American fighting man. I serve the forces which guard my country and our way of life. I am prepared to give my life in their defense.

---

**2.** I will never surrender of my own free will. If in command, I will never surrender my men while they still have the means to resist.

**3.** If I am captured, I will continue to resist by all means available. I will make every effort to escape and aid others to escape. I will accept neither parole nor special favors from the enemy.

**4.** If I become a prisoner of war, I will keep faith with my fellow prisoners. I will give no information or take part in any action which might be harmful to my comrades. If I am senior, I will take command. If not, I will obey the lawful orders of those appointed over me, and will back them up in every way.

**5.** When questioned, should I become a prisoner of war, I am bound to give only name, rank, service number, and date of birth. I will evade answering further questions to the utmost of my ability. I will make no oral or written statements disloyal to my country and its allies, or harmful to their cause.

**6.** I will never forget that I am an American fighting man, responsible for my actions, and dedicated to the principles which made my country free. I will trust in my God and in the United States of America.

The article noted that the Defense Department committee concluded that prisoners of war who became Communist collaborators "weakened because they lacked sufficient knowledge of U.S. democracy. The committee therefore recommended, and President Eisenhower agreed, that U.S. fighting men must henceforth be fully grounded in the principles of U.S. democracy before they go to war, because 'the Korean story must never be permitted to happen again.' "

On August 15, 1955, *Newsweek* published a story entitled "No Bands Playing," telling how an Air Force Colonel Arnold had been subjected to "the kind of systematic barbarism which few in the West can understand or believe." Beneath photographs of Arnold before and after his confinement in Korea, the colonel himself explained how he had been tortured until he couldn't stand the pain. "I have had to leave a lot out. There are some things you don't want to talk about. I told those people things that would be better if they did not know. I am very much ashamed. . . . I was not proud of it, but I have to tell you they got what I had. . . . I was gone [unconscious] for thirty hours. There were periods of complete irrationality."

For two successive weeks in August 1955, the *Saturday Evening Post* ran a lengthy story written by Air Force Lieutenant Colonel Edwin L. Heller relating his experiences as a prisoner of war. Entitled "I Thought I'd Never Get Home," the article explained that, after long months of agonizing pain, mental torture, and solitary confinement, Colonel Heller became ready to "confess" anything. Heller and other Air Force personnel were coerced into signing germ warfare confessions, confessions that the Pentagon vehemently renounced.

The *New York Times Magazine* on August 14, 1955, published a story, "For the Brainwashed: Pity or Punishment," expressing bold sentiment on the issue:

Our Armed Forces are divided over how much a prisoner of war should be expected to take and what he should be allowed to say under pressure from a ruthless captor. Officials in Washington realize now that Americans of all calibers broke more or less under the rigors of brainwashing, professional soldiers, including one steeled by the training and traditions of West Point, as well as uneducated boys from divided homes.

. . . The Pentagon realizes all too plainly now that the United States, taking humanity, decency and justice for granted, and respecting the Geneva Prisoner-Of-War Treaty, failed to prepare its young men adequately for the conditions they might encounter under harsh captors.

While the men who were brainwashed await their fate under a shaken and divided American policy, the nation is groping toward a uniform code by which its troops can meet the sterner tests of any war in the future. In the Korean War, American policy governing the treatment of repatriated American prisoners split in two, with the Air Force and Army following quite different and antagonistic codes. Should our young men submit to enemy interrogation and sign confessions and prepared statements when captured, in the hope of sparing themselves mental and physical torture, indefinite imprisonment and perhaps death? Yes, said the Air Force. Or should the nation insist that its young be Spartans to the end, giving their captors nothing more than name, rank, and serial number? This is the only conscionable policy, says the Army.

In an effort to win public support for its decision to court-martial repatriated POWs (while the Navy, Marines, and Air Force refused to do the same), the Army sponsored an extensive public-relations campaign. At the heart of this effort was Army psychiatrist Colonel William E. Mayer. As late as 1962 journalists reacted to the Army's campaign. On November 10, 1962, *The Nation* criticized the American media as a whole for their "wide dissemination of Mayer's diatribe," and went on to say: "Mayer is given nationwide credibility by mass-circulation magazines. He speaks at hundreds of colleges and Harding College of Searcy, Arkansas, will even provide you with a do-it-yourself 'Flannelboard Speech Kit' for $29.50 so that you too can deliver Colonel Mayer's address if you are not influential enough to secure the Colonel himself."

In 1963 The Macmillan Company published a book by Dr. Albert Biderman called *March to Calumny*. Biderman had inter-viewed hundreds of Korean War POWs in 1953 when he served as project scientist for a study of Communist exploitation of the pris-oners. And his book claimed that the Army had seriously distorted the POW picture. Biderman wrote this book in order to refute the charges and implications of a book published in 1957, which had been commonly regarded as the truth about the Korean War prison-ers. The book, *In Every War but One*, published by W.W. Norton & Company, was an expanded version of an article that appeared in *The New Yorker* magazine in 1957. It was authored by a popular contributor to *The New Yorker,* Eugene Kinkead. In this book the Korean War POWs are portrayed as a group who yielded to their Communist captors, in some cases with ease and eagerness. They are distinguished by the fact that none, not a single POW, escaped enemy hands. In every war but this one, according to Kinkead, there had been successful escapes.

The book goes on to imply that the exceptionally high death rate among the POWs (thirty-eight percent) was attributable not to the brutality of their confinement or to mass executions, but to the POW mentality and a general desire just to give up.

*In Every War but One* enumerates the Army's version of the POW repatriation process and the study of POW behavior that led to the Army courts-martial. According to Kinkead, the Army learned early in the war that Americans held prisoner were engaging in pro-Communist acts. These acts supposedly included propaganda radio broadcasts and newspaper articles, and they were often brought to the Army's attention by South Korean intelligence agents employed to observe activity behind enemy lines. In Kinkead's book, General Arthur Trudeau, Chief of Staff of Army Intelligence and Security at the time, reacted to the information: "From the evidence procured in this way, it was obvious that a number of Americans were collaborating. We knew what this meant. It meant that upon repatriation of the prisoners there would have to be a complete, unbiased investigation into the whole period of imprisonment of every man."

Declaring that the security of the service demanded such an investigation, Trudeau explained that the Army made plans to examine its portion of the prisoners released from Communist captivity. The examination consisted of a general psychiatric evaluation with an emphasis on counterintelligence questioning, to determine the Communist techniques imposed on the prisoners and to find out who the collaborators were. The Army set up ten Joint Intelligence Processing Teams, each consisting of seventy-two specialists to handle the returning prisoners. The teams (one assigned to each of the nine Army transports bringing the POWs home and the tenth assigned to those in temporary hospitalization in geographic locations west of the United States mainland) questioned prisoners to determine if a man had yielded to Communist indoctrination and to what extent. Each team was headed by a board of seven men composed of four intelligence representatives, a lawyer, a psychiatrist, and a board chairman.

All questions, examinations, interviews, and tests by the Joint Teams were completed by the time the three-week voyage home was over. At that point the teams filed preliminary reports on the POWs. The reports were then disseminated from Sixth Army Headquarters to various field commanders to whom the repatriates would be assigned. After the commanders had the opportunity to review the files and add their own personal observations, the files went to the Intelligence branch of the Department of the Army, where the information in the files was correlated. Included in the information were statements by prisoners that named other prisoners as having committed acts of collaboration. Some files are said to have contained hundreds of names.

Of the thousands of men questioned and the thousands of files compiled, the Army decided that 215 of these cases of men still in the Army and 210 cases of men already discharged required further evaluation. In other words, these 425 men appeared most guilty of collaboration. The files of those 210 men already discharged from the Army were referred to the Federal Bureau of Investigation with the Army's recommendation that the FBI investigate them as possible security risks. The 215 files of men still in the Army were again reviewed by what the Army called "a specially selected group of legal, intelligence, and combat officers."

Kinkead assures the reader that these files were examined without bias by the Army. Eighty-two of the 215 cases were eventually approved for court-martial. Of these eighty-two, forty-seven were finally approved for court-martial by the Army's Board on Prisoner-of-War Collaboration, established in 1954 by the Chief of Staff and the Secretary of the Army. Fourteen of the forty-seven cases were ultimately court-martialed. The Army claims these fourteen were the most guilty.

Lieutenant Colonel Charles M. Trammell, Jr., a Plans and Policy Officer who served as Special Counsel to the Army's Intelligence Sector at the time, is quoted in Kinkead's book, when asked to comment about the justification for the courts-martial: "The trials were, after all, a matter of simple logic. The Army had formulated certain policies for the conduct of its personnel which it believed to be the right ones. . . . Once these had been agreed upon, the decision had to be supported consistently thereafter by all the disciplinary machinery at the Army's command — or these policies, and other Army policies, would become completely meaningless."

What surprised me was that Kinkead's book seemed to tell only the Army's official side of things, and that he had overlooked the truth which was so obvious to Ronald Alley — that the Army in Washington, D.C., was only *one* Army and was never to be trusted.

I kept reading about the war. Erna kept writing me letters. She had made it through another winter. She still talked about a book.

In April of 1979 I received a copy of the Alley court-martial transcript and an FBI file on Ronald Alley that I had requested under the Freedom of Information Act. The file contained thirty-six pages with a cover page labeled "Bureau File 100–363987."

I'd completely forgotten about the file. But when I sat reading it I discovered the name of an Army officer who had been involved in the process of repatriating POWs after the war. Most of the names and addresses in the file had been deleted with a heavy black marker, but his was still visible.

Within a few minutes I had reached Colonel Marion Panell by telephone. When I identified myself and explained why I was calling, the colonel seemed eager to talk about the Alley case, and quite confident of his recollections. He told me he had been on an Army processing board that had collected and reviewed all the material assembled by the Defense Department's Joint Intelligence Processing Teams. He had also been called as a potential prosecution witness at the court-martial in 1955. Commenting about this, Panell said: "I think I was called as a prosecution witness, but I was never asked to testify. I was called because I was on the main board that processed all the intelligence reports on the Korean War POWs. My board saw all the dossiers on all of them."

Colonel Panell remembered the Alley file, and when I told him that Alley had gone to prison, he replied: "He shouldn't have gone to prison. Maybe if a man hadn't cooperated with the enemy he and his men wouldn't have gotten out alive. That was the thing you never knew."

Panell went on to say that he did not think the Army had intentionally made Alley a scapegoat: "I think the times and the American people demanded that someone go to prison. This was one way to disprove Senator McCarthy's claims about the Army being soft on Communist sympathizers."

When I asked Colonel Panell how the Army could have narrowed down their suspected collaborators for the courts-martial, he replied: "We had names. Everybody was accusing everybody else. Almost all the prisoners had technically collaborated. They were all potential defendants."

Kinkead's book, I told Panell, had made it seem like the Army had legitimate methods of validating one prisoner's accusations against another. He replied: "We couldn't really validate the accusations. You don't know anything about the people making the accusations. Many of the people doing the accusing were also accused. They were all scared about what might happen."

Colonel Panell stressed the fact that he believed the Army had been doing the best it could to be fair, but that, in the end, accusations of guilt had been treated as proof of guilt.

Colonel Panell was convinced in his own mind that Major Alley should not have gone to prison. He spoke with no trace of doubt or ambivalence about this.

It was this conversation with Panell that made me begin to seriously question the Army's side of the Alley case. In Kinkead's book the Army had made the whole process appear so proper and efficient; Panell's statements placed all that in doubt.

And there was more. I discovered in the FBI file a memo written in 1960 to J. Edgar Hoover (then director of the FBI) from an agent named Lawrence Sullivan, who referred to Ronald Alley's campaign for the Bar Harbor Town Council:

Another Communist running for public office.

Regards,

L.S.

When I read this I called Erna. She was furious. She said that she and Ronald had suspected many times that they were being followed and that their telephones were tapped. "It went on until 1965," she said. "From time to time there would be this noise on the telephone, a clicking sound. It was like the noise before, in Schenectady." I reminded her that Ronald hadn't been accused of anything or run into any trouble until *after* they'd left Schenectady, and she repeated that there had been a clicking noise on her telephone there. She was certain. And there was more, she said. Something else had happened there, something she still hated to think about and had never told anyone but Ronald. "I can't talk about it on the phone," she said.

"Write it then," I said. "Write me as soon as you can."

Three days later her letter arrived, describing in detail what had happened.

It was in 1951, in the spring. We had spent Christmas in Maine, the children and I, and then we went back to Schenectady. I was downstairs in my friend's apartment. I had the children with me and she had her two. There was a knock at the door. A man asked to speak with me. He asked for Mrs. Alley. He was a handsome man, and very well dressed. He said he wanted to talk with me about my husband. I was so excited. "Do you know anything about him?" I asked. He nodded his head and asked if there was some place we could speak privately. We went upstairs to my apartment. My friend kept the children with her. I sat on my couch in the living room and he sat at one end of this couch. He said he was a POW himself and had escaped. He said he was the only one to escape. And he told me how he had gotten away. Then all of a sudden he said, "Why does a pretty girl like you wait for her husband to come back from over there? You'll have to face the fact, he probably won't ever get home alive. You know your husband is not well." I said, "What do you mean, not well?" And he said he had known Ronald in the camp and that he was sickly. He got up then and came toward me and sat right down next to me. And he changed completely. He put his arm around me and tried to pull me close to him. I struggled to get away. I said, "You have brought me all the more problems after what I have suffered! Don't you think I have problems already? You do this to me to shame me." I was humiliated. He straightened out and then he said he was sorry. It was later when my friend told me he had been around the apartment while I was away. He and another man had been asking questions about Ronald and me.

In the letter Erna wrote: "I still hope and pray for a book, Don. I have never lied to you about anything and I wish you could help us."

All through that summer of 1979 when I tried to work on my novel I felt like an impostor. I kept going back to the notes from my conversation with Colonel Panell and to Kinkead's book. It was his book that led me to a discovery that changed everything. His book noted that one officer had been sent to prison for collaboration. No name was given, and when I read this I thought it must have been a mistake. It was in August that I telephoned the Army Historian's office in Washington, D.C. Someone working in the office confirmed to me that this one officer was Major Ronald Alley. There were no others, he told me. It was several days later when I spoke with this person again, and he told me then that there had been no officers sent to prison for collaboration during the Vietnam War. None during World War I or World War II. "There may have been some during the Civil War," he said. "Our records aren't complete back that far. But in this century Alley is the only one."

I drove to Bar Harbor the next day and told all this to Erna.

"If I had known before," I said awkwardly.

"But now you see," she said.

"I want to spend a few days here," I told her. "I'd like to look up Ronald's parents."

I had waited too long. We went back to Ronald's grave that afternoon. Alongside his grave were those of his father and mother: Howard O. Alley 1896–1979. Thelma P. Alley 1901–1978. Within little more than a year after their son's death they too had died.

I looked at Erna and thought to myself, We're running out of time.

Before I left Bar Harbor I promised her I would find out why Ronald had gone to prison, why he had been the only one. "I'll write the book."

"I only want the truth," she said.

And for what seemed to be a long time we stood there speaking of this word *truth,* certain now that it existed, certain that it could be found and that I would find it.

# CHAPTER 7

J ohn Bradford and his wife were living in Washington now, and I called there right away to say I would be coming down. "I knew you'd meet our son sooner or later," John said. He wasn't surprised that I hadn't been able to let go of the Alley story. I told him I didn't have any answers yet, just too many questions to ignore.

That was exactly how it was. I'd made a decision without really making a choice. It wasn't that I'd said yes to this story, but that it was impossible to say no any longer. I believed then that I would go to Washington, find what I needed to find, and then write it all down in a book. There had to be Army files that held answers, the proof or absence of proof of Major Alley's guilt.

I wrote a few free-lance stories for money to help with the trip. Then, the day before I was to leave, Lee became ill. I was going to cancel the trip, but she insisted I go.

I rode a bus to Boston and then caught a train. I kept thinking how hard it would have been for me to cancel or even postpone this trip, how grateful I was that Lee had not held me back now that everything was pulling me toward Washington. It was October 1979, twenty-one months since I'd met Major Alley, and now it seemed unbelievable that I had not started months before. My reluctance seemed to have disappeared almost overnight. It was as if some part of me had been waiting all along to get started, and then — after Colonel Panell, the Army historian, and Kinkead's book — I couldn't have stopped for anything. At least by making this trip I was moving my feet again. On the train it felt good to be in motion.

I stopped in New York City on the way. Al Robbins, a producer for NBC News, had assured me I would be able to view the tapes of their 1976 television interview with Major Alley. John Cochran, news correspondent for NBC, had visited the Alleys in Bar Harbor and conducted several hours of taped interviews which were then used to produce a five-minute special for the "NBC Nightly News" program. When I arrived at the station, Al Robbins said he had disappointing information — somehow the tapes had been erased.

"All of them?" I asked.

"Yes," he said.

I thought to myself how this revelation would only make Erna more certain of some kind of conspiracy. I listened as Mr. Robbins explained how tapes were frequently erased. "The moon walk tapes were erased by accident, too," he said.

I stayed in New York only a few hours, then continued on to Washington. I had found, just prior to leaving Maine, that General Arthur Trudeau, the former Chief of Army Intelligence who was quoted extensively in Kinkead's book, was still alive and living near the capital. Trudeau had not promised to meet with me, but I was determined to see him and I hoped that if I just showed up at his door he wouldn't turn me away.

Those first few days in Washington I was like a man chasing his hat in a gale. In the Pentagon no one would discuss the Alley case with me. I was sent to various desks, and when I finally met the Army major in charge of Korea, he said, "I can't tell you much about the war. I wasn't even born yet, to tell you the truth."

General Trudeau did not see the point of a personal meeting. I waited for him one afternoon on the eighteenth green of the Chevy Chase Country Club and he politely waved me off.

I was working in the library of the *Washington Post* one morning, going through a file of old press releases on Major Alley's court-martial, when a man came up to me, looked down at what I was reading, and said, "I wrote most of those." He introduced himself as Charles Puffenbarger, an editor at the *Post*.

Puffenbarger explained that he had covered the Alley trial for the Associated Press: "I was just starting out then. I was twenty-five or twenty-six years old."

He remembered Alley, and told me his recollections of the court-martial at Fort Meade: "I think when the trial began we all felt Alley wouldn't be convicted. I mean, he may have been technically guilty, but we all felt that whatever he did, he did under pressure from the enemy.

"He looked like a soldier right down the line. I had lunch with him one day and got to talk with him. He was a very friendly guy, I remember. Very relaxed. You could tell he believed he'd be acquitted. He never believed he'd be found guilty, and neither did I. Even after the sentence came down I just figured someone would intervene on his behalf.

"I remember he just sat there and looked straight ahead, and then he stood at attention when they read the decision. I remember his wife broke down then."

Puffenbarger said that the trial never got much press attention: "Most of the papers just picked up my stuff off the wire. They weren't terribly interested."

After talking with Puffenbarger I telephoned General Arthur Trudeau again. He was certain there was no reason for us to meet, and in his voice there was more than a trace of suspicion. I asked if we could just discuss the POW interrogations conducted under his authority while he was Chief of Army Intelligence.

"You need to talk with Colonel Trammell," he told me. "He was in charge of the interrogations."

I asked if he knew where I could find Trammell.

"He may be dead for all I know," he replied. "Hell, you're talking about something that happened a long time ago."

---

I suggested we could discuss the Kinkead book. He said he had never heard of the book. I explained that the author had quoted him in it. He replied: "Well, a lot of people quote me. They used to quote me all the time. A lot of the time they quoted me incorrectly."

After a long silence, the general told me again that I should find Trammell. "And Senator Charles Potter. He's retired now, but he was in on the Army-McCarthy hearings up on the Hill. Speak to him and Trammell. I'd prefer to leave it at that."

Senator Charles Potter was retired from politics, but he now ran a business in the District of Columbia. On the telephone he seemed extremely interested in the Alley story, and he volunteered to have someone go through his files and check for any mention of that case.

When I asked Senator Potter if he knew anyone else who might have information on Major Alley, he said, "Find General Arthur Trudeau. And Colonel Trammell."

Someone doing a favor for a friend had obtained Trudeau's address for me. That same person checked the files for Colonel Trammell the next morning and found nothing. I was told that Trammell in all likelihood was dead.

I decided to telephone General Trudeau again. This time I took a different tack. I told him I had read that the Korean War could have been won if the Army had been tougher. "That's a lot of bull!" he declared. After that I asked if he would tell me his side of things, and he grudgingly told me to come to his house the next day.

The general, a soft-spoken, intelligent man with a cherubic face and white hair, sat with me in the second-floor study of his home in Chevy Chase, Maryland. The signs of a long military career were everywhere in the room: miniature cannons for bookends; the photograph of a younger, trimmer Arthur Trudeau at his West Point graduation; a framed full-page photograph of the general on a 1960 cover of *Missiles & Rockets* magazine. On his desk an opened book — *The Campaigns of Alexander.*

For the better part of an hour we talked about the Korean War, and then I switched the conversation to the POWs and Major Alley. When I told the general that Alley had spent time in Leavenworth, he grimaced and got up from his desk to walk over to the window.

He turned his back to me and began talking, almost as if he were delivering a soliloquy: "I had some trouble with the Army myself. Dulles was head of CIA. His brother was at Defense. As intelligence chief I was concerned about security in the new Bonn government when our classified documents were about to pass to them as a new NATO partner. I expressed that fear, that the Communists had infiltrated the government in Germany. I was eventually proven right, but it was rough on public relations, and so I was transferred and made Chief of Research and Development. Here, you can read all about it." The general handed me a copy of Richard Helms's new book, *The Man Who Kept the Secrets*.

"I warned the German chancellor about Communist agents in his organization in 1954. Dulles went to Eisenhower and demanded my transfer. Ike was soft. A good general, but soft."

We talked awhile about the Army-McCarthy hearings. He said he believed McCarthy's hunches were accurate but his tactics were wrong. When I asked if he thought it was possible that the Army might have sent an officer to prison in 1955 in order to dispel McCarthy's accusations about the Army being soft on Communists, he answered: "I don't know what I can say. I hope not. I'd like to know myself. You've got to get the intelligence records and you have to get Potter's files. If Trammell is dead, that's too bad. But honestly, it was Trammell who knew about the interrogations. I had nothing to do with them on that level."

After the meeting with General Trudeau I spent several hours in an Arlington restaurant talking with a Washington attorney, Colonel Ford Young, who had answered a letter from me about the Alley case. I'd discovered his name in a newspaper clipping and had read that he'd assisted Alley's defense attorney, Colonel Logan (now deceased), at the 1955 court-martial.

Colonel Young, in his seventies now, characterized the Army's prosecution of POWs as an outrage.

"No other branch of the service prosecuted those poor bastards after what they'd been through in North Korea. The Army had done ninety-seven percent of the ground fighting, and the war had not been won. I was there. I was a captain myself and I know. The Army needed to blame the loss of the war on someone. It was a disgrace that they were allowed to get away with it, and that the press and the public went along."

He shook his head and fell silent, then continued. "How can you condemn a soldier for something he said or did while the enemy held a bayonet at his throat?"

Speaking about the Alley case, Colonel Young explained this element of Colonel Logan's defense strategy in the court-martial: "My role in that — hell, I was just a young man then. I was just following through on a plan that Alley's defense counsel had come up with. It was a brilliant plan. I filed a writ of habeas corpus, saying in essence, 'You have the body, we want the body,' to take the trial out of the military's hands. To put it in a civil court. Well, we lost. The federal judges were too damned hard-nosed. They hadn't fought in Korea and they were content to just leave the whole matter up to the military. The Army's charges against Alley, in our view, amounted to treason, and treason had to be tried in a civil court. But the Army said it wasn't treason, but something *akin to treason,* whatever the hell that means. Those are their words, 'akin to treason.' The federal judge went along with it."

That night John and I were up late talking when the telephone rang. John answered it, and said it was for me. There was a man's voice on the line, and when I asked him his name, he said: "I know some people at the Pentagon. You should talk with the Army Board for the Correction of Military Records."

He waited while I wrote that down. I asked him a second time for his name. "That's not important," he said. There was nothing menacing or melodramatic in his tone of voice. In fact he was cheerful in a way. "Just follow this up" was the last thing he said.

Lying in bed when sleep would not come, I turned over in my head all the people with whom I'd ever spoken about Major Alley. In the morning I awoke thinking about Senator Potter. There had been something sincere, a concern bordering on contrition, about him when we'd spoken five days earlier.

Later that morning I waited in the offices of Maine's Republican Senator William S. Cohen, until one of the senator's staff workers got an assurance from the Pentagon's Congressional Liaison Office that this time I would be allowed to meet with someone to discuss the Alley case. A representative of the Army Board for the Correction of Military Records would be waiting for me, I was told.

In Washington they use words like bright, precocious, and polished to describe Senator William Cohen. Known as a man of exceptional poise and integrity from his early days as a congressman in Washington, he became a senator with the reputation as a mover and a shaper of events in the capital, a man who could get things done, his way. He was much too careful a politician to speak out publicly about the Alley case or to do battle with the Army over it until he had the facts, but for several years his staff had kept a file on Major Alley, and the senator made it clear to me he was willing to help open doors in my search for the truth. This morning there was a door at the Pentagon he was going to push.

It was just after eleven o'clock that morning when I presented myself at the information desk in the Pentagon concourse next to the metro exit. I was waiting for the officer on duty at the desk to get off the telephone when a woman with teased hair and a pink carnation corsage pinned to her bosom walked up to me and said, "You're back for another try?"

On half a dozen previous visits I had not managed to get any farther than this desk. I explained to the woman that this morning I was going in to see someone on the Army board. I said they would be calling the information desk any minute. She just nodded and walked away, disappearing in the crowded concourse.

At the end of an hour one of Senator Cohen's workers telephoned to say they were having trouble with the Congressional Liaison people. "You'll have to stand by. We're trying."

After another hour I telephoned the board myself. A woman informed me that all calls from the press had to go through Public Affairs. She had just hung up when a call came for me from another woman, in the Public Affairs office. She was calling simply to underscore the fact that all requests to talk with members of the board, the Army's highest review board, must be channeled through Public Affairs.

By two o'clock there was still no word from the Congressional Liaison office, though the woman in Public Affairs had called the desk for me every half hour to repeat her instructions.

I'd been waiting three and a half hours and I was about to give up when I spotted the woman in the pink corsage walking toward me. She smiled knowingly. "What in the world are you after, anyway?" she asked.

I told her in five minutes everything I knew about the story of Major Alley and his wife. I told her I had come all the way from Maine to find some answers for the major's son.

"Oh, dear God," she said. She paused for a moment, looked around, then took hold of my arm and led me through a crowd of people, off to one side of the corridor. "Come with me," she said. "When we get to the guards, just lean against me and put your arm around me like this."

From a distance of about fifty feet I saw the entrance to a long, battleship-gray corridor leading from the concourse into the central area of the Pentagon. I saw the glass doors and then the beginning of a tiled ramp. Two guards in stiff uniforms stood silently at these doors. One was searching a briefcase while the other glared straight ahead. I watched them hypnotically until we were within a few feet of the doors. Suddenly my escort pulled me close to her chest and blurted out, "Hey, Sammy, how's the bowling?" We didn't wait for an answer, but swept past them as Sammy, totally disarmed by the pleasant greeting, waved cheerfully.

At the far end of the corridor we stopped by a water cooler. She quickly drew a map of the building, tracing the maze of hallways and ramps that led to the basement wing where the Army board was quartered. "Just walk like you know where you're going, and don't tell anyone how you got here," she said.

I presented myself at the basement offices of the Army Board for the Correction of Military Records, where a receptionist sat at a desk in front of a wall-size map of Vietnam. She looked up at me, and when I told her who I was she told me I had no business being there. I was taken immediately to see her boss, a man named Plant.

Mr. Plant stood in a sparsely furnished office behind a desk the size of a billiards table. He held a match to the end of a stubby cigar which was clenched between his teeth. I told him who I was, and he interrupted, "I already know who you are." I began to explain why I had come, and he interrupted a second time, "I know what you want to talk about."

I started right in again, telling Mr. Plant that Major Alley had twice appealed to this board to have his case reopened, and had been twice denied. I asked what it would take to reopen the case. My only intention, I quickly told him, was a thorough reexamination of the facts, which could bring the truth his widow was hoping for.

Mr. Plant sat down at his desk. "There's a correct way to discuss this," he said.

I asked what he meant.

"There's a right way and a wrong way to speak to me. You're going about it the wrong way."

"I'm sorry, can you explain?" I asked.

"Public Affairs. Go through Public Affairs."

"I've spoken with the people in — "

"I'm aware of that."

"I waited, and no one called back."

"Public Affairs called back."

"Yes, that's right, but I wanted to speak with you."

"You go through Public Affairs."

"I'd just like to ask you about the case of Major Alley."

"Look, now I've tried to be nice. I'm not going to discuss that case or any case with you. Is that clear?"

"We can't discuss the Alley case?"

"No."

"I'm not sure why we can't. It was a court-martial open to the public. The press was there."

"I've been pretty clear, haven't I?"

"Are you saying I have no right to be here?"

Mr. Plant slowly got up from his chair, circled his desk, and stood two feet away, facing me. "You have a right to be anywhere you want, I suppose. I'm telling you to go through Public Affairs."

"Then you're saying the board won't talk about the Alley case?"

"I didn't say that, did I?"

"That's what it amounts to."

"All right, then."

There was a silence. Mr. Plant puffed on his cigar.

"What's your title, sir?" I asked.

"My name is Francis Plant. That's P-L-A-N-T. I'm Deputy Assistant Secretary of the Army in charge of military review boards and personnel security."

"Then you *are* the person I need to speak to."

"You won't speak to me like this," he said.

Five minutes later, while a staff worker from Senator Cohen's office was still trying to get me *into* the Pentagon, I was escorted *out*. In the concourse the woman at Public Affairs was on the telephone waiting for me. "You should have gone through this office," she said. "The people on that board aren't used to dealing with the public."

I wasted two more days at the Pentagon trying to find someone who would discuss the Alley case. "The word is out," I was told in Senator Cohen's office. "They know you want to talk about Alley."

The senator's office wasn't making any progress securing Major Alley's Army 201 file. Army officials were claiming it could not be located.

I wanted to see the stockade at Fort Meade, Maryland, where Ronald Alley had been locked up after the court-martial, awaiting his transfer to the prison at Fort Leavenworth. Senator Cohen's office had telephoned the Public Affairs office at Fort Meade and had been told my visit would pose no problem. I made a call to the Public Affairs officer there.

"You're going to write about this?" he asked.

"That's possible," I said. "Senator Cohen's office contacted you."

"That sort of eludes me. I don't recall speaking with anyone."

"Well, will you check on it?"

"Sure thing, let me call you back."

"When will you call?"

"Give me a couple of hours anyway. What did you want to see up here?"

"The stockade."

"You're writing about the stockade?"

"Someone who was locked up there. Major Ronald Alley. In 1955."

"That happened a long time ago. I wouldn't count on taking any pictures. I mean, that probably won't be allowed."

"No pictures. I just want to see the stockade."

He called back an hour later.

"Ah, Mr. Snyder, it won't do you any good to come to the fort. We built a new stockade in 1958."

"Really?"

"That's right, and you wouldn't be allowed to go inside."

"Why not?"

"Regulations."

"But Senator Cohen's office already checked that out with your people there."

"I don't care what was checked out. I'll read you the regulations. Right here it says — "

"No, please, don't bother reading."

He read anyway.

"Why does that apply to me?" I asked. "I want to see the *old* stockade, the one that's no longer in use. So I should be able to go inside."

"That I didn't check on," he admitted. "It's probably torn down by now anyway."

"Well, will you please check on it?"

"You can look at the new one from the outside. Wait a minute."

He left the telephone and then returned. "Yeah, you can see the new one from the outside."

"I need to see the old stockade. The one Major Alley was in."

"When?"

"1955. November 1955."

"No, no. When do you want to see it?"

"Today. Now."

"I'd have to get a date. I don't know how long that could take."

"Well, why don't you go find out. I'll hold."

"Look, you can see the new stockade from the outside. No pictures. I don't know where the old stockade is."

"You don't know where it is?"

"That's correct."

"Well, there must be someone at the fort who does. Will you please find out?"

He left the telephone and the line went dead. When I called him back he began reading the same regulations to me again. I told him I found it hard to believe that no one there knew where the old stockade was.

"Look, I read you the regulations. Now, you can see the new stockade, today. From the outside only. No pictures."

"I understand that. But where is the old stockade? And why can't I see it?"

"The man who knows where the old stockade is isn't in today."

"Will he be in tomorrow?"

"Maybe."

\*     \*     \*     \*     \*

"Public Affairs has a trick," I said to John that night. "They keep you moving around the outside, hoping you'll give up from exhaustion before you get anywhere."

Late that night I got a phone call from the same person who had telephoned me before. Again he wouldn't give me his name. "You can't afford to get the board angry at you," he said. "Write an apology to Francis Plant."

I took the train back home and forgot all about writing to Plant. I didn't think I had anything to apologize for anyway.

My first week back in Maine I found a book by Senator Potter in the Portland library. In it the senator had written about the Mc-Carthy hearings and about his personal role in them. I called his Washington, D.C., office to ask him if he had been the one who'd telephoned me anonymously. The senator, I was told, had passed away only a few days after my trip back to Maine.

# CHAPTER 8

I tried to make Erna see that I had really gotten nowhere in Washington. I had no Army files. I had met neither a single soldier held prisoner with Ronald, nor anyone who had testified at the court-martial. I had not found anyone in the Army who would discuss her husband's case, or even the Army's official policy toward Korean War prisoners.

"I'm so angry," she said. "I cannot sleep I'm so angry."

I tried to console her. I told her it was only a matter of time before something good happened. I concealed things from her. I didn't tell her what the officer in Public Affairs at the Pentagon had said to me when I'd asked her what the Army policy was governing

POWs now, and if it had changed since Korea. She didn't know, she said. Then she added: "Policies change over the years. The Army shot a man for something he wouldn't be shot for today. That's life — policy changes."

I was angry myself. I had lost some innocence at the Pentagon and I'd begun to see the Army as an adversary — exactly as Erna had portrayed it. "Something good will happen," I told her.

"I've spent my life waiting for that," she said.

A few weeks later this letter arrived from a German police officer who had known Ronald after World War II:

Eric Mauch
Chief Executive of the German Police Academy for the
County of Baden-Wuerttemberg

Dear Mr. Don J. Snyder:

You have the intention to write a book about Ronald Alley's life. I want to thank you for that. In 1945 I was released by the Americans. This is when I had my first contact with the US Troops. Between August and September 1945 I did preliminary work to organize the German Police for the US Military Government in Stuttgart under the public safety officer Lt. Col. Perry. The first of October 1945, I worked with the newly organized police in the US part of Wuerttemberg-Baden. Through my work I got to know all the nineteen county Military Governors. Captain Alley was the youngest of the nineteen governors, and he worked for the County of Crailsheim. From the beginning he had a very clear sight into the German police which was at that time in very bad condition; no uniforms, and no weapons and everyday stealings from the farmers.

During the summer of 1946 I became County Police Chief in Crailsheim because Captain Alley was not happy with the one he had and had to let him go. I found Captain Alley was a very energetic officer. His first order was to make sure that the people have food and have been properly taken care of. Captain Alley understood the many problems the German people had.

Because of the no-fraternization policy it was difficult for a US officer to do the right thing for both parties. In his work it

---

**100**

was Captain Alley's duty to help the children of the county. He started football clubs and have been in close contact with German mayors. Captain Alley showed a lot of understanding for the poor people, and his congenial approach was very remarkable. In the progress of the Democratic endeavor of the US Military Government in all counties, approximately sixty villages, hearings were held under the direction of Governors and also participation of all German governmental leaders. Those hearings have been a great success to help remove the suspicion of occupied forces and the German public. Captain Alley had an interest also in partnership between Crailsheim and the English city, Wurthington [sic], to establish one of the first partnerships in Germany.

Captain Alley also had a very close contact with the churches. Especially one whose minister had been persecuted by the Nazis. He later became Minister of Education for the County Baden-Wuerttemberg.

Very distinguished was the way Captain Alley handled justice: He immediately recognized people with bad character and if one did not do the right thing he had to take the punishment. As Police Chief it was also for that reason easy to work for Captain Alley. With a clear conscience I can say that we never had any difficulties in working together. The following will show how much justice meant to him: We had to arrest a gristmill owner who had poached with a German military rifle. The gristmill had about thirty deer hides and fresh deer meat. The American Military Court found him guilty and his sentence was three years in jail. Another gristmill owner who owned a large parcel of land for hunting purposes only had hidden his and his friends' guns and received a six month jail sentence. This was certainly punishable. An anonymous person had reported him. Captain Alley found the great difference in the sentences unacceptable and he sent a complaint to the headquarters to the US Military Government. And this complaint was the reason for Captain Alley's transfer to Nuertingen. The judgement and the difference in both penalties was the cause of a revolt in the County. The judgement of Captain Alley expressed the feeling of the community.

If anybody says that Captain Alley has any Communistic

leanings, it is absolutely ridiculous. There were quite a few Communists put in very important positions by the US Military Government. Some people in the Military Government thought that those people were reliable Democrats. The District President of the community himself was a former Communist. I know that Captain Alley made quite sure that this man would not be able to influence people with his Communist politics. After the first free election this man was not re-elected again. At the same election Captain Alley made sure that a former Nazi was not allowed to run as a candidate.

In conclusion, we in Crailsheim have to say that we have been very fortunate in our relationship with Captain Alley as Military Governor. He had an energetic interest in running the Military Government; silly little requirements (and there were some of them) he judged by his own rules. And he had a heart for the German population, especially the kids and the elderly. Several years ago I initiated a reunion of the former police officers and their families which I'm sure was a very happy occasion for Mr. and Mrs. Alley. To the best of my knowledge this was a once-in-a-life-time occasion in the German Republic. It showed that Captain Alley was accepted by the German people for his humanitarian behavior and on the other side because he ran the Military Government in a correct way. All of us hope that justice will be done even though he has passed away.

Eric Mauch

On December 12, 1979, John Cochran telephoned me in Portland from London, England, in response to a letter I had sent him. He was on assignment there for NBC News. Cochran had come to Bar Harbor to interview Ronald and Erna in 1976, and Erna had spoken to me often about that time, how excited she and Ronald were and how sensitive and down-to-earth John Cochran had been. They had cleaned the house and gone to town for whatever was needed to replenish the liquor supply, and then John had said he preferred a glass of beer. The only thing they didn't have. He joked that he was surprised that the kitchen of a German woman would not contain at least one bottle of good beer.

---

Cochran remembered the interview: "I had just left the Pentagon, had been what we called the Pentagon correspondent, or the closest thing to it that we had then. Carl Stern had passed on to me a letter from the Alleys, and I was immediately impressed that it was a good story. I got news film from the trial and a record of the court-martial transcript. I didn't know if Alley had been guilty of collaboration or not, but it seemed to me curious that he had been the one officer to go to prison. My piece focused on the fact that the times had changed since Korea, because of Vietnam. I talked with John Warner, who had been Secretary of the Navy, and Bo Calloway, who was Secretary of the Army. That was the angle — that times had changed and we had treated the Vietnam POWs so differently.

"Alley was an interesting guy. Maybe he had good reason to feel the way he did, that he had been singled out for some benefit to the Army higher-ups. I remember that my story concluded that he'd had one heart attack and that time might be running out for him. I had the feeling that unless something happened pretty quickly he'd drop dead one day. We talked about that. I'm afraid I muddied up the story; I was impressed by the personal side of it.

"Alley claimed there hadn't been any leadership in the POW camps, and so he stepped forward to keep people alive. He filled a vacuum. He seemed like the kind of man who would do that.

"My story ran on a Saturday night for five minutes on the evening news. This was during the last days of the Ford administration. I got quite a few calls; it provoked some interest. I contacted some people in the Ford administration about the case, but maybe they had other fish to fry or they were all out looking for jobs. Nothing came of it. And then I got tied up with other things, other stories.

"I'm amazed that my tapes have been erased though; not that my story was that good or anything. I'm just surprised."

Erna Alley was fond of Cochran. When I told her I had spoken with him, she recalled his visit to Maine: "After he did the interview, he told Ronald he would go back to Washington and see what he could do to help us. Early in January 1977 he called and told Ronald that he wanted to help him write a letter to President Ford. Mr. Cochran had just returned from a skiing trip with the president in Colorado — I remember seeing him on the news from there. He said he had a chance to speak with President Ford about Ronald's case.

He said the president wanted to do something. Mr. Cochran gave Ronald the address of a man to write to who worked in the White House. He said the letter would go through the channels to the president. I typed Ronald's letter that same evening. I believe it was January fourth or fifth. We waited, and we received a card saying that the letter had been received. But then nothing happened. We heard nothing. A few days before Mr. Ford left office John Cochran telephoned again and asked Ronald what had happened: 'Why didn't you write that letter?' he asked. He said the president had been waiting for it. Ronald was surprised and confused. He told Mr. Cochran that he had sent the letter and even had a receipt, and that the president should have gotten it a long time ago. It was after President Ford left office that we got a letter from an Army general who had been stationed at the White House. We never found out why it had taken that long for him to reply, but by this time it was too late for President Ford to help us. Ronald was very discouraged about this."

In February of 1980, I wrote a short article about the Alley story for a Maine newspaper. I was paid two hundred dollars for the piece, and we needed the money. The story prompted a letter from a retired Army colonel living on the coast of Maine.

Colonel Clifford Young wrote to tell me he knew a great deal about the Alley case and was willing to meet with me whenever it was convenient.

We met in the Portland library, and I explained that I would be taking notes. "That's fine with me," he said.

Colonel Young, a barrel-chested man with an austere manner, explained that he had held two positions in 1955, both bringing him in contact with Major Alley. Working on a Defense Department secret program called Operation Alert, Young was assigned to the Executive Office Building adjacent to the White House, where Army and civilian officials were working on a secret plan to move the White House — lock, stock, and barrel — to the inside of an undisclosed mountain cave in the event of a nuclear attack along the eastern seaboard. He described an elaborate plan.

"That was the sort of thing that was going on in those days," said Young. "People were scared."

While at the Executive Office Building, Colonel Young heard about the impending court-martial of Ronald Alley. "At the White

House and the EOB I was a walking, listening observer. I mean the fellow, Alley, was from Maine, and so was I, so I was naturally interested in his case. It didn't take long before I got the story. The attitude as far as Alley went was that they had to get him. Someone had to be sent to prison. Now don't get me wrong here; I was not a POW in Korea and so I have no comments as to the merits of the case. I never *did,* for that matter. But once Ike had come out with his new Code of Conduct, it became clear that Alley had been targeted as a major role in enforcing that."

Colonel Young gathered momentum as he spoke; it had bothered him that a man from Maine had gone to prison, and he had apparently spent much time over the years thinking about this.

"I can tell you this much," he went on, "at the White House I had good contacts with high-ranking people, and I saw through the subterfuge. I can tell you that it suited everybody that Alley had no connections to come to his defense. He was perfect — a round peg that fit in a round hole. I could never prove that Ike and Nixon had been in on the decision, but you have to remember that Mr. Nixon had gained his power in that sort of game, the red-baiting game. And there was no doubt around the EOB that Alley would be portrayed as a Communist sympathizer, a 'progressive' is what we called them in those days.

"So then I got to know Alley. It was strange how it happened: I was stationed at Fort Meade, and the post commander brought Alley to me and I was told to keep him occupied, to keep him busy until the trial began. I'd heard that I was chosen for this because I was also from Maine. When I found out Alley was from Bar Harbor, I said, 'You must know my brother then, he's a dentist there.'

"Alley was a friendly guy. I remember him as a big fellow. He had a domineering appearance, and yet there was something about him that wasn't like that at all. He was fairly fluent, but no intellectual, that's for sure. He couldn't seem to see the steamroller that was about to run over him. He was so damn confident that he'd be found innocent. Funny, the rest of us could see what was coming, but not Alley.

"Once I told him he ought to try and get his court-martial moved to Fort Devens, in Massachusetts. Get it out of D.C., where there were all these politics going on. I told him that people in the White House had questioned me about him, whether I knew if any activist groups from Maine were going to come to his defense. There weren't any activist groups in Maine. I said, as far as I knew, Alley was standing alone.

"But the thing is, he was so cocksure that the Army would stand by him. You know, he was a rube. That's it — a rube! I reminded him about the Slovik case when Ike had made an example of Slovik even though he hadn't been more guilty than any of the others. Nothing got through to Alley. And I wasn't going to go around beating the drum for him; I mean, I wanted to get my twenty years in. But in an odd way I felt a kinship for him. Probably because we were both from Maine."

Young remembered Alley's defense counsel, Colonel Logan, as a mild man who didn't want to make waves. Young thought Logan had made a big mistake in not allowing Alley to take the stand in his own defense. He believed this might have turned some of the jurors against Alley.

Colonel Young and I sat in a small restaurant on Congress Street and spent another hour going over the notes I had taken. Several times I asked if he was sure that Alley's case had been discussed at the White House in connection with President Eisenhower's Code of Conduct; from the beginning I had thought the court-martial might have served as a perfect way to buttress that new pronouncement. Young was sure.

"If you write a book, I have no stake in it," he said. "And I do have a stake in the Army. I believe in a strong Army, so if we had to take sides I'd go on the side of the Army. But I remember what I remember. In my opinion, the pressure against Alley was also exerted from the FBI. It was opaque and you might never prove it, but it was there. There was lots of pressure at the EOB. And when Alley was sentenced to prison, oh, there was great relief around the place. There was a feeling that now things had been taken care of.

"More than anything, I felt sorry for Alley. He was like a person carrying a cross up a hill. He wouldn't let anyone help him. He thought it was all going to be all right. But once he got to the top of the hill, they crucified him. It was just too bad."

By now I had filled six notebooks with details of my interviews on the Alley story. I typed these notes onto 127 pages, then sent the pages to Pennsylvania to be proofed and retyped by a professional typist. This was the first step toward Erna's book.

Four weeks later a package containing the original and one copy arrived at our apartment. The upper-left-hand corner of the package had been ripped open, and the original manuscript had been crudely folded down the middle. When I went through the pages I found that three of them were out of order in the original; they were the pages containing notes of my 1978 *Bar Harbor Times* article detailing plans of Erna's suit against the Army for three million dollars.

Later that month a very clearly defined clicking sound began to occur on our telephone. I had never heard the sound before on this or any other telephone.

As the weeks passed the sound persisted. In the spring of 1980 we moved to a small house outside the city, in the town of Cape Elizabeth, and no sooner had telephone service been installed than this clicking sound returned. Again it was clear and distinct.

The telephone company in Portland could not explain the sound, but after they sent a repairman, who heard the sound himself and shrugged his shoulders as he listened, we were assured there was nothing to be alarmed about.

I made up my mind to say nothing of this to Erna. Then, two weeks later, when I sent the manuscript to an agent in New York City, it disappeared in the mail. I waited three weeks, then sent a copy by registered mail. This time it got through.

I hoped to hear good news from New York. I was waiting for good news just as Erna was.

On March 11, 1980, Erna sent me a registered package in the mail, and she enclosed the following note:

I wanted to call you on the telephone but I can no longer trust it. The clicking noise comes all the time now.

Here is a letter which came to me from a Sergeant Wilson. It came yesterday, even though it says he wrote it at Christmas. Why did it take so long to reach me? This letter means so much to me. You tell me, Don, that you must find the people who knew Ronald. I knew him best. And here is a man who knew him. Does this sound like a traitor? I am going to see Gary this weekend and I will take this letter along. I hope we will have a book soon.

Love
Erna Alley

At the bottom of this note Erna wrote: "If the Army reads this letter, then I tell them this. I will not give in to you, no matter what you do to me."

I read the letter from Sergeant Wilson.

Dear Mrs. Alley:

Sorry to bring up sad memories at Christmas time. I have only recently learned about all your husband's misfortunes and his passing on.

I was with Captain Alley when we were first captured in December 1950 on the Chosin Reservoir in North Korea. It is hard to understand why a few was [sic] singled out for punishment. If an individual intentionally caused harm to a fellow POW, I could see some type of punitive action, but that was not the Captain Alley I knew. The first month on the Chosin was the worst of the thirty three months I was a POW.

I was in the same house as Captain Alley that first month and I will be honest in saying that he helped many of us to survive. The majority of us was [sic] seriously wounded. All had frost bite or frozen limbs. It was impossible to get anything organized.

Captain Alley, with the few that could walk, chopped wood, carried water, buried the dead and helped anyway they could. One night he and a few others slipped out and braved the fifty-degree-below-zero weather and went back down to the area where we had fought that week before. They returned with a few first-aid packets, clothing and what little else that had not been burned.

The majority of the enlisted men were young and helpless. I can remember Captain Alley literally getting into shoving matches with the Chinese about treatment according to the Geneva Convention. He demanded food, medicine and heated huts for us. It was a difficult situation. The Chinese finally moved the walking wounded which included Captain Alley and one other officer on to another camp. Had he been allowed to stay with us there would have been more survival in the spring of 1951.

Captain Alley should have been awarded a medal for his leadership and help with the wounded the first month of our captivity as far as I am concerned. I am in the process of trying to locate some of the survivors of the so rightly called "Death Valley," Chosin Reservoir area, December 1950.

I will help in any way to clear the record of one that suffered along with us in Korea and then had to suffer all over again after his return to the States. I was shocked to hear that Captain Alley had been court-martialed and sorry to hear of his passing on.

Again, wishing you and yours the best for the coming holidays. Good luck and God Bless.

Respectfully Yours,

SFC Clyde Wilson Jr. (RET)
Co. B, 1st BN. 32 Inf. Regt.
7th Infantry Division, Korea
POW Korea 1950–1953

PS Please excuse the grammer [sic] and typing. I was a good field officer but this typing is something I picked up after the Korean War.

# CHAPTER 9

One morning in early spring of 1980 Lee and I were out of money completely. I was wading through a new draft of the manuscript, this time for an editor at William Morrow & Company in New York City. The only hope I had was to get a book contract from a publisher, and along with it enough money to finish my research. There was a long way to go. Twelve publishers had already sent me rejection letters. No one wanted to pay for a book whose ending was uncertain.

This particular morning I sat at my desk going over the 1,500-page court-martial transcript. Lee was at the bottom of the stairs. I told her we would have help soon.

"That's what I've heard you telling Erna for two years now," she said.

I kept going through the pages, turning them over unconsciously and thinking how on earth two years could have gone by. Lee called up the stairs that she was was going out to look for a job. I heard the door close behind her.

Two days later I borrowed money from John Bradford and took the train back to D.C. This time I was meeting with a POW from the Vietnam War, a soldier who, according to sources in Washington, had faced Army collaboration charges in the early 1970s. It seemed unbelievable that twenty years after the Korean War the Army was once again bringing charges against their own men.

We met in a crowded office off Dupont Circle.

Robert Chenoweth, a soft-spoken and scholarly young man, did not exhibit any of the stern, intrepid qualities one might consider necessary to endure imprisonment by the Vietcong. He had been shot down in an Army helicopter in the jungles of North Vietnam in early 1967, when the war there was going full tilt. After spending five years and two months with the North Vietnamese he had been brought home a hero. Chenoweth said he was surprised at the time, and uncomfortable with the role of hero: "I was not a hero. I didn't know anyone in our village who was. I think the Pentagon made us out to be heroes because there needed to be some bright spot in the war. Heroes could divert attention from the defeat in Vietnam."

Held captive in a number of jungle villages, Chenoweth readily admitted that he and his comrades did whatever their captors asked of them. He explained that he felt no compunction about having cooperated with the enemy, and he told me that he and the POWs he knew seldom gave any thought to the matter of name, rank, and serial number. "The Geneva convention regulations and the rules outlined in President Eisenhower's Code of Conduct were almost never discussed. We were never prepared for captivity and the rules governing it. Certainly the North Vietnamese wouldn't have cared about these rules anyway."

What Chenoweth was saying could have brought him a prison sentence in the early 1950s. When I told him this, he said: "When we were prisoners we used to joke once in a while about the name, rank, and serial number thing. Some of the men may have been worried about retribution by the Army, but most of us were not. If I was ever concerned, my concern disappeared when we came home as heroes. How could the Army turn around and prosecute its heroes, the only heroes they had?"

But there had been an effort to prosecute at least some of them. In May of 1973 a man who had been a senior officer in the POW camp outside Hanoi where Chenoweth had been held brought charges against Chenoweth and seven others on the grounds of collaborating with the enemy. One week later, one of the men charged, a Marine, committed suicide. Then the Army was ordered by the Secretary of Defense to drop all charges of collaboration.

Chenoweth contended the Army had no choice. "If they were going to court-martial us for giving more than name, rank, and number, they would have had to court-martial everyone."

When I explained to him what happened to Major Alley, Chenoweth shook his head. For a moment he couldn't speak. Then he said, "He was a prisoner in the wrong war. In Vietnam he would have come home a hero."

I took a long walk from Dupont Circle to Capitol Hill. I thought about everything Robert Chenoweth had told me. The war, to him, had been a myth. Heroes, too, were part of this myth. Heroes and convicted collaborators served the same purpose for the Washington Army. They were used to prop up the myth. The Army had the power to honor or dishonor its soldiers, whichever was required to keep the myth from collapsing.

On Capitol Hill I went back to Senator Cohen's office. I had given him a list of thirty-seven names, the most influential prosecution and defense witnesses at the 1955 court-martial, and members of the jury. I needed to find these people, and I was hoping Cohen could come up with addresses.

Someone on the senator's staff met me in the hallway. There were no addresses yet. But there was some good news. I had been granted permission to return to the Pentagon to discuss the repatriation of Vietnam POWs with the Air Force. I had wanted to talk about *Korea,* with the *Army.* This was as close as we could get.

At the Pentagon I asked why I was talking with the Air Force. Claude Watkins, an intelligence specialist with the Air Force and chief of the Code of Conduct Training Branch, gave me a candid and forceful reply: "The Air Force is the executive agent, Department of Defense, for all POW affairs now because the Army fucked things up so badly after the Korean War, and then they tried to screw up again after Vietnam."

"The Air Force decides Army policy now?" I asked.

"Affirmative," Watkins said.

I spent half a day in the Pentagon with Watkins and his staff, all Air Force personnel. He spoke in unambiguous terms, telling me that the case of Major Alley was well known in the Pentagon as something of a watershed case in the history of POW affairs. This case in 1955 had been studied by the Air Force and carefully considered by the new task force that eventually recommended changes in the Code of Conduct at the end of the Vietnam War.

"The idea, or myth," said Watkins, "that American GIs give only name, rank, and number was finally abolished after 'Nam. From now on prisoners are expected to just do their best, *period.* Future POWs will be expected to help each other as best they can, and they'll be instructed that the United States government stands behind them, not to condemn them, not to court-martial them, but to support them unequivocally."

To this end, and because of the collaboration trials of the 1950s, and then the Army's plans to hold more trials after Vietnam, President Jimmy Carter officially ordered the Code of Conduct changed on November 3, 1977, by Executive Order 12017.

President Carter explained the need for these changes by writing: "Experience indicates that certain words of the Code have, on occasion, caused confusion resulting in training divergencies. . . . In order to clarify the meaning of certain words Article V is hereby amended."

President Eisenhower's Code declared: "I am bound to give only name, rank, service number and date of birth. . . ." The new Code reads: "I am required to give name, rank, service number and date of birth. I will evade answering further questions to the utmost of my ability. . . ."

There was a need to change this, according to Watkins: "Eisenhower's Code was taken from Article 17 of the 1949 Geneva convention, which said every prisoner of war when questioned is *bound* to give only his surname, first name and rank, date of birth, and serial number. This was lifted and put into the Code of Conduct in 1955 and completely misinterpreted by the Army. The Army said, 'Give them that and nothing else or it's your *ass!*' When in fact it was written to mean that, as a prisoner of war, you were *bound* to give the enemy something. The original reason for this was to help the POW, not to put pressure on him. Hell, man, the Japanese would just kill POWs, take them out and cut off their heads when they refused to answer any questions. The Geneva convention intended to authorize some form of communication, that was all. But the Army exploited it. It was a matter of semantics."

Changing the Code of Conduct had a broad influence on military justice. The Articles of War and the Uniform Code of Military Justice under which Major Alley had been court-martialed in 1955 could now be interpreted differently: those sections forbidding "unauthorized communication with the enemy" would never be the same, because now a soldier could present an arguable defense simply by claiming that his communication was not unauthorized according to the new Code of Conduct. So long as he had done his best to avoid communication, all communication would be what Watkins called "quasi-authorized."

Claude Watkins was fearless of speaking on the record about the Alley case. He said, in his buzz-saw, hard-fisted style, that the Army had used Alley as a scapegoat — "in order to get old Joe McCarthy off their back." He also said that by today's standards Major Alley would never have been court-martialed.

"With the Air Force in charge it won't ever happen again, thank God. The Air Force told its people in Korea to give the enemy any ███████ thing he wanted; there wasn't any information that could compromise our position in the war, the Air Force knew that. But the Army held this hard line. It was ███████ stupid, and its purpose was only political. Why, hell, if you tell a man he can't do *this,* and he can't step over *that* line, I can make him step over the line in thirty minutes. After that, I own him."

Watkins acknowledged that there was still opposition in the services to these changes: "There is some resentment, some knee-jerk reactions from the dinosaurs around here. But they are generally uninformed."

Before leaving the Pentagon that day I had lunch in the dining room with Watkins. We walked together down the long, gray corridors, past the harrowing photographs that showed scraps of bodies and dead American soldiers in Vietnam and Korea. We stood for a minute or so in the Hall of Honor. It was all so moving, and in such sharp contrast to the happy faces and the cheerful atmosphere of the cafeteria — to the soldiers, many of them very young men and women, in crisply pressed uniforms, to whom the idea of combat and imprisonment must be only a vague abstraction. This, in a way, is what Claude Watkins was trying to make me see; he railed against the Army policymakers for making rules to apply to situations so far from here, imponderable situations they could not begin to understand.

*    *    *    *    *

In Washington I received a curious reply to the letter I had written an old friend of Ronald's. I had written to see if he remembered any officers who might have held a grudge against Ronald Alley for one reason or another. In his reply he wrote: "Sorry. Too many years have passed to give you details about this."

I telephoned him and asked him to explain. On the phone it was obvious he was frightened of something: "I'm not going to rack my mind about something that happened twenty-five years ago."

"But Ronald was your friend," I said.

"I'm not saying anything. I can't give you anything."

"I only want to know about names," I said.

"I don't want . . . I can't answer any questions about this."

"But didn't you know him well?"

"You know I did."

"Close friends?"

(Pause) "Yes."

"Weren't you in Germany together?"

"Yes. And that's all I can say to you."

"Weren't you in the military government in Germany with him?"

"Look . . . I know what you're doing. You're trying to get me to answer questions. I'm not going to answer anything. Nothing else."

"I just want you to be reasonable — you could help an old friend," I said.

"I've been called a Communist and everything else because of this. . . . You're probably taping every word of this. . . . The FBI. That again!"

"I'm not taping, you have my word."

"I don't trust that. I don't trust anyone when it comes to this. I'm hanging up."

115

He hung up. Two hours later I called him back. His wife answered this time. "He won't speak with you," she said. "Please don't call back ever again. Please leave us alone. He's been through too much already because of this."

Much of the summer I was preoccupied working on a story for Mel Allen, a senior editor at *Yankee* magazine. I had written proposals to dozens of magazines, but only *Yankee* was interested in commissioning a story. I locked myself away in a room day after day and wrote with great hope. I believed this one story would rescue all of us. It would bring in some money. If I could make it good enough it would surely lead to a book contract. It would prove to Erna that she had placed her story in the hands of a competent writer. After the last two years I needed proof myself.

Out of the blue in late July Erna learned that POWs from the Korean War were going to hold a convention in Louisville, Kentucky. The night I told Lee about this she had just spent ten hours on her feet working in an art gallery.

"How do you know there's anything there?" she asked. "You've gone back and forth to Washington for essentially nothing."

I told her there would be several hundred Korean War POWs in Louisville. "I have to go," I said.

She looked at me. She already knew that I would go.

"I'm going to use the money from the *Yankee* story," I said. "I'll have to use all of it."

\* \* \* \* \*

The Ohio River is brown and brooding in Louisville. It muscles its way around the city and off through the sea of blue-green grass where heavy white mansions sit like ships at anchor.

It was a hundred and five degrees there at four in the afternoon when I arrived on August 1, 1980. The sky was a smoky gray, and everyone was watching the big black clouds standing in the west, hoping they would move in and bring some rain. At the airport a green bus snarled at the sidewalk, waiting on several dozen boys in uniform bound for Fort Knox. They looked very young in their pressed khakis and mirror-finish boots, raw recruits with slightly puzzled expressions. Newspaper headlines told how the big John Deere plant not far from the airport had laid off another fifteen hundred workers this week — the sort of economic gloom that did wonders for the new volunteer Army.

I went on to the Holiday Inn a few miles south, just off the interstate. The receptionist at the front desk gave me a key to my room and directions to a banquet room reserved for the POWs. On the itinerary it was marked as "The Watering Hole," the place where I spent all but a few hours of two and a half days.

More than a hundred POWs showed up, many of them finding it difficult ever to leave The Watering Hole. They were balding and their stomachs were prominent, but they still thought of each other as kids — as they had been at seventeen and eighteen, when they had last seen each other.

There was some big talk here right from the beginning, talk that swelled with bourbon and gin. These were hard-bitten, bighearted fellows, and they came to talk things over, to have a few laughs and play some poker, and to cry a bit over the days when friends had died horribly on hills and in squalid huts they could still picture in their minds. They came to Louisville to talk about this and about the way so much had changed since those days.

They told me that being POWs from Korea meant two things. First, they were in the wrong place at the wrong time. And second, they were forgotten by their country. Long before America decided to forget about Vietnam, it decided to forget Korea.

There has always been a curious amnesia about the Korean War, and the men who did the fighting there still grope for a reconciliation between their own vivid memories and their country's need to forget. They are quick to admit there is no honor in being captured by the enemy. Every man seems to owe his survival to another man and to someone who did not survive. And when they meet, many of them for the first time since their release from captivity in 1953, there is a handshake that lingers over the exchange of names and units, until the past and present converge, eyes fill with tears, and finally they embrace in that shy, gallant way men do.

"We need each other," said Tony Ryan, a gritty man with boyish good looks and dark, steady eyes. Ryan was forty-nine years old. He had spent his seventeenth birthday as a prisoner of war. "Just seeing these guys will get me through another year. What we went through we can't explain to anyone else, but we know we need each other." Ryan had been home from Korea only a short time when he got into a brawl at a pool hall in West Virginia. "I heard this kid saying he didn't need any friends, he didn't need anybody. He was a rough kid, and he was going on and on about not needing nothing, and I tried to tell him he was wrong, but pretty soon I found myself shaking him by the shoulders and yelling at him."

With a crusading zeal and a deep, modulated voice, Paul Atwood of Kentucky, a career man in the Army and a veteran of Korea and Vietnam, tried to put into perspective his relationship with the other POWs. "I have a brother who I've tried for years to tell about Korea, about what happened to me there. I know he can't understand, but I keep trying to ███████ tell him. I don't know why. . . . In a way I love these guys more. I know they would die for me."

Tom Adams, a strapping black man from California and the father of seven children, said he just had to come to Louisville to

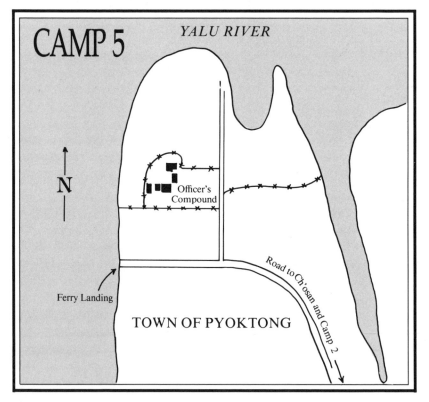

*(Based on a sketch drawn from memory by an ex-POW.)*

---

share something with these men. In addition to fighting in Korea, Adams had also led a Special Forces team for three years in Vietnam. "I wanted to see these men, to see if they'd made out all right. I see men I suffered with, and in their faces I remember the faces of others we buried in Korea. At Camp 5 the ground was so hard, full of rocks, we could only dig the graves about a foot deep. When you'd come back a day or two later and the rocks had moved, the guy you'd buried would be staring up at you. I cry for those faces. I can't help it. We lost so many good men at Camp 5."

"When I came home," recalled A.T. Blake of South Carolina, "people asked me how I felt. I said it was good to be home. But inside I felt uncomfortable. I felt uncomfortable because America had surrendered . . . that we had surrendered after so much had been sacrificed. That we could have won if we hadn't given up. It broke my heart and spirit."

Using beer bottles, a little, brown-faced man from Alabama interrupted in order to elaborate: "We had them on the run, right here. We had them right up against the Yalu River," he said, placing a bottle down on the table with his right hand. "We would have driven them right into the damn river with MacArthur. Then we was told that we didn't want no war with China. We was told to just hold our line and not to shoot at any Chinese. Now what the hell kind of war is that?" As the little man spoke, his voice became stronger and smoother, like a man with a French accent when he suddenly starts speaking French. "Good God, the Chinese had other ideas, and they came over the hills, hundreds of thousands of them, and they pinned us down near Chosin Reservoir and they beat hell on us. For three days they beat on us. It was fifty below zero, and we had to piss on our machine guns to thaw them out, and it was too late. They outnumbered us seventy-five to one. We were cut down like fish in a barrel. And we could have won, mister. If they'd wanted us to win in Washington, we could have won."

Tony Ryan picked up the conversation, pushing his way to the table. "And then the POWs come home and, hell, you're guilty of something just because you survived. You know what I mean? There had been so much talk about POWs giving in to the Chinese, we were all under suspicion when we came home. You could tell that people were looking at you, asking, 'Now, I wonder, did he collaborate or not?' They thought maybe you'd come home because you had been a collaborator. To them, collaboration meant giving anything more than name, rank, and number."

Ryan spoke philosophically about collaboration. "Every kid growing up in America has the idea that when American soldiers are captured they give only name, rank, and number, no matter what. But let me tell you this, the first thing the Chinese told us was that they hadn't been to the Geneva convention and they didn't care what the Geneva convention said they were supposed to do. I know of men who were murdered for not cooperating. In my mind there was never an excuse for collaboration, and by that I mean doing something that would hurt your buddies. Or your country. But there was a lot we had to do just to survive. We had to write what the Chinese called 'self-criticisms.' Hell, they were a joke to us, and they kept the guards off our backs, so we wrote them. Is that collaboration? No way, man!

"A man does what he has to do. So far as I'm concerned the Code of Conduct was a joke. Who wrote it? People who had never been prisoners.

"First of all, we were kids, without any training about what to do to survive capture. That was a mistake. The other mistake — and this I'll never forgive the Army for — was putting POWs on trial before boards of officers who'd never spent a day as a POW. They should have been judged by their peers. I'll stand up for the Army any day, but when it comes to talking about those collaboration trials, it was a joke. It's possible that I'm alive today because some officer I didn't even know collaborated."

From these men I learned of prisoner abuse, a subject the Army never officially recognized after the POWs came home.

"People died every day," related Richard Phippin, a thin, nervous man who lives in Pennsylvania. "Dysentery was so bad your bowels would move forty or fifty times a day with nothing but blood and mucus. We were all beaten. I know men who were put inside fifty-gallon drums and kept there for days while the guards beat on them with sticks. Then there were the so-called hospitals; the death houses. Once a man was taken there he didn't have a chance. They were using us for medical experiments."

Charles Harrison of Virginia sat in a wheelchair, his nerves ruined from beriberi. During the time in the POW camp, he lost sixty-five pounds. "I went to Korea not knowing it was more than some police action. I thought we were going to patrol the streets or something. That's all. But I gets there and seen the blood pouring from the backs of those trucks and I knew. . . . They tied wires around my arms and legs and cut off my circulation. I was bayoneted and whipped with the stock of a rifle. I was interrogated many times. I didn't tell them nothin'. I just didn't care no more; I didn't care what they said they would do to me. I figured I wasn't gonna live long anyway. But I was scared, though. I messed my britches; yep, a couple of times I messed my britches I was so scared."

Ernie Jakes, a medic in Korea, saw an American executed at a place called The Mining Camp. "James Lewis Emerson was his name. He had frozen feet and could barely move, but he was a happy-go-lucky sort of fellow. The Chinese accused him of war crimes. They had a trial for him which lasted an hour, then they brought him outside, and his wrists had been skewered so they could put a piece of wire through them and tie them together. He was bleeding profusely from his wrists. They set him up and asked him if he wanted to run. He said no. Then they asked him if he wanted to be blindfolded and he said, 'I've watched you people screw up everything else since I got here. I want to watch you screw this up, too.' He stood there while they fired eight rounds into him. . . . His body . . . his body flipped backward. . . . I still can't tell this story, even after all these years," said Jakes, weeping.

Because this group of men had been enlisted men with the Army they had no knowledge of the officers held at Camp 5. No one could tell me anything about Ronald Alley. They didn't recognize his name. "The first thing the Chinese did," one man explained, "was separate the enlisted men from the officers. They wanted to break down our chain of command."

Tom Adams, the black man who had done so much fighting in Vietnam, talked with me privately about the soldiers charged with collaboration. "After Korea, and then after three years in 'Nam, I've matured. I've come to learn that you don't judge another man for breaking. The name, rank, and number business is a myth that people who don't have to fight have enjoyed. Nobody knows why a man says what he says. Maybe one kick in the head changes everything around for him. And all men are different. I've seen too many men die to sit here and judge any one man. And there was a lot of judging going on over there in Korea, and back home later on. There was a lot of people who wanted to have a trial so they could get on with the hanging."

The men who came to Louisville did not come to complain. Concerned about America's future, they offered a prayer for the hostages held in Iran; they asked God to restore America's greatness. And in the last few minutes of their reunion, Robert Christian, a veteran who had helped organize this convention, fought back tears to share a memory with his friends:

"We were moving south a few weeks after we were captured, and we came to what appeared to be an old mining camp. The buildings were dilapidated, the walls were crumbling, and the place — we thought — was deserted. No movement could be detected. Then, to our amazement, we saw faces appearing. Pale, frightened, ghostly faces. They were unrecognizable. Then someone spoke up and said, 'My God, those are American soldiers.' When the Chinese decided to march us from there, they said only those who were able to move would be taken to the next camp. We carried as many as we could. Some of them crawled on their stomachs and only made it a few yards. They knew if they could come with us they would at least die among friends. . . . Each time . . . each time I see the flag flying in the sky I can still see those faces. I can . . . I can still hear them saying, 'Take me with you. Please take me with you.' "

My last night at the Holiday Inn in Louisville, a message was left under my door to meet a man named Girardi at the bar at 11:30. Girardi looked at me with dark, piercing eyes. He told me he was from Tennessee, and that he had taken time off from working on Ronald Reagan's election campaign to come to the POW convention. He had been a prisoner of war with these men in North Korea, but he said he was not a soldier. He had been with the CIA at the time he was captured in early 1951. He said he had followed the court-martial of Ronald Alley and other POWs.

Girardi didn't want to answer any questions. All he would say for the record was this: "I took notes in those camps for three years. They were all collaborators. All of them."

*   *   *   *   *

When I returned to Maine there was a letter from Senator Cohen's office. The Army was still refusing to speak with me about the Alley case. They would not discuss current policies concerning

---

122

the Code of Conduct, either to confirm or deny what the Air Force officials had told me.

There was worse news. The Army had just informed Senator Cohen that Ronald Alley's 201 file, the standard file kept on all servicemen, would not be available to me. The Army said it had been destroyed in a fire on July 12, 1973, along with many others.

# CHAPTER 10

In Louisville, Ronald Alley's story became a larger story for me, and more important than ever before. In the face of each veteran I met there, I saw what I had seen on Major Alley's face, a longing to have his story told. I came home determined to tell it.

But after Louisville, though I had come closer to Major Alley, to an understanding of what he had endured in Korea, I was no closer to knowing why he had gone to prison. That was the problem: Every trip to the Pentagon, every telephone call and letter in the past two years had brought me closer to the truth, so that I couldn't turn back, and yet no closer to any kind of proof that would persuade the Army to reopen the Alley case.

We waited for this proof. Erna waited in Bar Harbor. I waited in Portland. Her son, Gary, waited as well. Not long after returning from Louisville I telephoned him and told him how important his father's story was, and he said to me: "I just don't want this to kill Ma. Whatever you find, I hope it's what Ma's been waiting to hear."

Gary was not really waiting. He was going on with his life. He had two children now, and a good promotion. His life was going somewhere.

I learned soon enough that waiting is the hardest thing. There is a kind of sickness that strikes you when you suspend your life in order to wait for something to happen. You give part of yourself away each day, each hour you wait for the telephone to ring, the mail to arrive. Ronald and Erna Alley had waited for more than twenty years. She had her anger, her defiance to keep her going. And he had his faith, which is, I suppose, the ultimate expression of defiance — the ability to say, I believe the Army will clear my name, even though there is no reason to believe it. Still, the waiting had deprived them of a full life.

I was waiting for addresses from Senator Cohen. I was waiting for someone to believe in the story enough to help me complete the book. I said this over and over and wrote it in countless letters. The editor at William Morrow finally said to me: "This is an important book, as important as you believe it to be. But we feel the story is peripheral to the concerns of contemporary readers."

Soon after returning from Louisville I rode a bus to Manhattan with my unfinished book in my briefcase. I had a meeting with an editor at Harcourt Brace Jovanovich. She greeted me pleasantly, and then I watched her expression change as I told her about Major Alley's story. Finally she stood up behind her desk and adjusted her necktie. "I didn't realize this was Korea we were talking about," she said. "It's too bad your man Alley wasn't in the Vietnam War; nobody gives a damn about Korea."

I didn't say anything to her. I stood up and walked back to the bus station.

They were prophetic words. One publisher after another rejected the proposal. I had rewritten it in five different versions. I always made the same plea — for the assistance to finish my research.

By the fall of 1980 I gave up the letters. I sat at my desk staring out the window. I had taken on Ronald Alley's obsession to find the truth, and now I was waiting to be rescued. For a man with an obsession, the waiting is insufferable.

Finally Lee made up her mind that all of this had gone on too long and would not stop. The real world, beyond this book and my obsession over it and my waiting for the chance to finish it, was lost to me, and *this* was the only world for her. She didn't want to waste another day.

The day she told me it was over I spent the last money I had on a train ticket back to Washington. John Bradford met me at Union Station. We drove to a supermarket to pick up groceries. We walked up and down the aisles saying nothing at first.

"Your life falls apart and you end up in front of the soup display," John said. "That's America. That's life."

Later that night while we talked, I tried to explain to John, and to myself, why I couldn't give up Major Alley's story. I spoke about how I had never known him. And as I told this to John, it struck me how it had to be that way. I was on the outside; I was a nonbeliever. I was skeptical. I had to be drawn in to his obsession on my own, by the events, by what had happened to me in the two years after his death. The reasons to keep going were *my* reasons, not his.

I thought about his family and how they had all waited in their separate ways. Ronald Alley had spent most of his life talking about honor and waiting to get it back. For all of them it was a question of honor.

And now *my* honor was at stake. If I were to turn my back on them now, I would always have to wonder. Someday I might hear that Erna Alley had died, and I would have to wonder if maybe I could have made her life better, if just by finding all there was to find and finishing this old, old story, she and her son and daughter could have been free to live a better life.

In the morning I walked all the way to Capitol Hill and went to the office of Maine Congressman David Emery. I found myself explaining to a receptionist the problem I'd had getting addresses. "I have to find these people," I told her, and I handed her the list of names.

She looked it over, then said, "If there's anyone who can find addresses, it's Mike Danforth." She explained that he worked in the congressman's office in Augusta, Maine. She gave me his office and home telephone numbers.

I moved into a room in Portland, and two months later things began happening. Michael Curtis at *The Atlantic* wrote a letter on my behalf to the Fund for Investigative Journalism in Washington, D.C. Howard Bray, the director there, was interested in the Alley story. "We may be able to help you complete your research for a book," he wrote me.

Howard Bray wanted a thorough report of all that I had learned about Major Alley since I'd met him in 1978, plus a detailed plan for the remainder of my research. It took a week to complete, and when he received it in the mail, Bray telephoned to say he would take my request before his board the next time it met.

It was also at this time that Erna wrote me a long letter in response to a question I had asked her about her husband's duty in 1948 and 1949 at the reserve unit in Schenectady, New York. "The only person I can think of who might have held a grudge against Ronald from that time," she wrote, "was the new commanding officer who was brought in, Major Rauterberg. He was in his late fifties then, so I don't think there is much chance he'll still be alive for you to talk to."

Erna was right; he had died, but with her help I located a man who had known Rauterberg. Eliot Boice ran a funeral home near Schenectady. He had been assigned to the reserve unit in the late 1940s. When I first spoke by telephone with him, I asked him to check around and see if there was anyone who remembered Rauterberg and Ronald Alley and how the two of them got along.

Late one Sunday evening in early March 1981, Boice telephoned me. A woman employed at the reserve unit in the late 1940s was living in a town outside Schenectady. Boice asked how I wanted him to proceed, and I told him to call her up and ask her out to dinner. I suggested they might talk about Rauterberg once he had gained her confidence.

It was almost two weeks later when Boice called me back. Previously, he had had a mild manner on the telephone, but this time there was a hard edge to his voice. He stammered a bit as he spoke.

"I don't know how to start," he said. "I did just what you told me to do. I thought I was going to get somewhere, but, well, I went and found her. She was very pleasant. I talked with her a few minutes and everything was fine. You know, she was very nice. But then I asked her if she remembered Ron Alley. You wouldn't believe it —

the color drained from her face. She turned her back on me. I wasn't even asked to sit down. She said, 'I can't answer questions about that man.'

"So I pushed a little, and all she told me was that Ronald had been a loner there. She said he never went out for lunch with the other officers, and he was always in a hurry to get home. Then I asked her about Rauterberg and she got really cold. Stone cold. 'They come and go. I don't remember the names,' she told me, which was stupid. Of course she had to remember Rauterberg's name; he was her boss.

"I'm not likely to get her out for dinner like you wanted, but I can tell you one thing — she knows something that she's not letting on," he said.

I trusted Boice's appraisal. In my notebook that night I wrote down SCHENECTADY CONNECTION, drew a line under it, and then made these entries: Alley; Rauterberg; the stranger who came to Erna's apartment; the former secretary.

I remembered that Rauterberg had been called to testify at the court-martial, and suddenly his appearance at the trial began to seem more important to me. I pulled out the section of the court-martial transcript where the prosecutor had questioned Rauterberg about his relationship with Ronald Alley:

Q: And what was your relationship to the accused?

A: I was his commanding officer.

Q: And how long were you the accused's superior officer?

A: I didn't get that, sir. I'm deaf.
*(Counsel moved closer to the witness.)*

Q: How long were you the accused's superior officer?

A: For about from November 1948 until the early part of 1950 — Was that commanding officer, no.

Q: Superior officer?

A: Superior officer, yes, sir, correct.

**Counsel:** Request this be marked Prosecution Exhibit 8 for identification. *(The reporter did so.)*

Q: I hand you Prosecution Exhibit 8 for identification and ask you if you have ever seen this document before?

**1.** Escorted by an MP, Major Ronald E. Alley, of Bar Harbor, Maine, is led away after his sentencing on November 7, 1955. Convicted of collaborating with the enemy during the Korean War, he is the only officer in this century to be imprisoned for such a crime.

**2. Right:** The offices of the *Bar Harbor Times,* where Don Snyder, then editor of the newspaper, met Ronald Alley for the first and only time.

**3. Below:** Captain Ronald Alley, in 1949, swears in a recruit at the reserve unit in Schenectady, New York.

**4. Left:** Erna and Ronald celebrate daughter Evelyn's first birthday, September 26, 1949, in Schenectady.

**5. Below:** Soldiers pause en route to Chosin Reservoir in North Korea, where one of the bloodiest battles of the Korean War took place.

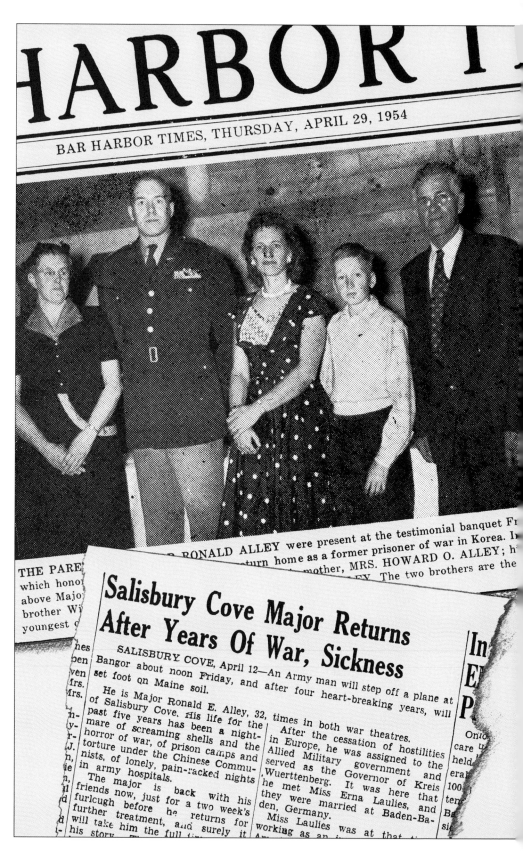

RONALD ALLEY were present at the testimonial banquet Fr

turn home as a former prisoner of war in Korea. I

mother, MRS. HOWARD O. ALLEY; h

EY. The two brothers are the

**THE PARE**

which honor

above Majo

brother Wi

youngest o

## Salisbury Cove Major Returns After Years Of War, Sickness

SALISBURY COVE, April 12—An Army man will step off a plane at Bangor about noon Friday, and after four heart-breaking years, will set foot on Maine soil.

He is Major Ronald E. Alley, 32, of Salisbury Cove. His life for the past five years has been a night-mare of screaming shells and the horror of war, of prison camps and torture under the Chinese Commu-nists, of lonely, pain-racked nights in army hospitals.

The major is back with his friends now, just for a two week's furlough before he returns for further treatment, and surely it will take him the full ti

his story.

times in both war theatres.

After the cessation of hostilities in Europe, he was assigned to the Allied Military government and served as the Governor of Kreis Wuerttenberg. It was here that he met Miss Erna Laulies, and they were married at Baden-Ba-den, Germany.

Miss Laulies was at that working as an i

**6. Opposite page:** Major Alley was guest of honor at a testimonial banquet held in Bar Harbor for returning POWs on April 23, 1954. Pictured from left to right are his mother, Thelma Alley; Major Alley; his wife, Erna; his brother, William; and his father, Howard Alley.

**7. Above:** Erna's German Motel, just outside Bar Harbor. With no means of financial help from her husband, who was still a prisoner of war in North Korea, Erna Alley opened this tourist business to support herself and their two children.

**8. Above:** Erna Alley was as shocked as her husband when he was found guilty of the charges brought against him by the Army in November 1955: "I was told that if I went to the press it would only make things harder on Ronald when he got to Leavenworth Prison."

**9. Right:** Colonel John Herzig, who was a captain in Army Intelligence in 1955, claims that the investigation of Ronald Alley and other Korean War POWs was not conducted fairly and that the evidence collected was "misrepresented."

**10. Below:** Winter gets a grip on the Korean countryside as US soldiers prepare to move further north, higher into the mountains, where ice-covered roads and frozen ridges would hamper their progress.

**11. Right:** Don Snyder was instrumental in getting the Army to reopen its case against Major Alley. Here Snyder leaves the Pentagon after testifying on February 10, 1982.

**12. Below right:** Captain Charles L. Peckham in September 1953. He and Ronald Alley spent their long captivity together in various POW camps, during which time Peckham suffered irreparable damage to his health.

**13. Above:** Colonel Robert Wise (right) in December 1953, three months after he was released from a North Korean POW camp. Wise was selected to serve as technical advisor in the movie "Prisoner of War" by MGM in which Ronald Reagan (left) had a role.

**14. Right:** John Cochran, NBC News correspondent, at the console in his New York office. Cochran interviewed the Alleys in 1976 for a segment on "NBC Nightly News."

**15. Above:** In August 1980, Don Snyder attended a POW reunion in Louisville, Kentucky, where copies of this photograph were handed out to those in attendance. It was said to be a view of Camp 5 in Pyoktong, North Korea.

**16. Left:** Erna and Ronald Alley at a party in Bar Harbor in 1971.

# Collaborator' Devoted to the Army

By Sara Rimer
Washington Post Staff Writer

The Army was Ronald Alley's life, and even after they court-martialed him at Fort Meade for collaborating with the Chinese who held him prisoner during the Korean War and sentenced him to 10 years of hard labor and disgraced him with a dishonorable discharge, he still believed in the Army and thought it would some-day do him justice.

He had, he declared again and again, committed no crime during his 33 months of captivity. He did 3 years and 9 months at Fort Leavenworth, Kan., and when he got out in 1959 and went back home and found work as a Fuller Brush man, he still had faith that the Army would see its mistake, restore his honor and welcome him back into the ranks.

Twice he applied for a hearing before the Army Board for Correction of Military Records, and twice they turned him down. His congressman offered to help him try to get a presidential pardon, but Alley declined that offer, say-

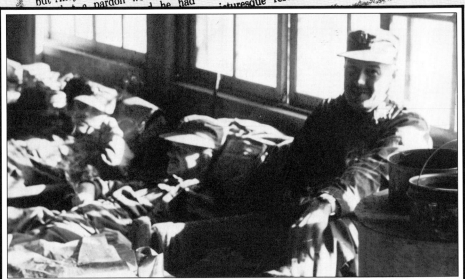

By Lucian Perkins—The Wa

Ronald Alley's wife Erna and son Gary testified here in effort to clea

Alley was a tall, husky, opinion-ated carpenter's son with a high school education, the oldest of eight children raised in Bar Har-bor, Maine. To the people of that picturesque resort island, which

he left so hopefully when he enlisted in th came back to in disgra after Leavenworth, h as a man with an o

**See OBSESSION,**

**17. Opposite (top):** When Colonel Herzig read this article in the *Washington Post,* he called the reporter, Sara Rimer, to say he had information that "could help Alley." Rimer contacted Don Snyder immediately, told him about the conversation, and put him in touch with Herzig.

**18. Above:** Erna Alley and her lawyer, Gerald F. Williamson, leave the Pentagon after the hearing in February 1982, which they hoped would clear Major Alley's name and restore his honor. Erna returned to Maine, where she spent the following five months waiting for a decision from the Army board.

**19. Opposite (bottom):** Captain Ronald Alley (right) in Untaek, North Korea, on Thanksgiving Day, 1950. Two days later he and his unit began moving north toward the Yalu River and Chosin Reservoir.

**20. Below:** Ronald and Erna Alley in Salisbury Cove, Maine, in 1973. Twenty years after his court-martial, Ronald Alley had the opportunity to apply for a presidential pardon, but he refused the offer. Pardons were for guilty men, he said, and he was not guilty.

**21. Left:** The cottage in Oak Point, Maine, where Erna and Ronald planned to live after his retirement. He died in January 1978, a year after they bought the place.

**22. Above (left to right):** Colonel Robert Wise, Erna Alley, and Colonel Charles Peckham gather at the Pentagon for the February 1982 hearing. Both men, who had been POWs in Korea with Major Alley, flew in from the West Coast to testify on Alley's behalf. Colonel Peckham died on May 13, 1986.

**23. Above:** Ronald Alley, flanked by two of his grandchildren, Timothy and Michael.

**24. Below:** Maine Senator William Cohen believes Ronald Alley was made a scapegoat and deserved an honorable discharge.

**25. Above:** Erna Alley and her son, Gary, at the hearing in Washington, D.C. "This is the chance my dad wanted," said Gary Alley. "I think a part of me always prayed that someday I'd be down here doing this for him."

**26.** Ronald Alley asked Erna to promise that, when he died, she would have him buried in his uniform, and she kept her word. "I did not have 'Major' engraved on his stone," she said, "for I hope that someday I will be able to put 'Colonel' on instead."

**A:** Yes, sir.

**Q:** Where did you see it, colonel?

**A:** It came into the Schenectady office in the regular routine of business.

**Q:** If you know, did the accused ever see that circular?

**A:** Yes, sir.

*(Defense counsel asked to see the document.)*

**Q:** What if anything did you do with this circular after it came into the office?

**A:** I looked it over and took it in person to Captain Alley's desk and asked him — I told him —

**Q.** That's enough. After you showed this circular to the accused, what if anything did you say to the accused?

At this point the defense counsel interrupted.

**Defense Counsel:** Mr. Law Officer, we object. At this time we feel that the matter concerning which the government is about to examine the witness is far removed from any issue in this case.

The law officer (judge) asked to see the circular and then he announced that the court would recess for ten minutes.

**Law Officer:** I would like for the court to leave the courtroom. There will be a closed session upon this matter.

*(The court members withdrew from the courtroom at 1014 hours, 25 October 1955. The closed session commenced at 1015 hours, 25 October 1955.)*

The law officer called the closed session to order. He asked Colonel Rauterberg to leave the courtroom. The prosecution spoke next.

**Prosecution:** Let the record reflect that the law officer, the accused, counsel for the accused, counsel for the government and the security adviser are present in court, that the court has been excused, are not present, but that the session is open to the public.

---

**The Law Officer:** Now, you object Mr. Counsel for the accused. Do you desire to state your ground for your objection?

**Defense Counsel:** Yes, sir.

**Law Officer:** First I think it would be advisable at this time if we elicited from the counsel for the government what he intends to do with Prosecution Exhibit 8 for identification so as to make it clear in order that you may understand what he attempts to do.

**Defense Counsel:** I think I know what he intends to do but go ahead.

**Law Officer:** You don't have to come up here. You can argue from back there.

**Prosecution:** Sir, Circular 338, DA, dated 28 October 1948 contains a list of organizations considered by the Attorney General to have interests in conflict with those of the United States. We intend to prove through this witness that when this witness showed this circular to the accused, he circled the following, that is, the Socialist Workers Party, and at that time when he circled that, told the witness — that is the accused said at that time and I quote, and I believe these are the exact words the witness will testify to, "What in hell is this god damn Army coming to? I'm a member of the Socialist Workers Party." That is what we expect to elicit from this witness.

**Defense Counsel:** Mr. Law Officer, we feel that that is irrelevant to any issue in this case, that it is an attempt to prejudice the accused with the court by showing an alleged prior act of misconduct entirely unconnected with any matter before the court. Further however, another ground of my objection and on this I will have to request the advice of the Security Adviser as to whether the further ground of my objection may be classified — may I have a conference with him?

**Law Officer:** You may.

*(Defense counsel conferred with the security adviser.)*

**Defense Counsel:** I am advised that it is classified and I will therefore have to ask that the court be cleared.

**Law Officer:** The spectators will leave the courtroom.

*(The spectators withdrew from the courtroom at 1018 hours, 25 October 1955.)*

---

The transcript covering the closed session was originally not available to me, but then was ordered declassified after I requested it.

**Defense Counsel:** That Major Rauterberg reported the matter to higher headquarters in a letter in which he praised himself very highly as being on the lookout for subversives of all kinds, that as a result of his report there was a classified investigation of the accused and that investigation disclosed not the slightest evidence that the accused was or ever had been a member of the Socialist Workers Party, and that the investigation was eventually closed without discovering the slightest evidence in support of the allegation. We feel that if the government is allowed to bring out this alleged statement by the accused that we should be permitted to produce the file of the investigation. The inference we draw from the investigation is that Major — now Colonel then Major Rauterberg was mistaken in his understanding of what the accused had to say. We feel that in any event that to bring out this alleged statement is improperly to attack the accused's character and very strongly to prejudice him before the court.

After this vigorous appeal by Major Alley's defense counsel, the prosecution once again stated its position that the testimony by Rauterberg was central to its case against the accused:

**Prosecution:** . . . We intend to prove, if permitted, that the accused circled this organization on this circular that you have before you, which organization is listed in about 2 or 3 places there not only as subversive but communistic and holding to the violent overthrow or the overthrow of our form of government by violent means. Hence, since they have interjected it into the trial we should be permitted to show in rebuttal the exact type of socialist that the accused is.

The closed session went on and on with the same arguments being advanced and repeated. What is most revealing is that, after Rauterberg had allegedly heard Ronald Alley's statement about the Socialist Workers party, he notified higher officials and an investigation was initiated. Also, by virtue of his own statement, the government prosecutor considered Major Alley to be a Socialist and was going to attempt to make this a central part of his case against him.

Eventually the law officer refused to allow this matter to be reopened in the courtroom. But by then the court had already heard about the nature of the circular, and damage had been inflicted on Alley's defense.

Reviewing the trial transcript that Sunday evening, and tracing the names I had included under what I was calling the "Schenectady Connection," it was clear that Alley's troubles with Rauterberg could have come back to haunt him. The efficacy of the government's effort to portray Alley as a Socialist or Communist sympathizer was obvious; anything like that, no matter how specious or unsubstantiated, would have given weight to the charges against him in 1955.

And then, too, there was another revelation in this incident. It had to do with Major Alley's temperament. It seemed utterly stupid that he would make such a statement to his superior officer at a peculiarly sensitive time in the Army's history, no matter how irresistible the urge to anger Rauterberg. Alley had been an officer in the Army long enough to know that acrimony between them might get him in hot water. But his obstinacy had apparently gotten the better of him.

So there had been trouble in Schenectady. And that could explain why Ronald's closest friend had been frightened to speak with me. He told me on the telephone that he himself had been accused of being a Communist because of his association with Alley.

I made a pot of coffee, put on Brahms's "Requiem," and began going through the FBI file that I'd obtained under the Freedom of Information Act two years earlier. I took notice once more of the memo to J. Edgar Hoover from the field worker assigned to observe the Alleys in Bar Harbor. "Another Communist running for public office," the agent had written. I'd grown tired of reading that memo. But after going through the file for about an hour, I discovered something I hadn't noticed before. There was a notation at the bottom of one of the mimeographed pages: "865 pages withheld by the Department of the Army." I couldn't believe what I was looking at, and that I'd never seen this before.

Monday morning I wrote Erna to say that I was going to make an urgent request through the Freedom of Information Act, to try and get these pages from the Army. I wrote Senator Cohen of my plans. And I sent requests to both the FBI and the Army Intelligence Office, which was located, ironically, at Fort Meade. In my letters to both agencies, I said I would be traveling to Washington, D.C., later that spring and would plan to come by personally to pick up the new information.

Over the next few days I thought a lot about the former secretary in the reserve unit in Schenectady. By now I had her name and home telephone number. I called her at nine o'clock one evening.

"I can't remember anything; I already told that to Mr. Boice," she said nervously.

"Well, can you just tell me what Alley was like?"

"You knew him," she replied.

"No, no I didn't. We had met only once, for a few minutes."

"He was a friendly person. But I can't say anything else one way or another."

"*Is* there anything else?" I asked.

She didn't answer this question. And it was apparent that she wasn't going to answer any more questions unless I took a different approach. So I did the only thing I could do — I stretched the truth in order to get at what I hoped would be the truth. I told her I was working to prove Ronald Alley had been one of the Communist sympathizers within the Army. I said I needed to put together all the information on him I could find.

There was a long stretch of silence before the woman spoke again: "*I* was never a Communist. I want to get that clear. I was never in the Socialist party. I hate Communism."

"I'm sure you do."

"Alley was not full-time Army. He was a reservist ordered into active duty. Major Rauterberg was full-time Army. He was in charge, rightfully so. And Alley was his own person, if you know what I mean — independent. Now, I want to make it clear that this is only hearsay; but people said he recruited for that organization, he recruited for the Socialist Workers party. People said this. I mean, what do you do when you hear that, run to the FBI? I just let it roll off my back. But with some, with some it was different."

"Do you think he was a Socialist?"

"I don't . . . I shouldn't talk with anyone about these things and if this gets me in trouble. . . ."

---

"It won't. I've already told you I won't ever use your name in connection with anything you can tell me. But was there any proof, any proof you knew of?"

"Not that I know of. But Major Rauterberg believed he was. The Army was after subversives then. Things were different."

"Did Rauterberg go to the FBI?"

"I don't know that. A person like Rauterberg, you never get to know that much about. And I was young then."

"What did you think when Alley got court-martialed?"

"People here really began talking then. We — they all figured the 'over here' part was one shade, and it got darker over there."

"So you *do* believe Alley was a Socialist?"

"I don't have anything to say about that. I just want to end this conversation, okay?"

"Tell me one more thing."

"What?"

"Is there anyone at the reserve unit, or anyone in the area, or anyone you know who has proof of this? Any evidence on Alley."

"I told you already that people said a lot of things, that's all. I don't know of anybody who had any proof. And I just want to stop here. I would like to get off now. You made me trust you, and I have to get off now."

What had started as a guess about some connection between Ronald's fate in 1955 and his assignment in Schenectady in 1949 now seemed clearly defined and certain.

In April of 1981 I went back to Bar Harbor with good news for Erna. I had not been back in almost two years. I walked along Cottage Street and stopped to stare across the street at the *Bar Harbor Times,* where someone I didn't know sat at the editor's desk in the front window. I walked through town to our old house. It had seemed for so many weeks and months that nothing was happening, that I was only waiting for something to happen. Now suddenly it seemed that a great deal had happened, and much had changed.

I found Erna at her cottage. She told me she was waiting for spring.

"There's something I need to tell you," I said.

We sat out on the porch. I told her that I had received a grant from a foundation in Washington. And that Mike Danforth had come up with addresses of the court-martial witnesses. "I'm going to take a long trip. There are a lot of people I need to talk with."

"This is what we've waited for," she said hopefully.

"I've got to be sure you can accept the truth," I said to her. "You and Gary."

My fear had always been that there was someone whom I would find who would take hold of my arm and say, "Listen, this fellow Alley was as bad as the Army said he was. You're barking up the wrong tree."

Now, after all that had happened I feared this even more. I had reason to be afraid. I had telephoned a retired Army major just before coming to Bar Harbor. He was one of the names on my list, one of the former prosecution witnesses for the Army's case against Ronald. When I spoke with him he made it clear that he wanted nothing to do with my search for the truth. "Why would you want to dig up those old bones now?" he asked. "What the hell good could come of it?"

I asked him if he had any regret for having testified against a fellow officer.

"Regret?" he said. "Why should I? I was following orders."

"Well, I want to come interview you," I said.

"Forget it. You show up here and you can interview my attorney," he replied.

From then on as I planned this trip I lied to the prosecution witnesses; I said nothing about Major Alley's trial. I introduced myself simply as a writer who was working on a book about the Korean War.

Erna said she wasn't afraid. "This has been bad for you, I know, and I feel to blame," she told me. "Don't worry about Gary and me. This is what Ronald would have wanted you to do. Finish your book."

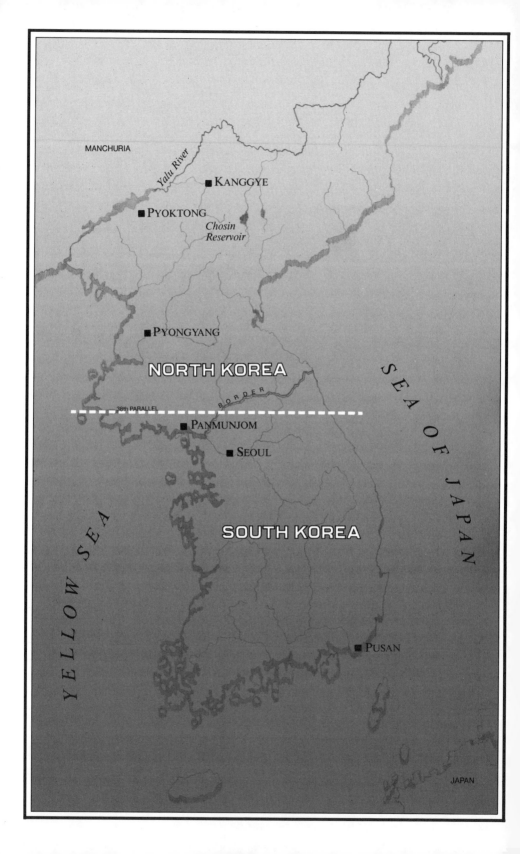

# PART · TWO

# CHAPTER 11

T hree weeks later I was ready to leave for the West Coast. My first meeting was to be with retired Army Colonel Charles Peckham in California. He had been held prisoner in North Korea with Ronald. They had spent all three years of confinement together. "I have a lot to tell you," he'd said to me on the telephone.

The night before I was supposed to fly to California I got a phone call from a friend of Colonel Peckham's.

"They've taken Charlie into the hospital for another open-heart surgery," the friend said. "He wants you to get here as fast as you can. Come straight to the hospital."

---

I landed in San Francisco, picked up a rental car, and drove as fast as I could to San Jose, to the O'Connor Hospital. I ran from the parking lot to the front desk and then to the fourth floor. A nurse in the intensive care unit told me Colonel Peckham had come through the surgery but was in critical condition and could have no visitors. I was so relieved to hear he was alive that I did not press her to be allowed in. I explained the urgency of my visit, and she told me to call the next morning. She would see what she could do.

I had other business in San Jose. The daughter of a former member of the court-martial jury had responded to a letter of mine, saying her father was dead, but that she would be willing to talk with me. When I arrived, Paula Shoemaker said she had not had a chance to go through her father's things. "At first when you wrote I wasn't sure I should trust you," she told me. "But if there is a possibility this man Alley should not have gone to prison, then I'm sure Dad would have wanted me to help."

We pulled several large crates down from shelves in the garage and began sorting through the papers. Colonel Shoemaker had been a career man in the Army and he had kept copious records of his years in the service. His daughter was quite sure he had kept a diary — she remembered him at his desk writing in it — and this was what we were looking for. While we hunted, she recalled her father as a man who tended to see things in black or white, a man who followed a rigid code of honor, a complex person who was outspoken and would not be silenced on issues he felt strongly about. A photograph of him showed a man who looked trim and tidy, more like a banker than a soldier.

As we were examining the contents of a three-drawer metal file cabinet, the telephone rang, and Paula went in the next room to answer it. In a few seconds she returned to the study. Whoever was calling had hung up when she picked up the receiver. "That's happened several times in the last few days," she said anxiously. "Ever since you first called me." I excused myself, and went to the driveway to lock the car, which held my notebooks and cassettes of taped interviews.

Colonel Shoemaker had kept everything under the sun. The Army had published papers on every imaginable topic, and he had dutifully saved them all.

In one drawer we found the flag, folded in the faultless military triangle, that had been draped over his casket. Under the flag we found the diaries. They were composed on loose pages and held in chronological order in black notebooks. Under the year 1955 there were five entries written over two pages:

October 28, 1955

Both Govt and Defense rested in the trial of Maj Ronald E. Alley, charged w/collaborating w/enemy in N. Korea camp 5 Pyoktong N. Korea. Defense was in final stages of its summation when session ended at 1515 hrs today

30 October

Paula went w/Francis trick or treat tonight. Brought her sack back and dumped it on the floor in front room

1 Nov. 55

Doris came down for Paula's birthday cake tonight. I had a bracelet from the PX. Pearls and rosy colored stones and she rec'd a sweater and slip from Lewiston. She was a delighted child.

2 Nov. 55 Wed

The defense in the trial of Major Ronald E. Alley began calling witnesses in extenuation and mitigation. The trial was recessed shortly before noon until 1000 tomorrow. Physical exam this afternoon. Weather: clear and warm during day.

3 Nov. 55

The Major Ronald E. Alley trial ended today. Sentence was arrived at with difficulty as the nominations for sentences were not adhered to by officers who voted light sentences. Thus when 6 votes were cast for a particular sentence, as the light sentences of none years confinement, 1 year, 5 years, 8 years, 10 years, etc. were defeated, the persons casting ballots for light sentences would vote down the heavier sentences starting with 8 years, which is not cricket. It rained at noon.

This was all there was. The last entry indicated that there had been some discord among the jurors as to the severity of the sentence imposed, but this out of context revealed nothing conclusive.

I made two visits to the O'Connor Hospital, a massive concrete-block structure bulging on the west side of San Jose, and was told both times that the doctors didn't want Colonel Peckham to be disturbed. None of the nurses could countermand those orders, and they were not sure when I might be allowed to see him. They said Colonel Peckham was weak, but coming along.

On Tuesday evening I went back again. I didn't stop at the nurses' station this time, but went right to the colonel's room. To my surprise I found a man sitting up in bed watching television and looking very alert. "Colonel Peckham?" I asked. "Nope," he said, pointing in the direction of a white curtain which separated him from a roommate. "If you're that writer, you'd better go ahead and wake him up. He's been talking about you in his sleep."

Colonel Peckham lay on his back sleeping. The sheet and covers were pulled down to the foot of the bed, exposing a deep purple gash that had been opened on the inside of one leg. He had been cut open and stitched in several places, and except for his snoring there was no sign of life.

His face was freckled, his head completely bald, and on the chair next to the bed hung a maroon robe with a patch sewn on it that read "American Ex-Prisoner of War." I had seen this same patch in Louisville, Kentucky.

I waited beside the bed and called his name several times before he opened his eyes and lifted his hand slowly from the sheets. He seemed to figure out instantly who I was. "You got here," he said.

I told him I was staying in town and could come back when he was feeling stronger, but he waved his hand deprecatingly: "No, no. I've been through this before. This is the fourth one. You sit down and let me tell you what I know."

He said he had never met Erna Alley, but because he had known Ronald from the first day of capture to the last, he felt he had to try and help if he could. He spoke slowly in a thin, hoarse voice that collapsed at times, interrupted by paroxysms of coughing that caused him to grimace in pain and press a pillow against his chest to keep his stitches from tearing open.

"Before the trial I was commanding officer of troops at Fort MacArthur, California. One day I got a call from the district CID office; they told me — they didn't *ask* me, but they *told* me — I was to report there. I arrived and was taken into a room where there were three agents in civilian clothes. They began telling me what I knew about Ron Alley. They made statements. . . . They said *you know* he was a collaborator, and *you know* he helped the Communists. After about five minutes I told them that I would be glad to testify to anything I had seen or heard, but not to hearsay. Then they told me that I could get into trouble for not helping them. I stood up; I was mad, damn mad. I told them that someone had better bring out an ID card showing he was a full colonel or higher up or I was going to leave, and if anyone tried to stop me I would knock him on his butt. I knew what they were after. They could scare people into saying just what they wanted to hear. I wasn't buying any of it."

Peckham had been ill when he was summoned to Fort Meade just before the start of the court-martial. He remembered that the defense witnesses were put up in a barracks at the fort:

"It was a condemned building, no heat and no hot water and no way to safeguard our stuff. The prosecution witnesses were together in the Hotel Willard in Washington. It wasn't hard to see what was going on. . . . I gave my deposition to the defense and I answered questions for the Judge Advocate people. But I told them the whole thing was ridiculous. Ron Alley hadn't done anything the rest didn't do. And they dismissed me from the court-martial; I don't know why. But I never testified. I came back home."

Colonel Peckham had no contact with Alley over the years following the court-martial. He finished his career with the Army, and it wasn't until he read about Ronald's death in the Salinas newspaper that he realized he'd actually been convicted and sent to prison at Leavenworth. When he told me this, his eyes filled with tears and he couldn't go on.

During my subsequent visits to his hospital room, Colonel Peckham described the confinement and suffering in the POW camps: "Camp 5 was the worst. We were starving, we were covered with lice. There was practically no sunlight, and we slept like sardines in huts with mud floors. Everyone was scared out of his mind. Death was all around. You couldn't get away from the smell of it. . . . The Chinese had the guns; there wasn't any question who was in charge. There were men tortured there. We saw Major Hume tied to a stake, and when he came back from interrogations he was crazy — out of his mind. He died the next day. You knew who was in charge all right. They put me in a hole. They put Alley in the same hole. You couldn't sit or stand. You had to just hold yourself in that bent-over position until you felt like your back would snap. They wanted us to confess. I finally realized I was going to stay there until I confessed. So I confessed that I had a hostile attitude. Why not? Was that collaboration? What harm did it cause the Army?"

It was during one of our last talks that Peckham began to bring me closer to Ronald Alley. It was a Saturday afternoon, and I was standing by his bed again, waiting for him to awaken.

"I have to leave tonight," I said.

"You have a long way to go. I wish I could help," he said. He pulled himself up and propped his head against the bed rail. He placed the pillow on his chest and folded his arms across it. He seemed to know there was something else I had to ask him. "You met the man's widow and kids?" he wanted to know. I told him I had. "It must be rough on them," he said.

"They want to believe him, or believe in him. But it makes you wonder why Major Alley was the only one. Unless there was something, something you or somebody can remember."

There was a long silence before Peckham began again. He explained that in Camp 5 prisoners were often taken outside the camp compound for long interrogations by the Chinese. Some would remain outside the camp overnight, or for several days. By this time, after a year of confinement, it was commonly agreed among the POWs that there was nothing they could divulge to the Chinese that would compromise the Army's position in the war.

"The trouble was," Peckham said slowly, "Ron had pissed a lot of people off. He didn't care what you thought of him, and he did things his way. The Chinese held these discussion groups, and Ron was one who spoke his mind, and this bothered a lot of the men. It got pretty bad after a while; you saw men talking with the Chinese guards, eating an apple or something, and it didn't matter. But if you didn't like the man, then you watched him eating his apple and you maybe figured he'd told them something. Rumor spread fast. There was a lot of rumor."

"Am I going to find anyone who would have proof that Major Alley collaborated?" I asked.

Peckham answered emphatically: "No. I believe I knew him better than anyone else over there. We were together practically the whole time. It was just so damn easy back here in 1955 for people to blame someone like Ron. A kid from Maine, a guy who spoke up and seemed to want to take charge. He was the kind of guy who would do anything for you when you got to know him, but he was outspoken and he had some enemies."

When we were saying good-bye, he told me not to worry. "Ron Alley was no collaborator," he said. "They had no right to send him to prison. You tell that to his widow and kids for me. . . . The night that I read about Ron Alley's death I cried. I just cried. I just couldn't believe that he would be dead without the Army granting him his honor. Oh — it was just too goddamn sad to believe."

From San Jose I drove on to Watsonville, California, a small rural town with low-slung houses and old appliances left to rot on dilapidated porches. This is a farming town of underpaid migrant workers, and off in the distance for as far as you can see the deep brown earth is crisscrossed by tractors that move along like pieces on a game board. Fred Smith grew up here and retired here after his career in the Army.

It was a fine, sunny day but the curtains were drawn in the Smiths' living room and reading lamps were turned on. On a coffee table and on the piano there were photographs of the children at their high school graduations.

Mrs. Smith was not well. When Fred left for Korea she was having trouble walking. By the time he came home she was completely paralyzed.

Unable to move even a finger, when she needs help she groans and her husband attends to her. Somehow he seems to know what it is she wants.

Major Smith, a soft-spoken, apologetic man with patches of white hair and a smile that hints of a good sense of humor, seemed eager to steer me away from a serious discussion of the POW camps where he had spent three years of his life.

"Has anyone told you about Rotorhead?" he asked, grinning. "Oh gee, Rotorhead, now there's a story. People did all sorts of things, crazy things to get at the Chinese. Guys shaved their heads, and this fellow Rotorhead, a helicopter pilot, drove around the camp on an imaginary motorcycle. One day he was called out for interrogation and he hopped on his motorcycle and screeched down over the stairs and flattened one of the Chinese guards. Oh boy, it's a wonder they didn't shoot him on the spot! Vrrooooooooom! He went flying down the stairs. The commandant came over and he said, 'You leave that motorcycle right where it is.' It bothered the Chinese; they thought we were all going crazy. Maybe we were."

I realized soon that Smith, who kept glancing over at his wife, was doing this for her benefit. He didn't want to talk about anything that might upset her. I moved across the room and sat down next to him and told him I had to know about Major Alley.

Over the course of an hour, this is what he told me: "Nobody figured there would be courts-martial. We'd lost about half of our men at Camp 5, and then things got better when the Chinese figured out they could use us for political reasons, to affect the truce talks. After that, word came in through Air Force senior officers that now there wasn't anything we could tell the Chinese that would hurt. Most of us figured that we'd tell them as little as we could. And this seemed harmless.

"Alley's court-martial, well it was a joke. A bad joke. I hated going to Fort Meade to testify. I hated the whole idea, just like I hate talking about it now. I was supposed to testify that Alley had given the Chinese information about Army artillery, information from technical and field manuals. I tried to tell the prosecutor that Alley and I, we were in the hut *together,* and I knew what he'd given. We both tried to give them [the Chinese] false information. We made a heck of a good try, but then they showed us they already had the manuals. They were in stacks in one corner of the hut! They'd got them from the United States during World War II. I tried to make the prosecutor see this, and I remember the law officer at the trial kept saying, 'Irrelevant, just answer the question.' It was obvious they wanted to hang someone."

I told Smith that Peckham had a theory it was Alley's own personality that caused him to be singled out for a prison sentence. Smith nodded his head.

"I remember there was a group of us sitting around, and Alley just piped up and said, 'I voted Communist back home in Maine.' He just blurted it out like that with his big, loud voice, and that accent. I looked around, and the guys were disgusted — they walked out. I talked to Alley later and I really let him have it. I said, 'What the hell did you say a foolish thing like that for!' He looked at me like he couldn't understand what I was making of it, and he said, 'I didn't like the other two parties' candidates and I knew the Commies wouldn't win anyway, so I voted as a protest.' That was Ron Alley, a stubborn, hard-headed guy. He thought he had a right to speak his mind one way or another. He didn't seem to have any idea how much a statement about voting for a Communist could hurt him."

He paused and we both sat quietly. He turned toward his wife, then looked back at me. He said he was certain that Alley hated Communism as much as anyone else did. Major Smith knew him well enough to be sure of this.

"But what about the others? Did they know him that well?" I asked him. He looked sad and shook his head no.

"And then there were some who thought he was too serious about the Chinese discussion groups. He would stand at attention when he was called on to read their propaganda. He played it so seriously. That was just his way. But other people figured he was getting favors in return. It wasn't true. He did a lot for the rest of the guys. He made a lot of bunk beds in the carpentry shop. And I remember a riding crop that he worked on. He hollowed out the inside, and he was going to put a list of every POW alive and dead in it so there'd be a record of us all, just in case."

I listened to Major Smith tell me about his travels with his wife. They had been all over the world with church groups. For a long time I sat and listened to the animated accounts of their trips to Russia and Europe. Smith spoke so earnestly, he seemed glad to be done talking about Korea. "I hope it will all end," he said as I got up to leave. "I've been trying to forget. I've never even told my children about this. I've been trying for a lot of years to put it out of my mind."

I had plans to meet an Air Force colonel three days later at a motel in the Bay area. I had read his testimony from the court-martial transcript, but on the telephone when we arranged this meeting I said nothing about the Alley case. He had been one of the Army prosecutor's key witnesses against Alley; he had stated under oath that he had actually heard Alley telling a Chinese guard about Army artillery procedures. His testimony had been persuasive, even though during cross-examination some questions arose. In the first place, he, prior to the trial, had mistaken a photograph of the assistant defense counsel for that of Alley. Also he had admitted that he knew very little about Army artillery procedures, and so it might have been possible that the information Alley was giving the Chinese was purposefully inaccurate. One other question I had in my own mind, and would never ask him, had to do with the circumstances of the alleged collaboration. He testified that he was on one side of a partition in a hut and Alley was on the other with the Chinese guard. They were separated by a wall made of paper or a paperlike material. He said he could hear through this partition. He later testified that he knew Alley had drawn a grid, an artillery grid, for the Chinese guard. He was never asked to explain how he could have described this grid in such detail without being present in the room.

The colonel was a neat, little man. He drove a waxed brown Mercedes and wore a baby-blue Banlon shirt and one of those big elaborate wristwatches that Air Force flyers are partial to. He spoke with a studied indifference. He told me without batting an eye how he had been shot down in the early spring of 1951, how he had fallen a thousand feet and his parachute had opened just as he hit the ground.

"You're lucky to be alive," I said.

He shrugged his shoulders and said, "I broke a foot." Then he smiled and ordered more black coffee.

The colonel spoke about his captivity: "I was taken to a place called Pak's Palace, named after the man who ran the place. There were fifteen to twenty Americans there, most of them officers. The interrogation was continuous, men were beaten around the shoulders, but it wasn't anything a man couldn't bear. At times I was the senior there; I recall protesting for better food. It didn't do any good. There were Russians there as interrogators, too. The Russians were low-key, but they were around the camp."

I interrupted, "Did you see any collaborators?"

He lit a cigarette. He fiddled with the package for a minute and then said that, as far as he remembered, the name-rank-serial-number rule had held up. "Obviously, if you had to go to the bathroom, you had to ask. But I personally tried to get the guys to hold as close to the line as possible. In my own case, I didn't even answer questions about family when asked."

"Did you think at that time that you would get into trouble for giving more than name, rank, and number?"

"Well, if you did, you deserved to get in trouble."

"Did you know any collaborators?"

"Not really, no. We suspected that within the camp some of our men were giving information about escape plans, and that was much more serious." He paused to brush off the table a long coil of ash that had fallen from his cigarette. "There were trials, you know, afterward."

"Yes, I know. Did you testify at any?"

"Yes, at a couple. But I'd never caught anyone red-handed. I don't know what happened to those guys. I think some may have gone to jail."

"Did you ever spend time at a camp that was the center for Chinese indoctrination?"

"Yes, but I can't recall what we called the camp."

"Camp 5?"

"Yeah, that's it. Up on the Yalu."

"Did you see much collaboration there, Colonel?"

"No. I would say there was no collaboration there, not to my knowledge. I didn't see any."

"Did you have to march in any 'Peace Parades' or write newspaper articles?"

"No."

"Did you sign any propaganda statements?"

"No. I just refused."

"You're aware that some Air Force officers signed germ warfare confessions there?"

"Yes. My theory on the confessions is that if you were shot down before the first of January 1952, you were just an enemy. After that you were accused of germ warfare. I didn't know any personally who signed. I don't know how I feel about those who did. I wasn't in their shoes. I didn't have that kind of pressure."

I asked the colonel if he had ever been to Maine, where I was from, and he said once, when he was working at the Pentagon and had just been promoted to colonel; he had flown up to Maine to get some lobsters to celebrate. We both laughed.

Then I turned back to Camp 5 on the Yalu River. "Did you feel the senior officers took over at Camp 5 and organized the men?"

"No. Looking back I must admit that there was no military organization in the camps."

"Did that lack of organization encourage collaboration?"

"It may have. The people we felt were collaborating in camp we just ignored. They were ostracized. In my case, there were only four or five people I trusted, and I ostracized everyone else. I don't know

---

why I didn't trust the others. I can't say. It was just something you felt about them."

"Did you feel the collaborators should be punished?"

"I think the Army was right to punish those men. I felt at the time that the guys who ratted on their men should be punished. But the others should be ignored. I still feel that way."

"Can you remember anything about the trials you testified at?"

"One was a little white-haired colonel, but I don't remember the other."

"Was the other a man named Alley? A Major Alley?"

"Yes. That's right," he said with surprise.

"I knew Alley. He was from Maine," I said.

"Oh?"

"You were sure Alley was guilty?"

"I was absolutely positive in my mind. I assumed he had received favors from the Chinese, I remember that. But it was just an assumption on my part."

"Did you *see* Alley do anything wrong?"

"No. At the time it was the sort of thing — where there was enough smoke there had to be fire. It was that sort of thing."

"But nothing you actually observed?"

"No, not that I recall. I'm hazy about my testimony, and those trials. I think I was just there at Alley's trial to help set the scene. If I'd been on a jury at the time I would have found Alley guilty."

We spoke off the record about other collaborators, even a Marine general whom he named. He did not like to use the word "collaborator," he said once. But he could name the men who had collaborated. He had many names. I asked him once more if he had heard or seen Major Alley do anything that was, in his mind, collaboration. He answered: "I never saw anything specific. I have no knowledge of specific acts by Alley." Then he added, "I do feel those trials were important to set an example for those who came after."

The colonel wished me well with my research, and we parted company. I watched him walking toward his car and I wished, as I had wished many times, that Ronald Alley were alive and that I could have brought these two men face to face to talk about his testimony at the court-martial in 1955.

That evening I flew on to San Diego, where another retired Air Force colonel met me at the airport and drove me to the Marine

Recruiting Depot for a meeting with a group of POWs. He was a rugged man with a cowboy face and drove a fast red sports car. The keys to the ignition hung on a chain made from his dog tags — a metal plate with his name, serial number, and the word NONE for religious preference printed in raised, braillelike letters.

We all sat around a table in the officers' dining room and talked first of the war in Korea. There were vivid accounts of the fighting and of atrocities committed against American GIs. In October of 1950, more than one hundred fifty POWs, survivors of what was called the Seoul–Pyongyang Death March, were herded onto a train and taken to the Sunch'on Tunnel. Late one afternoon the prisoners were marched to an open ravine, where they were told they were about to be fed. Several trucks backed up to the ravine, their rear doors dropped open, and machine guns fired until all the prisoners were dead.

Other stories told of Army chaplains being murdered while they tried to comfort dying prisoners. Wounded GIs held by the North Koreans were commonly dumped from stretchers and shot in the head or bayoneted and left screaming on the frozen ground. In the camps the sick were taken to crude hospitals where they were used in medical experiments and then left on dirt floors to die, covered with maggots. There was widespread torture, torture with heated bamboo spears, starvation, and rats.

All this was told only after much beer and many cigarettes.

No one here knew anything about Major Alley, but I stayed an extra day with these men because, now that they had begun talking about the horror of the POW camps, they had a great deal to get off their minds.

On April 10 I left Southern California and flew to Seattle, where I hoped to meet with another prosecution witness who had testified against Major Alley. This man had been an Army medic in Korea, and he now practiced medicine in the Seattle area. When I telephoned him from a motel near the airport he told me he really didn't have time to speak about Major Ronald Alley. "I would be happy to send you a minitape or something like that," he said, "but I don't know what we would accomplish by getting together."

I explained how I had been in California meeting with other former POWs, and that I was eager to find out what Alley had done wrong, and why he'd been singled out for a prison sentence. I said I only needed a few minutes of his time.

---

151

"I don't know how I can help you there," he replied. "I don't know what I can say. As an old Army man, I'm sure the Army did the right thing."

Curiously, he was one of the few POWs quoted in Kinkead's book, *In Every War but One*. In that book he appeared to share the Army's official perception of the POWs: "[There was] a regrettable lack of Yankee ingenuity, you might say. . . . [The POW behavior] was also, I think, the result of some new failure in the childhood and adolescent training of our young men — a new softness."

I decided to ask my questions over the telephone:

"What was it like for you, testifying at the court-martial?"

"It was hard on the liver," he replied.

"Why do you suppose Alley was brought to trial?"

"It would be speculative on my part, but, well, Alley was not very well liked. He didn't have many friends. He would go his own boneheaded way, regardless. He was a typical martinet type, an officer, but a reserve officer, so he didn't have West Point to save him," he said.

"Did you ever see him collaborate with the enemy?" I asked.

"No, not that I can recall."

"What was the trial like? Or, more specifically, did there seem to be an attitude that Alley had to be found guilty?"

"That would be quite an accusation. . . . I can say that the prosecutor was a junior-Senator McCarthy type who used all sorts of flamboyant tactics. . . . He gathered us together every morning at the Willard Hotel and we talked; he discussed his plans. . . . You might be right about Alley's trial, about the fact that it was over before it began."

"Alley was really bad, though," I said.

"Actually, I personally didn't know Alley that well. I spent a little while with — — — [another officer put on trial], though, and I personally would have loved to see him behind bars. He was a total wish-wash. Personally I didn't feel that way about Alley. As I think back on it, I wonder why I was called to testify. I don't remember testifying at Alley's trial. But the way I felt about — — — , well, I have no knowledge that — — — collaborated either. But many of us at the time felt that West Point saved him from prison. And like I said, I didn't feel the same about Alley."

"You never saw him do anything wrong?"

"No. And as I said, I wonder why I was called to testify."

I said nothing to the doctor about the record of his testimony at the court-martial. It read as follows:

As monitor from his squad the accused made a statement which was contributory to the indoctrination program [at Camp 5] as advocated by the enemy. . . . As I recall, the accused made the following statement, in substance: "The members of my squad are not cooperating with me in this program." I do not specifically recall what his recommendation was. It was, again in substance, something having to do with forcing each man within the squad to contribute, personally, to the indoctrination program.

This testimony had been very damaging at the trial. I had already been told by one former juror, whom I reached on the telephone, that the word "forcing" had made an impression on him.

I thanked the doctor and told him I would be in town for a while and would like to meet him if he had the chance. He told me again that he felt a meeting wouldn't accomplish anything constructive.

The next person I spoke with was Colonel Robert Wise, a wiry, brown-eyed, hell-for-leather Army infantryman. We met at the Holiday Inn, where he drank strong coffee and used his hands to underscore the urgency of what he had to say about Major Alley: "I'll tell you why Ron Alley got in trouble — because he was a tough guy. You know what I mean? One of the biggest problems we had in those camps was we didn't have many combat veterans and there wasn't anyone willing to organize things. Alley took things into his own hands right off the bat, and he made a lot of enemies for it. There were senior Air Force people telling us that we had nothing the enemy could use against us and so go ahead and tell the slopeheads what they wanted to hear. It was a big joke! Then the Army went after its own men when we came home. I'll tell you why — because somebody was trying to make himself look good. The guys who came on strong against Alley had their own hides to worry about."

Wise had been a prisoner of war held by the Germans in Poland during World War II. He recalled that conditions in that POW camp in Poland were much better than in Korea: "It was a different story in Korea. Oh, sure, you could get outside the camp compound, but what good did it do you? As soon as you set foot in the countryside you'd stick out like a sore thumb and you'd be picked up. We didn't blend in with the people in North Korea, and so how could we escape?"

Colonel Wise spoke at length about Alley's general court-martial: "I went to Fort Meade, to Washington. I couldn't believe the Army was actually pressing those charges against him. And it was clear to me and to others that this guy Alley was going to get stuck, and so we'd better get with the program. There were plenty of bitter feelings against Alley, but they were personal things, small things the Army managed to exaggerate and take out of context. . . . I never even got the chance to testify, because I was qualified as a hostile witness. The prosecution lawyer had questioned me and he said, 'All right, let's write it up as a statement and you just sign it.' I did. But then in the courtroom he started taking parts of what I'd said out of context. I had said stuff about Alley's interest in Socialism, and that was true. But Alley was always clear about one thing: He was always clear that the Socialism he thought was all right had nothing to do with the Communist crap the Chinese were dishing out. He said there was a big difference. But the Army never allowed that to come up at the trial. They thought it was all the same thing anyway. And in the courtroom I got angry. I let it be known that the truth wasn't being brought out. The whole trial stopped, and I was termed a *hostile witness* and dismissed. Logan, the defense counsel, tried to get my explanation put on the record, but it wasn't allowed."

Wise listened while I named those who had testified against Alley. "Hell," he said angrily, "those guys were put up in the Willard Hotel with the prosecutor, drinking every day and getting their stories straight while the Army picked up the tab. What the hell! This was the Army's big chance to tell Joe McCarthy how tough it was by nailing a Communist collaborator. It was ridiculous."

Just as Wise was certain Alley had been railroaded, another former POW who joined us at the Holiday Inn was not certain at all. Al Ellis, an impressive man dressed in a tweed jacket and gray flannel slacks, listened to Wise with an expression of incredulity and comic amusement. Then he described his own capture in Korea: "It never crossed my mind that I'd be captured. I figured I'd just go down fighting. I'd rather be dead than live under Communism. I drew my carbine and tried to shoot my way out, but the Chinese surrounded me when the carbine jammed."

Ellis spoke with self-assurance about Alley: "When I first saw Alley at Camp 5 I thought he was a Marine. He had on a Marine cape and he seemed to appear with the Marines. I'm not sure who was collaborating then; no one really knew. And yet there was no doubt that some were. So anyone who came into camp was under suspicion. Like Alley, some could never shake that suspicion. . . . I had heard Alley speak about Socialism; he talked about how he'd been stationed in Germany after the war and how he'd seen socialistic programs work. It bothered me to hear him talk like that. I never knew him to collaborate, but he made enemies with his talk."

Ellis told me he was from Maine himself. "It's always hurt me that a man from Maine was sent to prison. I mean, maybe that's part of the reason I didn't go back to Maine. I don't know."

Both Wise and Ellis told me there were two men who would be in the best position to know what Alley had done. They gave me the names — Ralph Nardella and Walter Mayo.

In my motel room that night, I tracked down Nardella and telephoned him. He spoke in a gravelly voice: "Listen, buddy, if I had anything on Alley I'd tell you up front. You understand? But I don't." At his request we left it at that. But reading through the court-martial transcript later that night I came across Nardella's testimony. He had contradicted testimony of eleven other prosecution witnesses who stated that, among other things, Major Alley had made many speeches exhorting men to sign a Peace Appeal circulating through the camp and written by the Chinese. Eventually the prosecution elicited from Nardella a "Yes" when asked if Major Alley was on the "yes side" of a debate over the Peace Appeal that showed the United States was the aggressor in Korea. Then the defense counsel attempted to show that all the officers in Camp 5 had been on the "yes side."

But the prosecution objected, saying: "And to which we object. No senior officer or any other officer except Major Alley here is on trial here before this court, and [it] is certainly an immaterial and irrelevant issue. Only the accused is on trial for the communication and other things and intercourse with the enemy. What a senior officer did or what any other officer did at Camp 5 is immaterial. Only one man is on trial, not the whole camp."

Before he hung up, Nardella told me I should talk with Walter Mayo. It was the second time that day I had heard Mayo's name.

That night I lay awake a long time, trying to picture what this man Mayo was like, wondering if he would be the man who would have proof that Alley was guilty as charged. I got out of bed after a while and telephoned Erna Alley in Bar Harbor. "I want to ask you about a man named Mayo, Walter Mayo," I said.

"Where are you?"

"In Seattle, Washington. What about Mayo?"

"He was at the trial. Ronald hated him. He hated Ronald. Have you found him? Is something wrong?"

I told her there was nothing wrong and that I hoped to be home in a week.

The last person I met with in Seattle was a retired Army major, Joseph Blanchard. We met on the golf course at the McChord Air Force Base in Lakewood, Washington, a suburb of Tacoma. The major still had golf privileges here, and we played nine holes together while he told me everything he could recall about Major Alley: "I was with him in Camp 5, and then Camp 2. He was with a small group of prisoners taken out of the camp for interrogations. The rumors were that they were constantly interrogated because they were cooperating. But I never knew of anything he did, and in Washington, D.C., I really had nothing to tell the prosecutor. They called us to the trial, and they were just fishing. They didn't know if we had anything on Alley or not. I remember that they were trying to build a case against him; that was obvious."

Blanchard, a soft-spoken, unassuming man with a deliberate style, finally volunteered his own theory on Alley: "I kept a low profile in the camps. That was the best way. But not Alley. I think he was singled out because of the widespread belief that he was a Socialist. Now, I could be wrong. But he was always talking about Socialism and trying to make people understand that there was a difference between Socialism and Communism. It was resented, and on the boats on the way home with many feeling guilty, and the Army doing things to *make* them feel guilty, well, it was easy to name Alley."

Major Blanchard gave me two names — Harry Palmer and, again, Walter Mayo.

I was able to reach Palmer by telephone that afternoon. When I asked him about the atmosphere of the court-martial, he spoke like a man with something to get off his chest: "Like most people, most of us went down as prosecution witnesses. I did. I had a young captain visit me for pretrial investigation. They took a statement from me. When I was on the stand, Kelly [the Army's prosecuting attorney] was disturbed with me because I didn't give him the answers he wanted. They were trying to get me to say things about Alley that I couldn't remember. . . . Kelly was openly aggressive. He was an energetic bastard. I can remember a very profound statement by Kelly that really pissed me off. I can almost remember it verbatim. We were walking toward the mess one afternoon, and he said, 'You know we have a stick of dynamite up this guy's ass, and we're going to light it any minute now.' It was an obsession with him to get that conviction, and he made it clear he wanted us to get with the program and to remember things that Alley had done. I couldn't, 'cause I didn't know of any, and so I was dismissed as a hostile witness."

Palmer also remembered hearing Alley talk about Socialism in the POW camp: "He seemed a little too sincere. And we had some self-styled heroes in the camp who took it upon themselves to go around saying who was a collaborator. Alley didn't have any friends among them. . . . And then on board the boats on the way home those guys were encouraged. We were days and days on board those ships, and it pissed me off the way those cloak-and-dagger types went around asking questions. They wanted to come up with something. Alley might have been finished off right on the boat."

There was no one left to see on the West Coast, and I was practically out of money, so my plans were to go straight back to Maine. But there was the name Walter Mayo; I had to talk with him.

I found out that Mayo was living in the Washington, D.C., area, so I telephoned him and asked if we could meet. I said nothing about Ronald Alley. He agreed to see me on Sunday morning after church.

I left for Washington that Saturday, and on the plane heading east, I read Colonel Mayo's testimony against Ronald Alley. There it was as plain as day: Mayo had told the jury that Alley was an informer, that he had informed the Chinese about the POWs' alerting system, the system they had for warning each other that guards were approaching. It was bad, the worst testimony against him.

# CHAPTER 12

A fter arriving in Washington, I spent the rest of the day walking around the city. I went to the Lincoln Memorial and down along the Potomac River. There were pick-up softball games everywhere. Spring had come.

Sunday morning I followed Walter Mayo's directions up the George Washington Parkway. At the second traffic light I turned right, a wrong turn, and in a few hundred yards the road narrowed through a heavily wooded area and then stopped short against a square concrete building. A uniformed guard hurried out a side door. He raised his hand for me to stop.

"I guess I'm lost. Where am I?" I asked.

---

"Just off 123," he said.

"Yes, I know. But what is this? This building here?"

"You'd better turn around," he said. He looked at the briefcase on my front seat.

"All right," I said. "But where am I?"

"This is CIA," he said.

I turned around and drove away.

A few minutes later I arrived at Colonel Mayo's. He greeted me at the door and brought me into the living room, where we sat down in front of a fireplace. Two large artillery shells had been converted into andirons. Another artillery shell had been turned into a lamp and stood in one corner of the foyer. The colonel's ten-year-old Chesapeake Bay retriever curled up on a couch by the window.

Mayo spoke with a discernible, somewhat patrician, Boston accent. Boston was the city where he had been educated, and the youthful, intelligent look of his face made it easier to picture him as a college professor in that city than a foot soldier in the mud and snow of Korea.

While we spoke of politics, of Cape Cod, and of anything but Ronald Alley, I sensed he was anticipating that at any moment I would change the conversation. He smoked cigarettes rather rapidly, holding them between thumb and forefinger and stabbing them in the air when he wished to underscore a point.

An hour went by, and when I finally asked how he felt about the court-martial of Major Ronald Alley, which I was researching for a book, he answered without hesitation: "I think you have to look at it in the context of the time it occurred. You have to remember that the Army had its problems then. They had trouble with McCarthy . . . . And looking back on it now, I think you could say the Army was on a witch-hunt, looking for Communists."

"And do you think Alley — "

"Yes, I think Alley might have gotten caught up in all that."

I had expected Mayo to oppose me vigorously, or at least to be defensive and vague. Instead, for the next forty minutes we spoke openly. He was informative and forthright. When I asked why Ronald Alley had been singled out for a prison sentence, he said, "Alley helped hang himself with his abrasive manner and his talk about Socialism. You can't go around telling people to look at the positive things about Socialism when their buddies are dying like

**159**

flies. You can't expect to get away with that in a Communist POW camp."

Mayo characterized Alley as being "different." He explained: "He was from Maine, and those people are just different. He had that crazy Down East accent and a very stubborn manner. He was a loner, without many friends."

"Was he a collaborator?" I asked.

Mayo paused, then replied: "I define collaboration as a sympathy for your captor and a philosophical belief in their system. Alley was not a collaborator. He should not have been found guilty. He should not have gone to prison."

He lit another cigarette. I let some silence fall between us over those last sentences. "But in 1955," I began slowly, "you testified against him. You said things that were very damaging. Did you believe he was guilty at the time?"

Mayo looked straight at me and answered directly. "What I said then might have been reinforced by what others told me. I was young, very young, and shared a guilt complex with the others. Not that we had done anything wrong, but the Army, the way the Army handled this thing made us all feel guilty, guilty for just having survived and returned home alive."

He continued: "The Chinese carefully planted the seeds of suspicion among us all. Alley had no friends. None. He was his own man, always keeping to himself. It was easy to be suspicious about someone who was an outsider."

In the following minutes I listened to Colonel Walter Mayo say what I knew Erna Alley had prayed someone might say one day about her husband: "*Then* I thought Ronald Alley was guilty. *Today* I know I was wrong."

Colonel Mayo had been a young officer in Korea. But in Camp 5 he had exhibited precocious nerve among the officers. I'd been told by others how Mayo had smuggled a movie camera and film into Camp 5, and how he had taken great risks to photograph the dying men. He would strip them so he could get on film their cadaverous faces and their arms and legs swollen with beriberi to the point of bursting. Mayo had risked a lot then, and I felt he was again risking a lot in order to help me get at the truth about Ronald Alley. He hadn't had to say anything at all to me. Others had refused to comment. He could have easily forgotten about Alley now. Or perhaps he just wasn't the sort of man who could have backed away. He said he wanted me to know the truth. And before I left he said he wanted Alley's widow to know.

I was ready to return home now, and with a sense of accomplishment. I was eager to tell Erna Alley about all this, but even before I left Washington I drafted a letter to Colonel Mayo confronting him with his court-martial testimony of 1955. I decided not to say anything to Erna until Mayo had answered this letter, explaining the contradiction. I had not done this with other prosecution witnesses, partly because they were not as crucial as Mayo was. Also, I was more interested in hearing their current versions of the story, versions that would not be influenced by the court-martial transcript. I was persuaded that the story told at the time of the trial had been deeply and dramatically shaped by the political atmosphere surrounding the trial. I wanted all the distance I could get from those events and that time; Major Alley had already been judged in that context. I wanted a new examination of the facts and I wanted, as much as it was possible, to strip away the prejudices of that time that might have obfuscated the facts and obscured the truth.

But now, after what Mayo had told me, I felt I had no choice but to confront him with his position in 1955.

At the trial Mayo had been put on the stand by the prosecution to show how he had overheard Alley having a conversation with a Chinese guard named Sun. The courtroom exchange went as follows (the Army prosecutor asking questions):

**Q:** When you observed the accused and Sun sitting on a bench, what, if anything did you do?

**A:** I grabbed hold of a brush broom and sort of swept myself towards — swept myself — swept a little path over to him, near where they were talking.

**Q:** Could they see you?

**A:** Their backs were toward me but, if they turned slightly to the right rear, they could see me.

**Q:** Why did you do this, Captain Mayo?

**A:** Well, we knew there was information leaking out of camp. We knew there were people who were informing. I suspected —

**Defense Counsel:** We object to suspicions, Mr. Law Officer.

**Law Officer:** He is testifying as to why he did it. Your objection is overruled.

**A:** I suspected Major Alley of being one of them. I thought it would be a good opportunity to find out exactly what he was telling Sun, so I went over there, got within earshot, and they were arguing rather loudly, so I didn't have to get too near to them to hear them and I sort of moved around a little bit.

**Q:** Did you get close enough to hear what the accused and Sun were talking about?

**A:** Yes, sir, I did.

**Q:** Will you please tell the court what you heard?

**A:** I heard Major Alley tell Sun in these approximate words: "What can I do? Every time they see you and me coming they have a lookout who gives the signal 'Bird Dog' and they all sit up and study." Sun replied, "You must make them study." And that's, in effect, what I heard.

**Q:** Did the accused tell Sun how the method of signalling worked?

**Defense Counsel:** We object to that as leading.

**Law Officer:** Overruled.

**A:** Yes, sir, he did.

Of the thousands of pages of court-martial transcript, the page containing this testimony by Mayo had always been the hardest for me to read. It not only pointed a finger at Alley, but represented him as a contemptible, despicable man, a man who would inform on his fellow prisoners. It had been the one page I had read many times over the past three years; when I had most felt like I ought to give up my search, it was because of Mayo's testimony.

I wrote Mayo about this portion of his testimony, which, I told him, was a blow. I was relieved when his letter came to my house in Maine. In it, he assured me that Alley had never informed the enemy about the POW alert system. Mayo remembered the incident described in the court-martial transcript, and he told me the Chinese probably already knew the alert system and that Alley just blurted out, "What the hell can I do, they have an alert system," after the Chinese guard had been prodding him to persuade his men to cooperate in the study sessions.

———

Walter Mayo's letter cast a different light on Major Alley. I took it to Bar Harbor and showed it to Erna. "After all these years," she said softly. "What this would have meant so long ago to Ronald."

*　　*　　*　　*　　*

In the months following my meetings with Colonel Mayo and the other former prisoners of war, I waited to hear about the intelligence files I had requested from the Army. Those were the files containing nearly nine hundred pages missing from the FBI report on Ronald Alley. I wrote several letters to Senator Cohen's office concerning these files, and — curiously — replies from his office began arriving already opened. Soon after I notified Sally Lounsbury, one of the senator's aides, of this tampering, the Army sent me official word that the files had been located and that I could come pick them up at Fort Meade, Maryland.

I arrived at Fort Meade on April 17, 1981, and was introduced to an Army captain who agreed to take me to Intelligence Headquarters. First, however, I persuaded the captain to show me around the fort and to help me find the building that had housed the courtroom in 1955. No one seemed to know where that building might be, and as we went from place to place I had a chance to tell the captain what I had learned about the Alley case. He listened and didn't say much at first, and then, over lunch in the Officers Club, he leaned across the table and said, "So you think this major was a scapegoat?"

Because I was relying on the captain's help, I was reluctant to say anything disparaging about the Army. He sensed this, and offered his own view.

"Seems entirely possible to me," he said. "You wouldn't believe what goes on around here. There aren't enough rifles to go around this place. During drills, some men march with yardsticks on their shoulders."

The captain went on to tell about rapes and assaults at the fort. He described an alarming disciplinary problem and a very low "level of intelligence."

"In one barracks, a group of soldiers had to be given an instruction sheet on how to operate the television. And we cover all this up. *We'd* get busted if we let on how bad things really are. No one wants to know how bad things really are."

With the help of a civilian engineer at the fort, we did manage to find the building that had contained the courtroom where Major

163

Alley had been court-martialed. It had since been converted to security offices, with banks of file cabinets and locked drawers on rows of metal desks. But records showed that it had been a well-appointed courtroom in 1955, with a plush red carpet and an exquisite mahogany railing across the front of the room a few feet from the table where Alley had sat with his defense attorney.

Finally, with the captain leading the way, we went to a basement room in the Security and Intelligence Command where two officers handed over 869 pages bundled and wrapped in plain paper. The officers stood silently at the table as I signed release forms of some sort. They said nothing when I thanked them. There was an eerie silence.

Outside, I told the captain how strange it felt for me to finally be here at Fort Meade, the place where Alley's life had changed; where he had first learned of the Army's charges against him, where he had been put on trial, convicted, and sentenced, and where he had been locked in the stockade before being sent away to prison in Kansas. I said it was ironic to think that his personal files were still here.

"You're really into something," the captain said. "Did you see the way those guys looked at you? I know these types. I could tell by the way they looked at you, they know everything you're up to. They know a lot more about you than you'd want them to."

The intelligence files contained a vast amount of information. They were like reading a book on Ronald Alley. The files told how he had requested a transfer from the reserve unit in Schenectady, where he was having trouble with his commanding officer, Major Rauterberg. There were letters from Rauterberg to the Army's Counter Intelligence Command, pointing out in a self-aggrandizing paragraph how he (Rauterberg) had always been vigilant and reliable to keep his eyes open for subversives, and how he was sure this man Alley was one of them. Alley was then investigated by the CIC (Counter Intelligence Command) and the FBI. His mail was examined, his residence was "checked," and his neighbors were interrogated at length. In the sanitized report the names had been deleted, and people whom the FBI questioned at the time were referred to as "Informant 1," and so on, right up through "Informant 15."

The investigation continued while Ronald was in Korea. It concluded that there was no proof or evidence to confirm Rauterberg's charges. But Alley was characterized as "someone worth watching."

When he returned home from Korea, and while he was hospitalized for two years, his mail was continually examined. He was again the subject of an investigation that lasted right through preparation for the court-martial at Fort Meade. And for eight years after his release from the prison at Fort Leavenworth, his private life was monitored by the FBI, who sent periodic reports to Mr. Hoover in Washington, D.C.

The intelligence file contained dozens of accusations against Ronald by fellow POWs who said, among other things, that he was most likely a Socialist. This is the one thing that seemed to tie all the accusations together. The charges had been collected by Army Intelligence interrogators when the POWs were repatriated. For twenty-five years the Army concealed the identities of these POWs from the Alley family.

There were also dozens of reports by men who said Alley had been a loyal officer and a good soldier. And many of the worst accusations were directly contradicted or explained by extenuating circumstances described in detail by other POWs. But the Army had enough to press charges and to order a general court-martial.

Reading these hundreds of pages and studying all the material I had collected in three years of research, I began to see a vivid picture of Major Alley and what had happened to him in Korea. I wasn't at all sure what my next step would be, but I began writing a long narrative on the POW camps. When it was finished, the heart of the Alley story had emerged. It was a heart full of disease and filth and suffering. A heart of darkness.

# CHAPTER 13

For Ronald Alley and several hundred other American soldiers the darkness fell in earnest during the last week of November 1950. The war was still new then, and GIs, having been assured again and again for several weeks that they would be home by Christmas, were suddenly surrounded and trapped in the frozen mountain passes of North Korea. Hundreds of thousands of Chinese troops had entered the war, decimating the UN forces that were positioned in the region of the Chosin Reservoir. The UN troops, comprised mainly of American Army and Marine units, were overrun and taken prisoner. Nearly a thousand men were captured as they retreated from the battle at Chosin.

Up until this time the enemy had been North Korea, and the American soldiers had heard plenty about what it would be like to be captured. They had heard of the mass executions and of the ghoulish tortures performed on prisoners. It was not just the North Korean *troops* one had to fear; in the tiny dilapidated villages scattered across North Korea, civilians had participated in the slaughter of Air Force pilots shot down and ferreted out of the dark hills. There were hideously mutilated corpses left behind as evidence of the antipathy for Americans.

What was it like to be a prisoner of the North Koreans in December 1950? First, there was the feeling of exhaustion. The fighting at Chosin Reservoir had gone on and on, through the days and nights for more than eighty hours. It had been the worst kind of fighting, much of it hand-to-hand, as hordes of fresh, well-trained Chinese troops burst through defense lines and artillery positions. Many who died were killed at point-blank range.

Those who escaped and were hunted down and taken prisoner felt their exhaustion and pain give way to terror. Expecting to be shot, they were, instead, prodded with bayonets and herded into groups in the woods. Held at gunpoint, they were at the mercy of a bizarre enemy that screeched and jabbered in a strange language and dressed in foolish-looking brown quilted uniforms with caps that buttoned down over their ears and around their faces, concealing all but their eyes.

The prisoners were marched along the roads throughout the night and then pushed back into the woods and made to lie down in the snow during the daylight hours. They were given no food for days. Those who were wounded received no medical attention; they were helped along by their comrades, and when they could go no farther they were summarily shot.

To be a prisoner then was to be a man without any hope of escape. There were no lines being held, no pockets of friendly forces. At night the prisoners were marched in a seemingly aimless pattern through the woods. And each day, while they were huddled in the snow, the UN troops that might have rescued them fled farther south, until soon the ground no longer shuddered from artillery fire and in the sky all the planes disappeared.

What Alley and the rest of them knew then was that they were stranded, and that they had to walk when they were ordered to walk or they would be murdered. Eventually the enemy felt secure enough to march their prisoners in broad daylight and to shoot them in broad daylight and leave their bodies lying in the open roads.

Among themselves, the prisoners began to admit that they were on a death march not unlike the infamous marches conducted by the Japanese in World War II. And this march was going nowhere but in mad, endless circles. Every day there were more prisoners rounded up and more wounded shot. Gradually, those who could reason at all began to see that their captors were just killing time. The North Koreans, too, had been surprised by their fortunes at Chosin Reservoir. Suddenly they had hundreds of prisoners on their hands and no place to put them. And now that the Chinese were in control, new orders had gone out that these prisoners, at least those strong enough to survive the march and those who would cooperate, were to be kept alive for some future purpose.

And so they were kept alive, barely alive. Eventually they were fed cracked corn and boiled cabbage and they were thrown into small huts that had been abandoned weeks earlier when the UN forces were confidently pushing north. Every day the prisoners and their captors were amazed to see how many American GIs were being rounded up in the woods.

While they were still in the proximity of where the fighting had taken place, a few prisoners managed to sneak off at night and carry back C rations that had not been stripped from the frozen corpses. There was no plan for escape, because there was no place to escape to, and so those who had sneaked away always came back to help the others.

Ronald Alley saw his first prisoner-of-war camp in a bombed-out village approximately thirty miles northwest of Chosin Reservoir. The Koreans called this place Kanggye. The GIs named it "Death Valley." There were many death valleys in North Korea in those days; each was a place that had once supported life, however primitive, and modest hopes and plans, but now contained only gruesome signs of death and terror.

There were two dozen GIs held in the same floorless hut with Alley at Kanggye. Inside this hut he saw flesh tear off the bones of men's frozen feet when they pulled off their ice-packed boots. Uniforms were spotted with dark clots of blood. There was new death every day. Provided only with a wooden cart, the prisoners carried the bodies off into the woods, while their captors followed indolently behind them with machine guns. Sticks and fallen tree limbs were thrown on top of the dead, for there were no tools for burial.

In those first days at Death Valley, Captain Alley was the senior officer in his hut. He had an infected gash on one leg and blisters on his feet, but he was better off than many. He had done nothing to distinguish himself so far except to help a wounded GI get to his feet and walk when a Korean guard had pointed a gun at the man's head during the long march. Alley was twenty-six years old and scared to death. When he sneaked out of the camp one night and brought back a frozen leg from a mule's carcass and sticks to keep a small fire going inside the hut, he had no heroic intentions. He was just a scavenger, cold and starving and wanting to stay alive. He just wanted to stay alive a little longer.

He came back to the hut and reported to his comrades that there was an English-speaking guard in the camp; he had heard his voice a few hundred feet away while making his way back through the darkness. To Alley this voice speaking in the darkness of Death Valley represented some vague prospect for hope. He said he was going to find a way to get closer to that voice, face to face with the man speaking. It seemed to some of the others like a brash and stupid thing to do. They were lucky to be alive, and all they wanted was to be left alone in the hut, some said. But Alley took a different point of view; he said they wouldn't be alive much longer unless someone did something.

In Death Valley in January 1951 soldiers were living in terrible conditions. The war they had come to Korea to fight had gotten out of hand. The Army they had sworn their allegiance to had retreated and run many miles away from them. Soldiers were dying needlessly, and no one was doing anything about it. If one soldier could change this, then Alley had to be the one. He was an officer, the senior officer in his hut, and it was up to him to decide what to do.

For several days Alley argued with the guards posted at his hut, shouting at them and gesturing wildly with his hands, until somehow he managed to be taken to the man who spoke English. He stood facing this man and he *ordered* him to comply with the rules outlined by the Geneva convention. There were rules, he argued.

He was told that North Korea had not been a signatory to any of the Geneva agreements. He was told that all those rules were no good anymore. And then, instead of being shot or beaten for his insubordination, he was, miraculously, brought in out of the cold to the hut where this English-speaking man lived. He was given a chair to sit on. Soon someone brought him a cup of hot tea and an American cigarette. And before long someone else appeared at his side to light the cigarette for him.

Speaking in fluent English, the man identified himself as the commander at Kanggye. He asked Alley where he was from. Alley got up abruptly from the chair, stood at attention, and began rattling off his name, rank, serial number, and date of birth. The commander laughed and told him to sit back down. He told him he was a Chinese officer, and that he had fought with the Americans against the Japanese in World War II. You Americans never seem to understand, he said, smiling. You think everyone plays by *your* rules. Your soldiers tried to do the same thing with the Japanese; they stood there giving name and serial number and they got their heads chopped off for it. One head after another. A whole row of American heads on the ground, and *then* finally they realized. Does it make any sense, the commander asked, to draw a line and say you won't step over it, just to make us push you over it?

Alley demanded to be told who the senior officer was in Death Valley. There are no senior officers, he was told. You are all the same rank, waiting to die in the middle of nowhere, and to be buried under a pile of brush. *Unless* — you want to discuss this situation sensibly.

The commander had an offer: No more American prisoners would die here if they could be persuaded to cooperate. If they could be made to offer no resistance and to understand that they were to obey the rules of their captors.

When Alley finally returned to his hut he explained to his men that he had some good news. He had managed to do some horse trading with the Chinese commander; there would be food and medicine for the prisoners and a promise that the severely wounded would be evacuated by truck, then train to the city of Hamhung. He explained that he had drawn up a questionnaire for the commander, a questionnaire he believed was innocuous, and that all the men should fill it out when their turns came. No harm would come to them if they listened to him.

There was then an argument in the hut which lasted for several hours. Among the enlisted men there was general agreement that

Alley's plan made good sense. But officers warned Alley that he was talking about breaking the Army's rules. The Army's rules don't apply here, he told them. The Army doesn't want us to die for no reason. I'll take responsibility, and the Army will stand behind me.

To his satisfaction, then, he was doing the right thing for the right reasons. He was going to do everything in his power to get them all out of Death Valley alive. And then, if he succeeded, if they lived through this, they could be of some future good to the Army. He told them he loved the Army and was doing what he believed was best.

In a group of more than two dozen prisoners of war, Ronald Alley from Maine had stepped forward to take charge. This is how he would forever assess his decision. He had distinguished himself as a savior to some, a traitor to others. And to him it never mattered what the detractors thought. He was going to get them all out alive if he could.

For two days the Chinese commander went from hut to hut with questionnaires asking for name, rank, serial number, date of birth, parents' occupations, religious affiliation, formal education, and duties in the American armed forces. And in every hut there was Alley speaking with this commander who had mastered such flawless English: Captain Alley and I have already discussed this, the commander would say. And Alley would then explain the deal he had worked out, assuring those prisoners who were reluctant to cooperate, that his way was the best way.

Many listened to him, some eagerly, others grudgingly. And many others just watched and swore they would remember: Not that Alley had a plan to save lives, but that he had been the first to collaborate with the enemy. That *they* had been willing to keep their inviolable silence until death, but Alley had compromised their position.

Winter went on, the days passed, and there were many more scenes of soldiers in ragged blood-caked uniforms pushing the wooden burial cart off into the woods. For a long time it seemed the deal that Alley had struck and the chance he had grabbed at would amount to nothing. There were more arguments between the officers. It was no longer just Alley's position, but that of many others of his rank and below, that the senior officers in Death Valley — those officers higher in rank — were exercising no authority. No chain of command had been established, no committees for escape. It was imperative that someone be blamed for this. Assigning blame would be a source of consolation. But always the consolation would come up short against the hard reality of Death Valley: There could be no chain of command here, for the enemy did not recognize rank. There could be no committee for escape, for everyone was too weak and sick to organize. And besides, there was still no place to run to.

Finally, in late March of 1951, this group of prisoners, nearly three hundred in all, was rounded up out of the freezing huts and herded out onto a snow-covered road. For a few minutes it seemed to Alley and to others that the English-speaking commander might finally see to it that they were taken south to that city he had spoken of, and that trains might be sent to evacuate them.

But out on the road they were prodded again with bayonets, and they walked just as they had walked before. They walked along as best they could for several days, marching through the nights, losing more comrades, until at last they could see, down in a valley, rows of huts pressed up alongside a river. From all over the countryside prisoners in shapeless formations marched toward the valley and the river that sparkled in the sunlight. And, when they got close enough to the huts, they saw that this was not just another village, but a prison camp surrounded by barbed-wire fences. The sinister, brutal look of this place filled them with apprehension. They might have been walking into Auschwitz or Birkenau.

This place would become known as Camp 5 in Pyoktong, North Korea, on the banks of the Yalu River. And, to the prisoners approaching the barbed-wire fence for the first time, there came the realization that this place was not here by accident or coincidence: It had been constructed for *them,* as if they might not be leaving here for a very long time.

Already there were prisoners here, with pale, terror-stricken faces and emaciated bodies — hundreds of them, and the numbers swelled every week. They were all packed tightly into dozens of floorless mud-and-stick huts. Packed so tightly they slept like sardines, no one able to stretch out his legs. It was an arctic place, with little sunlight and no warmth. At night the rats burrowed between their bodies to keep alive. The prisoners' cries for food and water were ignored. There was no medicine to kill their pain. At night they prayed for the wind to howl hard enough to drown out the sounds of men vomiting and weeping. Below the sound of the wind there were death rattles to awaken them.

Camp 5 was a miniature holocaust. The Chinese were in charge of this subjugation, carrying out a program of systematic torture and torment that went on day and night. Prisoners were thrown into holes in the ground too shallow and narrow for them to lie down or stand up in; for days they were kept there, crouching and calling out. They were kept in cages and stabbed with sharpened sticks by the passing guards. As a form of entertainment for their captors, they were tied with ropes and strung up on wooden beams in such a way that when they moved involuntarily they would die by hanging themselves. There were prisoners with their eyes gouged out of their skulls, and others with limbs missing. Twice a day they were given a meal, but here, too, it consisted of cracked corn like chicken feed. They were covered with lice. There was pneumonia and beriberi and dysentery. Men had dysentery so bad that their bowels moved every half hour for months. Every night there were more horrors, and in the morning more men to bury, their bodies already gnawed upon by the rats. Those wounded prisoners who had made it this far submitted to the Korean "sickhouses," hoping for refuge. Instead, they were used as guinea pigs for indescribable medical experiments.

Again, in those early days at Camp 5, there was no organization among the prisoners, no chain of command, no senior authority among the officers. Officers were held separately from the noncommissioned officers, who in turn were segregated from the enlisted men. Each man was on his own to face his own portion of this nightmare.

Many just gave up. It was discovered that death could be brought on by giving up. Soon there was a term for it the prisoners used — "give-up-itis." And everyone knew exactly what this meant: A man would move to one corner of his hut, he would refuse to eat his bowl of corn, and in a very few days he would be dead. Quickly the others would take his clothes, and at the next roll call they would try to hide the body, hoping to receive the dead man's portion of rations.

The idea of giving up was anathema to Ronald Alley. He talked about his wife and family and told the others he was going to make it home alive. He went from hut to hut preaching that they all had a duty to stay alive, for their families, for themselves, and for the

United States Army. He was always keeping after them, pushing food in front of those who wanted to give up, sometimes hollering at them.

In the woods outside Kanggye, Alley had found a green Marine cape that was in remarkably good condition. Standing with his shoulders filling out this cape, he looked and sounded like he was the one in charge, the one responsible.

He preached to them because he couldn't stand the sight of anyone giving up. It was as if he sensed that his own chances for survival were tied to the survival of those around him. He may have imagined what it would be like here if he were the only one to survive. He preached at them in the darkness of the hut at night, as if the sound of his voice could animate them and prevent their sleep from sliding into death by morning.

In the morning at roll call, the others could count on seeing Alley there first. He would stand at attention when his name was called. Somehow he'd gotten hold of a broom with half a handle, and every time the others turned around he was crouched over, sweeping out the frozen mud floor of the hut. He was seen everywhere in the officers' compound, sweeping and preaching and coughing; he was coughing all the time now and spitting up blood.

Toward the end of March, when winter had begun to subside, the prisoners at Camp 5 observed the sudden arrival of a number of Chinese officers, who moved their belongings into the headquarters building just outside the barbed-wire fence. These officers quickly took over the administration of the camp, and on April 1, 1951, all the prisoners were brought together for the first time for a "camp meeting."

A Chinese officer named Ding, who would earn the nickname "Snake Eye," proclaimed that the prisoners had been brought to Pyoktong for a purpose. They were here to study and to learn the *truth,* he said. They were here to learn that soldiers fighting for America were nothing more than cannon fodder for the imperialists of Wall Street.

Concentrating their efforts primarily upon the two companies of prisoners in the officers' territory, Ding and his associates initiated an intensive program of interrogation and indoctrination. Singly, or in small groups, the prisoners were taken at gunpoint from their huts out to the headquarters building, where they were held and interrogated for days at a time. During the lengthy interrogations the prisoners slept on the floor of the headquarters building. They were often walked around the barbed-wire fence so other prisoners could observe them. Public interrogations were important to Ding, who seized every opportunity to plant the seeds of suspicion among the officers; he wanted to pit them against each other and to destroy their mutual trust. As an officer was walked around and around the camp compound there would be English-speaking Chinese guards moving among the prisoners, pointing out how easy life could be if they too cooperated. Those who refused to answer questions during interrogations were put in holes in the ground until they acquiesced.

Alley was one of the first to be interrogated at length and to discover that it was not the answers that mattered to these Chinese officers. He was held at the headquarters building for several days with another Army captain and told to write down information about Army artillery manuals. For a while both prisoners wrote false, misleading facts, until the interrogator revealed several stacks of Army manuals on the floor in one corner of the room. Ding explained that these manuals had been left over from World War II, when China had been America's ally. He made it clear that all he wanted was cooperation. We want you to learn to cooperate, he said. We want to teach you the truth about Communism. And if you don't learn the truth, we will keep you in Pyoktong for twenty or thirty years to educate you; and if you still don't learn the truth, then you will die in Pyoktong, and we will dig a hole and bury you so you don't stink. Ding was a sinister man, and this was his favorite threat. He talked often about how the dead GIs stank.

Ding and another officer named Wong appeared to have insatiable appetites for interrogating the prisoners. Their energy was inexhaustible. They were ready at any time of the day or night to start in on someone else. And gradually the prisoners began to see that they could keep Ding happy by giving him information, even though he already had it. For many, this was what he meant about learning the truth, and it was a small price to pay to stay alive.

Ding's program of education accelerated. The officers were broken down first into squads that met for several hours every morning, afternoon, and evening in study groups. Usually the individual groups were comprised of the men in each hut. There were introductory lectures by the Chinese, characterizing America as the illegal aggressor in Korea. Communist literature by Marx and Engels was read aloud hour after hour, first by the Chinese and soon by individual prisoners. In every squad, one prisoner was appointed monitor. The appointments were made arbitrarily by the Chinese. It became the monitor's responsibility to conduct discussion groups and to force everyone in the group to participate in a dialogue about the lecture material. At the end of each class the monitor would require each prisoner to write an opinion of the material.

At first, all of this seemed like a preposterous joke to the prisoners. And there were many officers who believed the Chinese would abandon the program if they resisted. Then, one afternoon in one of the study groups, an American Army officer, a major, was forced to sign a "cognition," which amounted to a confession of guilt for his participation in the war in Korea. By now these cognitions were routinely requested and signed, but this officer refused, saying the damn thing wasn't worth the paper it was written on. The class was stopped. The officer was led away, and all night long he was interrogated at headquarters. He was heard screaming through the night. When he was finally returned to his hut he was insane, and soon afterward he died.

The idea of resisting now seemed pointless. The education program itself was ludicrous enough to be harmless, so long as you cooperated. Most officers agreed on this, and late that spring there was additional impetus to go along. Recently captured Air Force pilots, some of whose rank made them the senior officers in the compound, began telling POWs of the new, official Air Force policy concerning capture in this place. Air Force pilots had been instructed now that there was nothing they could divulge to the enemy that would hurt America's efforts in the war. They were told to say and do whatever was required of them by the enemy in order to stay alive.

Some officers took issue with this; they argued that cooperation was, in itself, fundamentally wrong because it gave the enemy the upper hand. Others argued that the enemy already had the upper hand, and that the Air Force policy was the only sensible way to handle things.

The Air Force policy made perfect sense to Captain Alley. He told others that finally someone in the Pentagon had come to his senses and realized that cooperating with the Chinese was the only

**176**

way for prisoners to beat their captors. For Alley, cooperation meant survival. And survival was the only victory at Camp 5.

And so he preached survival. He felt compelled to tell the others to cooperate. Just because a man reads their literature doesn't mean he has to believe it. This he often said. And he would go on: Who cares about their truth? Truth is what a man keeps to himself in his heart.

Soon Alley was appointed by the Chinese to become his squad's monitor, replacing a man who had died. He took this task seriously. When prisoners fell asleep in his class he woke them up and told them that staying awake in this class was the only thing keeping them alive. When they were ordered to write opinions and cognitions, he saw to it that they were written properly. If cooperation could keep them all alive, then he was determined to see that they cooperated, to the letter. This earnestness, this unremitting and irremediable earnestness was Alley's way, had always been his way since his first week of boot camp.

His way began to irritate some of the others, however. He began to be distinguished by this way of his. And when the Chinese took him out of the compound for interrogations, when he was led around the perimeter of the barbed-wire fence, prisoners began to believe that he could not be trusted.

The deaths continued throughout the nights and the colorless days, but there were some subtle changes. Prisoners were suddenly given the chance to write letters home, if they advocated the Chinese position on the war and if the letters bore the following return address: "Care of Chinese People's Committee for World Peace Against American Aggression." The theme was always the same — that Communism could bring peace to the world.

Soon the indoctrination programs expanded. One hut was converted overnight into a "library" and stocked with new hardbound volumes of Communist writings, which included *The Twilight of Capitalism* and *Bases and Empires.* On the stone steps of a bombed-out church in the center of the officers' compound, groups of prisoners were assembled each night to sing Communist party songs with names like "East Shines Red." Men were dying while the disjointed chorus of American voices filled the sky over Pyoktong.

Against a macabre backdrop, a game was being played between the prisoners and their captors. Not everyone knew exactly what the boundaries of the game were, and some men either refused to play along or refused to acknowledge to themselves that they were a part of it. The game was one of deception. The Chinese believed that the greater a prisoner's cooperation in the education program, the greater the chance that he might be used for propaganda purposes, which could influence the peace talks that would eventually be initiated. There was a belief among the Chinese guards that cooperation signaled brainwashing had begun to take effect, and that at the end of the war there might be thousands of Americans who would refuse to go home, who would become eager converts to Communism. Most POWs, however, cooperated in order to get the Chinese off their backs; they were willing to give the illusion of cooperation in order to increase their chances of survival. Some of the Chinese guards knew this, but were willing to tolerate this condition because it enlarged their own stature among their peers; they could win points in this game by appearing to be the kind of men who could elicit cooperation from the prisoners.

The indoctrination and education programs became more and more public as time went on. Discussion groups expanded from the squad to the company level. In the early evening hours, the prisoners were brought together to stand in a large semicircle while one officer after another was led to the stone steps to read statements denouncing the United States. Only those too sick to stand were excused. The rest would read aloud when they were told. They would read that President Truman was a vicious warmonger and that Secretary of State Dean Acheson was a pawn of the rich and greedy capitalists. Most of these speeches would be forgotten in the ludicrous monotony with which they were presented; most of the prisoners had learned by now that by going along they could make it easier on everyone. The officers also understood that the extent to which they could appease their captors would affect the treatment of the enlisted men and noncommissioned officers who were quartered separately at the other end of Camp 5. When officers began writing pro-Communist articles for the "camp newspaper" (which was called *Toward Truth and Peace*), medical officers were permitted to go into the huts of the enlisted men and administer what aid they could. A bulletin board was hung not far from the stone steps, and so long as there were anti-American statements hanging there, signed by the senior officers, the executions were postponed, and death was left in the hands of starvation and disease.

The speeches Ronald Alley gave made an impression and so did the articles he signed because he had distinguished himself again, this time as a rebel. Privately, he had begun to argue with other officers that the Army's role in Korea had been distorted by the Pentagon. The Army, he said, had come to Korea to drive the insurgents out of the South, back across the 38th parallel. This was *one* war — the war he had agreed to fight. But then there was another war, the war of the politicians, the war that endeavored to push the enemy all the way out of Korea to the Manchurian border. *This* wasn't the Army's war. And yet this was the war they had been captured in. Alley took it upon himself to explain that all of the soldiers held captive at Camp 5 were not military prisoners, but political prisoners. He was certain of this, and became unrelenting on the point. And when he was backed into a corner by officers opposing his position, particularly those officers educated at West Point, he held on stubbornly. In the presence of thirty officers he stated defiantly one night that he believed in the virtues of Socialism. He had been in Germany after World War II and he had seen Socialism work for the good of the people. And what about the programs of Franklin D. Roosevelt? Socialist programs had saved America.

When he was through talking that night, every officer who had heard him left in disgust. And this was one speech that was unprovoked. It was a speech they would not forget.

It was not long before the Chinese issued each prisoner a notebook bound with a red-and-blue cover. On the front there were Chinese characters and the symbol of a giant gear. Mao Tse-tung's picture was engraved on the inside, and there were many blank pages on which the prisoners were told to write their personal biographies. Most filled in five or six pages, writing what they knew would satisfy their captors. Alley told the men in his hut that writing was one of the things a man could do to stay alive, to keep his brain working. He had read once, long ago, that if you could write every day and exercise your intellect you could fight off the ravages of malnutrition, and your own sense of judgment would not atrophy.

He wrote a great deal. Word went around soon that Alley, the guy with the funny accent and the theories on Socialism, the guy who was taking all of this so seriously, the guy who at Death Valley had gone from hut to hut with the English-speaking Chinese commander, had written a biography of one hundred twenty-five pages — a damn book!

These days, when still more prisoners were dying senselessly, there were plenty of Air Force officers going off each day to sign spurious germ warfare "confessions" for the Chinese. There were prisoners participating in the Chinese "Olympics," posing with baseball bats and soccer balls in front of Chinese photographers. There were other officers drawing diagrams of tanks and airplane instrument panels — all of which the Chinese already possessed. They all agreed this was harmless. And yet, there was something about Alley, something about his seriousness and the way he seemed to know so much about Socialism; there was just something that made many of the other prisoners think, when they watched him standing there with his shoulders drawn back on the steps of the bombed-out church, that he might be one of them — he might be a Red. None of them knew that at this precise time the same suspicion about Communism was tearing through their towns and cities in America, and would be waiting for all of them when they returned.

Soon there appeared on the bulletin board at Camp 5 the transcript from what the Chinese said had been a broadcast over Peking Radio:

Our special correspondent with the Chinese People's Volunteer Corps in Korea has recently visited a prisoner-of-war camp of British and American troops. He reports that the prisoners he talked to all expressed amazement at the tremendous difference in the morale of the two sides fighting in Korea.

An American artillery officer, Captain Alley, in discussing the question of morale, told our correspondent that anyone who has been anywhere near the front can size up this difference at a glance. "I doubt that troops like ours could win any war."

When our correspondent asked for an explanation of this difference in morale between the two sides, Captain Alley replied, "It's clear the Chinese know what they're fighting for. That's why they don't seem afraid of any damn thing we throw at them. We are fighting simply because those are our orders.

---

We shoot because we want to save our skins. . . . When we meet up with any kind of setback or reverse we feel that the bottom has dropped out of everything. Then we just concentrate on finding some way to stay alive for another twenty-four hours. That's why I surrendered, and why most of the guys who got here gave up as soon as it looked like they were pinned down."

This statement is borne out, our correspondent writes, by the readily growing numbers of American prisoners of war who turn up at this camp each day.

This particular camp already holds several hundreds of American captives, largely from the 31st and 32nd Regiments of the US 7th Infantry Division. It was virtually wiped out.

Those who have been wounded get daily medical attention, and the prisoners are receiving as good if not better food than the Chinese People's Volunteer Corps. The camp is also surrounded by anti-aircraft batteries manned by the Chinese People's volunteers to protect it from the attacks of American bombers.

Another artillery officer, Captain Deere [phonetic] of the 67th Artillery Battalion told me that he had fought in both world wars, but that he had never fought against such a tough enemy as the Chinese People's Volunteer Corps.

"Our planes and guns have tremendous firepower," Captain Deere remarked. "I always thought nothing could survive our all-out barrages. Yet the Chinese would stand up to our heaviest bombardments, and even launch immediate counter-attacks with their machine guns and grenades. If I hadn't seen it myself time and time again, I would not have believed it possible. I hand it to you Chinese, you can sure fight."

A surprisingly large number of men, our correspondent says, when asked how they were captured replied, "In my sleeping bag."

One such account was given by a man named Scott who had been in the [1st] Company attached to the 31st Regiment. He described his capture as follows: "We had three medium tanks leading an infantry attack. We advanced on the Chinese positions with our cannons and machine guns going all out. The Chinese soldiers waited until we were nearly on top of them. And then, ignoring the fire, they rushed straight at our tanks.

---

They got two of our tanks at once by climbing on top of them, went to work on the turret covers, and threw hand grenades inside. When the hatch opened I looked up to see a Chinese soldier fumbling with the detonator of the hand grenade.

"That was enough for me," Scott said. "I got my hands up as fast as I could. And so here I am, still alive and kicking. And I must say I don't find it so bad. Some of the guys pity us because we aren't living the life of Riley we had back in Tokyo, but I've no complaints. I can see that the camp authorities are giving us the best they could ever give us, and I'm beginning to think that's probably a darn sight better than we deserve."

Our correspondent found that the prisoners seem to spend a lot of time complaining that MacArthur had not gotten them back to the States long before this, and that MacArthur's promise and predictions had all proved wrong. . . . And they usually wound up expressing thankfulness that at least they are now safe . . . and well out of the war instead of lying among the dead under some deep snow on the battlefield.


Day after day, new broadcasts were posted on the Camp 5 bulletin board, and many officers were quoted. The officers would deny having said any such thing, and they would be believed. Alley too would deny it, would tell them all to go to hell if they didn't believe him. And they *didn't* believe him.

Late in the spring of 1951 the Chinese turned the screws of their indoctrination program a little tighter. They brought all the officers together in the mess area to participate in what was called "The Great Debate." The subject of this debate was that America had been the illegal aggressor in Korea.

One hundred thirty-six officers were present when the debate began. All were on the side opposing the statement. For three days the Chinese ordered men to read prepared statements, and finally, when it became obvious that there was only one way for the debate to end, every officer moved to the side supporting the Chinese position. The Chinese seemed to consider this an important victory, and they immediately chose one officer from each of the fourteen squads to form a "Peace Committee." During early June these officers were taken outside the barbed-wire fence for regular meetings. Alley was among them.

After several meetings the Chinese presented the committee with a "Peace Petition" to sign, a petition they were told would be sent to the United Nations. The officers agreed to sign only if the malicious references to President Truman were deleted. The Chinese agreed.

The officers of the Peace Committee, believing they had scored a moral victory of some kind, took the petition through the camp compound until every single officer had signed. There were at least eight officers going from hut to hut, urging cooperation with the Chinese. The officer who would be remembered doing this was Ronald Alley: tall and thin, coughing all the time; they would remember him.

Within the month the following article appeared in the Russian newspaper *Pravda:*

The needless death of thousands of American boys in Korea is more and more convincing the troops that this is not a just war. The extreme unpopularity of the Korean War among the American and British soldiers was pointed out earlier this year by Joseph Stalin in his statement to *Pravda:* "Indeed it is difficult to convince soldiers that China, which does not threaten either Britain or the United States and from which the Americans appropriated the island of Taiwan, is the aggressor, whereas the United States, which appropriated the island of Taiwan and brought its troops to the very boundaries of China, is the party defending itself. It is difficult to convince the soldiers that the United States of America is entitled to defend its security on the territory of Korea and at the frontiers of China, whereas China and Korea have no right to defend their security on their own territory or at the frontiers of their State." That is the reason, said Stalin, why the war is unpopular among the Anglo-American troops. This is true to such an extent that many soldiers of the United States Army in Korea are surrendering.

According to the *China Monthly Review,* a peace rally of American soldiers was held recently in a prisoner-of-war camp in North Korea. About 300 soldiers turned out. Most of them from the 1st Division, United States Marines, and from the 7th American Division [sic]. One of the men who spoke is John Mooney, staff major of the 10th American Army Corps: "How many of us realize," he put the question to the other American war prisoners, "that the so-called United Nations resolution followed immediately after the American invasion of Korea? How many of us know what a threat to China an attack on Korea would be?"

The staff major then asked his audience how the United States would like a foreign invasion of Canada or Mexico. "The arrival of the 7th Fleet at Taiwan," he declared, "was a breach of the United Nations Charter."

"Our foreign policy," said the American war prisoner, "is leading us toward a new war in the Far East."

Major John Mooney concluded by declaring that the American war prisoners were united with all nations in the desire for peace.

The staff major was followed by Colson, an NCO of the 31st Regiment. The American division, Colson declared, and the American troops were fighting in an unjust war. "Yesterday," he said, "we were led around by the nose. Today we are fighters for peace."

A soldier of the 24th Infantry Division who asked not to have his name mentioned, for fear his wife and son might be persecuted back home, said he hated war. It tortured him, he said, to think of all that the Americans are doing in Korea.

"In my opinion," said the soldier, "Korea and China are fighting for real democracy and peace. The truth will surely be victorious and their cause is a right cause."

Along with these statements, the *China Monthly Review* published a list of American soldiers who have surrendered to the Korean People's Army and the Chinese volunteers. Here are some of the names. . . .

On this list were the names of the officers at Camp 5 who had signed the Peace Petition. Alley's name was first.

That summer, in a frail effort to organize some influence on the Chinese programs, a group of American officers requested and were permitted to form a "Daily Life Committee." They had intended to use this committee to push for medicine and better conditions. Within this committee officers were allowed to elect a medical representative, a rules and regulations representative, and representatives for food and sanitation. To this list the Chinese added an "education representative." This man would serve as monitor over all the study groups. He would read many prepared speeches on the stone steps and in the mess hall. He would meet frequently at the Chinese headquarters building. At speech "contests" sponsored throughout the summer of 1951 this man would be called upon to speak first and to introduce the selected topics for discussion. He would be named and appointed by the Chinese. His name was Captain Ronald Alley.

The Daily Life Committee was the highest point of organization attained by the POWs at Camp 5. Gradually, the members of this committee worked out an alert system that was used from squad to squad to warn of the approaching Chinese guards. Rudimentary tools were stolen from time to time and escape plans were discussed secretly. More than actually accomplishing anything, the presence of this committee restored for the prisoners a feeling, however evanescent, that they had regained some control over their destiny.

But the interrogations and beatings persisted, and those who managed to escape beyond the barbed wire were quickly picked up in the civilian population of Pyoktong and then punished.

At any time of the day or night prisoners were taken at gunpoint to the headquarters building, where there were threats, where a loaded revolver was often placed on the table in a room where guards stood watch. The interrogations had changed somewhat from the early months of captivity, however; the Chinese still asked questions about military intelligence, but now they were thoroughly uninterested in the content of the answers. By now they were looking only for indications that their indoctrination programs were succeeding. They began rewarding the prisoners with candy and cigarettes, even from time to time a raw egg. If a POW would write a lengthy cognition, saying he had come to respect the Communist line, he might be able to get enough cigarettes for the others in his hut and he might return to his hut something of a hero.

By midsummer word was spreading through Camp 5 that an exchange of the sick and wounded prisoners of war was imminent. In the officers' compound the Chinese commanders explained that the number of sick prisoners released from Camp 5 depended entirely upon the officers' compliance with the study programs. What the Chinese wanted first was a parade of officers through the village

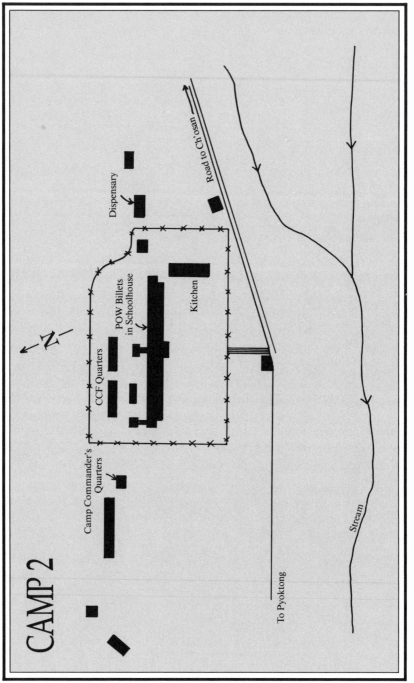

# CAMP 2

Camp Commander's Quarters

CCF Quarters

POW Billets in Schoolhouse

Dispensary

Kitchen

To Pyoktong

Road to Ch'osan

Stream

*(Based on a sketch drawn from memory by an ex-POW.)*

of Pyoktong, a parade with banners and slogans celebrating the benevolence and the infinite superiority of the Chinese people. All of the officers marched in the parade; it seemed a small, worthless concession that might ensure the release of many prisoners.

There was a game being played again at Camp 5, a game with life and death at stake, but a game that many of the POWs began to believe they might win now. After months of uncertainty, months of random death and torment, it seemed that the hell of this place was going to be relieved.

The game could be played, but the prisoners were to learn bitterly that they could never win it. There was no prisoner exchange that summer. It would be two more years before any of the sick and wounded were finally released. And that was far too late for the prisoners of Camp 5.

Not only could the Americans never win this game, but the Chinese could change the rules at any time. In early September 1951, both companies of officers were marched from Pyoktong to where there was another prison camp waiting for them. This one would be called Camp 2. In its starkness and smell it resembled Camp 5, and even in the warmth of September the mud walls and rock floors of the one-story huts promised that this winter would be as brutal as the last.

The prisoners were told they would be here for a very long time, perhaps forever. They were not merely being detained, they were being kept. They were told to forget their sick comrades left behind at Camp 5, for they would be dead soon. Not all of them would be dead, though — there were five officers who would soon be sent back to America. These five officers had been chosen by the commander of Camp 5 to remain at headquarters in Pyoktong to take part in "advanced studies in Communist theory." When they completed the course they were going to be sent back to American lines and used as "military advisors" spreading the truth. Even now these five officers were being cared for and prepared for "a better life."

The officers at Camp 2 had a name for the five who stayed behind. They called them "The Faithful Five." As the weeks went by, it was easy to believe that these five had betrayed the rest. Confinement at Camp 2 was as harsh and savage as before. More men had to be buried here. The harbingers of another arctic winter could already be felt. It was easy to blame The Faithful Five for the hopelessness of these new surroundings. So many of the prisoners had believed in their hearts that if they ever survived the horror of Camp 5 the worst would be behind them. Now they felt they had been tricked. And it was easy to believe that The Faithful Five were a part of that trick.

Six weeks after the officers had been moved to Camp 2, a mud-smeared truck pulled in there and stopped alongside the building that was being used as a mess hall. Two guards quickly jumped out and went around to the rear of the vehicle and pulled away the canvas flaps. That morning the prisoners had been told of a change in plans: the five officers had completed their instruction course in Pyoktong, but instead of being returned to American lines they were being brought to Camp 2 to work as monitors.

It was dusk, and in the prison compound there were many men milling around. All day they anticipated the arrival of The Faithful Five. And now, as the truck pulled away, they could see them at last outlined against the front of the mess hall. For a long time these five men barely moved. They turned their heads methodically and curiously, taking in the coarse details of their new surroundings and the dark eyes that were fixed on them. They looked for friends, for familiar faces in the crowd. The five men, officers in the United States Army, the Air Force, and the Marines, were prisoners just like the rest of the Americans at Camp 2, just like the scores of men standing there watching with blank, baleful stares. Except that these five men would never be trusted again. They would be ostracized and hated and remembered. And Ronald Alley was one of them.

The whole point of the Chinese captors' plan with these men was to use them against their will to engender more suspicion among their comrades, to throw them off balance, to discourage them. It was like a fraternity initiation trick, but it worked exceedingly well.

Finally Captain Alley put together the pieces; he didn't mind being on his own — that was his way. But he wouldn't be exploited by the enemy. He fought with two Chinese guards to be relieved of this duty as monitor. For this offense he was put in solitary confinement. He was very ill at the time. He had lost seventy pounds and was coughing up a lot of blood. An Army physician examined him in Camp 2 and told him he had either advanced tuberculosis or a tumor in his lung.

He knew he was ill. What he did not know was that South

Koreans employed by the Central Intelligence Agency had infiltrated the Chinese troops and had begun sending out their reports. In the Pentagon The Faithful Five had been identified, and an investigation of these men had already started.

None of the prisoners knew that by now official steps had been taken to organize armistice talks and that the Chinese were going to try to use prisoner "converts" as bargaining chips. POWs turning to the Communist side would be an embarrassment to the Pentagon, an embarrassment they might pay to avoid.

The Chinese had hopes for Alley and a handful of other officers. When, after three weeks as a monitor, Alley refused to go on, the Chinese grew impatient with him. They transferred him to the camp's carpentry shop. Alley should have refused this duty, too, because soon he was ordered to build desks and chairs for the Chinese officers — desks over which interrogations of the prisoners were conducted. Duty in this carpentry shop isolated Alley from the others. Their contempt for him deepened.

They needed to hate someone, to blame someone for what they were going through that winter of 1951–52. By this time many of the prisoners were deathly ill. At times during the lengthy study sessions the Chinese lecturers would be interrupted by the sound of a prisoner dropping dead on the ground. Guards would be called in to carry away the body, like butlers summoned to take away a guest's hat and overcoat. Even the healthiest prisoners began to doubt their ability to stay alive through another winter. Another winter without heat, without warm clothing and food. All of them had to consider the possibility that they might never go home. That their wives might not be able to wait for them.

The thought that they had been prisoners now for more than a year without anyone coming to their rescue led to overpowering depression. The longer they were lost, the more easily they would be forgotten. Depressed and hopeless, they longed for sleep. Sleep was an escape that might last; many went to sleep at night and were dead by morning. But even sleep could exploit their fears, sleep with terrible dreams. There was no coherence to the drifting days and fitful nights that came in endless succession. Colder nights now, and days with practically no sunlight reaching their huts. There was never a whole day without fear and pain. And seamless torment. There was never enough to eat. Day after day was consumed by the changeless sequence of death, beatings, and sickness. They died from bleeding bowels; nothing they could do would stop the bleeding. They died from vomiting and starvation. The air always smelled of these deaths. Through a blur of exhaustion, the days were accepted and finished as more days rose up to take their place. The days seemed to divide into blank hours and minutes — and then into more days, like organisms in a laboratory — until periods of time were indistinguishable. And there were always more days waiting. Dark, delirious days.

They were held captive in this darkness a whole year, and then a second year. Fear and illness robbed them of the codification that makes the memory work, and so the past became vague. Even the sharpest facts began to give way under the pressure of recollection. Nothing held its shape anymore. It took days to organize thoughts.

In the spring of their third year the indoctrination program stopped. It was as if the Chinese themselves had grown weary, too weary to continue. Peace negotiations began in Panmunjom and, miraculously, there was medicine and food at Camp 2, and the Chinese made a concerted effort to fatten up the prisoners and restore them to health.

In his own way Ronald Alley tried in this time to mend the tear, the lesion that had isolated him. He persuaded the Chinese to let him build bunk beds for the prisoners. He made a wooden leg for an officer who hated him. He secretly taught the rudiments of surveying to a group of prisoners, just to give them some reason to go on living.

Ronald Alley was smart enough to see the lines that had been drawn, the lines that separated him from the others. And he might have used the time that was left to change these lines and to reestablish himself among them. But by now he was far too ill. He would spend the rest of his time isolated again, this time in a sickhouse. He was unable to gain acceptance.

Perhaps he thought acceptance didn't matter now that the indoctrination programs had proved unsuccessful and they were going to be released. In his own mind he had done only what he knew was best for them. Stubbornly he had gone his own way; he always would. Sick as he was in late August 1953, when the prisoners were exchanged at Freedom Village, he was seen there, ordering a group of enlisted men not to tear off their lice-infested uniforms. Look like soldiers, he told them. He helped them into formation as they approached American officials. And then, just before he was taken away to a hospital he filed a report with a United Nations official, a report saying that the senior officers in the POW camps had neglected to do one single thing for the prisoners. He wrote out the names of these men, many of them West Point officers, and then he was quietly taken away to a hospital. He remained in the hospital while the others were shipped back to the States on Army transport vessels. On board these ships, sailing for home, Army Intelligence officials began asking questions of the ex-POWs. The officials did not want to know who was guilty of giving the enemy more than name, rank, and number; they knew everyone was guilty of this. There might be trouble for all of them unless someone could be held responsible for this. They wanted to know who among the ex-POWs could be blamed. Those who could be blamed were going to be called "progressives" and "collaborators" by the Army. The officials told them that this was going to be a big deal back home. The Army was going to make it a big deal. The Army wanted names.

Again and again on board those lumbering ships the name of Captain Alley came up and was written down in the notebooks of these new interrogators. He was not on board to defend himself, but even if he had been he might have let the opportunity pass. He might have believed he would never have to explain anything to anyone. For two years more he was hospitalized, and he said nothing. And then came his court-martial and he still said nothing. He was told by his Army lawyer not to take the stand, that anything he said would only be twisted and used against him. And so in the courtroom he said nothing. Day after day prisoners from whom he had been disassociated took the stand to blame him for the collaboration. They said he was a Socialist. They said he had fallen for the Communist line. They said he was a turncoat.

He sat there believing the United States Army would accept none of this; believing the Army would understand exactly why he had done what he did. He sat silently for more than two months while the trial went on. And he was restored to health now, he looked handsome and strong in his uniform, and there were many on the jury who, looking at this soldier, found it hard to imagine that he had ever suffered at all as a prisoner of war. Two years had passed; they were looking at a man who got up early each morning before the trial to have time to shine his shoes and polish his brass so he could look his best.

Only after he was found guilty and put back in prison did he begin to speak. He spoke for twenty years, asking that he be given a chance to explain, even begging for this chance. He would always believe he was guiltless, and that one day the Army would clear his name, restore his honor.

*   *   *   *   *

This was the truth about Major Alley. The truth was in hand at last. I could write all this about him and write it confidently. I had the picture of him now, a clear picture that would allow his widow and children to see exactly what sort of soldier he had been. They would be able to see that he was not a hero, neither was he a traitor. He had been young and frightened like the rest, he had been less careful than the rest. But he did not betray his country.

He was not unlike the figure in Robert Penn Warren's *All The King's Men:* he was a man who had stepped over the line — in this case the Army's line. Just a half step, which would normally have gone unnoticed. And then, because of the unique time in which he took his half step, he was left to fight his whole life for redemption, for the right to be allowed back to the Army's side of the line.

# CHAPTER 14

I rode the train once more from Boston to Washington, D.C., in June 1981. I had time on this trip to go to Arlington National Cemetery to stand for a few minutes at the graves of John and Robert Kennedy. It was a warm, sunny afternoon, and there was a great sense of order and solace in the cemetery, where tailored green fields sprouted thousands of white stone grave markers. Soldiers had been sent here from all over the world, from wherever they had taken their last steps and breaths, from wherever they had last taken stock of personal plans and held some vision of their lives going forward. So many thousands of soldiers lying in their uniforms; this much they had in common with Major Alley. At the

Tomb of the Unknown Soldier a young Army corporal, a boy who looked to be still in his teens, marched ramrod-straight in front of the concrete shrine. He didn't look old enough to know what his assignment on this green hill was all about. He marched on, expressionless and stiff, moving back and forth for reasons beyond his understanding, reasons he had nonetheless accepted.

Twice Ronald Alley had petitioned the Army Board for the Correction of Military Records — the Pentagon's highest review board — to reopen his case. The petitions had been rejected. The board had explained to him that, without new evidence, there was no reason to reopen the case.

But now, with all that I had learned, both Erna Alley and Gerry Williamson, the lawyer from Brockton, Massachusetts, who had kept an intense interest in this case, felt it was time to petition the Army board again. I had some initial misgivings; it had been more than two years since Francis Plant, the head of this board, had confronted me after my illicit entry into the Pentagon, but it seemed unlikely that he would have forgotten this.

After talking with Erna and Gerry, I decided to take the materials from my research to Senator William Cohen. I met with him in his office and told him what I had learned, and he agreed to study my documentation. We discussed briefly the possibility of a petition to the Army board, but the senator made it clear that he wanted some time to go over everything before committing himself.

I decided to go back again to the Pentagon and call on an Army lawyer on the Judge Advocate General's staff, whose name had been given to me by Senator Cohen's office. The lawyer I met did not wish to be identified for the record, but when I had spent almost an hour with him telling him all I knew of the Alley case, he surprised me by saying, "And now you want to petition the Army board for Alley's honorable discharge."

"How did you know that?" I asked.

He said it was just a guess, and he picked up his telephone to call someone he thought I ought to speak with. While he was waiting for the person to answer, he turned to me and said, "Your man may have had good reason to do what he did, but if you exceed the boundary of the USCMJ [United States Code of Military Justice], regardless of your motives to help others or what, you are still guilty, right?"

He didn't expect an answer. A few minutes later, another Army lawyer arrived in his office, a tall dark-haired man who said he had worked on the My Lai massacre case, prosecuting Lieutenant Calley. "Calley, Alley," he said casually, "quite a coincidence."

He listened patiently to my story, and I explained that Major Alley's widow wanted to have the case reopened and to petition the Army for an honorable discharge.

"Who's going to speak?" he asked.

I explained that Erna Alley would speak, that her attorney would speak, and that, probably, I would present to the board the results of my research. At this point the first lawyer repeated his earlier admonition about the USCMJ. The prosecutor was in complete agreement, and he went on to say, "What would it do to the USCMJ and its punitive strength if we exonerated all the turncoats convicted under it?"

"Well, that's assuming a lot," I said.

He didn't agree. "What I think is that you could bring God Almighty down here to testify for Alley, and it wouldn't do any good."

Senator Cohen took very little time deciding he would support a petition. This meant he was going to speak personally to the Secretary of the Army requesting that the case of Major Ronald Alley be reopened and an official hearing be held to review new evidence.

The senator's decision left Erna Alley ecstatic. Both she and Gerry were confident that the Army would finally grant a hearing.

It turned out that they were right. On October 2, 1981, the Army board notified Senator Cohen that the case would be reopened. And that Sunday, October 4, under the headline U.S. REOPENS CASE ON COLLABORATOR: WIDOW WINS HEARING IN EFFORT TO CLEAR MAJOR IMPRISONED IN NORTH KOREA IN 50s, the *New York Times* carried a lengthy story on Gerry Williamson's plans. The petition would ask that the original court-martial record be expunged, that Major Alley be granted a posthumous honorable discharge, that he be posthumously promoted to the rank of colonel, and that all his back pay and benefits plus interest accrued be paid to his widow.

I spoke with Gerry by telephone, and when I asked if he was worried, and if he thought the petition was asking for too much, he said: "Look at it this way. Senator Cohen calls the Secretary of the

Army and asks for a favor. The Secretary of the Army calls him back to tell him we've got our hearing. What are the chances the Army's going to get us all to Washington and then slam the door in Erna's face? I mean what sort of favor would that be?"

Gerry said Erna was entitled to everything he had requested, and he was going to do his best to see that she got it.

In the *Times* article Erna had been quoted as saying that she hoped she could "fulfill my late husband's wish to clear his name." She was excited when we spoke about this. And also disappointed that the *Times* had used a photograph of Ronald taken not long before his death. "I don't know where they got that," she said. "It makes him look so old. I wish they had shown him in his uniform."

There was no way of knowing when the hearing would be held, but Erna had already begun preparing. "I'm going to just tell the Army everything Ronald wanted to tell them. I want them to know how he suffered and how he loved the Army."

She said to me, "I probably shouldn't have, but I went out and bought some clothes for Washington. I want to look nice. I just don't want to look old. . . . The last time I was there I was a young girl, you know."

Soon Mike Danforth in Congressman Emery's Augusta office contacted me to report that Emery would join Cohen's forces. He was going to write a separate letter to the Secretary of the Army.

I spoke with Senator Cohen by telephone in October. The senator and his staff had been of great help to me during the course of my research, but neither the senator nor anyone on his staff had ever told me how they actually felt about the case. This time, Senator Cohen did. "It looks to me like the court-martial in 1955 smacked of a kangaroo court," he said. "On the surface, this looks like a gross violation of justice."

I conveyed this news to Gerry Williamson, who in turn passed it along to Erna. He wanted to do everything he could to bolster her hopes and strengthen her for the hearing in Washington.

Over the years other politicians had written letters and made statements on behalf of Erna and Ronald. The letters had never amounted to anything, and the statements had been quickly forgotten. But this news of Cohen and Emery's support invigorated Erna. During the next weeks we spoke frequently by telephone, and she grew impatient with me when I cautioned her that we still couldn't be certain of anything. "But with Emery and Cohen on our side," she said, her voice straining, the pitch creeping higher, "the Army will have to listen! They will have to do the right thing this time."

The more we talked the more she made me see that this was the chance she had always wanted. "You told me I had done my best, I had kept my promise and buried Ronald in his uniform. You told me that was enough. But I always wanted more. I always wanted to just go to the Pentagon and make them see."

To her it was a matter of love and honor: the love Ronald had for the Army, the honor he had cherished and lost, and the love and honor she had for him. Love and honor were at stake. "I want my son to be there," she said emphatically. "This will be a great day. Gary will be there beside me. He will see that he can be proud."

I knew what she wanted, but I also worried about her. I worried that, because of her faith, she would be destroyed. Faith had distorted Ronald's perception of the Army. It had led him silently to his court-martial and then to prison. Just as his struggle and his obsession had taken the life slowly out of him, it was his faith, powerful and unreasoning, that had prodded him on and helped kill him. He had been worn away on the inside from following this faith. I wanted to see Erna survive, and so I wanted her to acknowledge that there would have to be an end to all of this, that someday she would have to stop. She was always grateful for my concern, but always firm. "You worry that the struggle will kill me, but if I stop now what life will I have? Help me get to Washington. I have to do that much."

Gerry Williamson closed his law office in Brockton, Massachusetts, for the long Columbus Day weekend, drove to Portland, Maine, with his family, and stopped at the Sheraton Inn just off Interstate 95, so we could talk before he continued on to Bar Harbor to spend two days with Erna. His station wagon was loaded to the roof, and as he pulled into the parking lot, children began spilling out all the doors. "You're loaded like a troop ship!" I called to him. "Did you bring all five kids?"

"Five? Hey, we've got an even half dozen now!" he said, pointing to his wife, who held the new baby.

From the first time I met Gerry Williamson in July of 1978 I had thought of him with fondness. I had been struck by his boyish energy, an energy that was not burdened by any of the affectations of his profession. He was a country lawyer, with no classic wardrobe and no cunning air. He was most content when his children were around him.

Gerry had already been in touch with the Army board, and he figured it would be another month before a date for the hearing was set. He was optimistic. "The executive secretary of the board, this fellow John Matthews, was very helpful on the phone. Very cooperative. He made it clear that this is Erna's hearing; she can have anyone she wants to speak for her. It's an administrative board, not a court of law, so the typical rules of evidence don't apply. Anything goes."

I asked if he was sure I would be able to recount my interviews with the POWs.

"Absolutely. They're going to give us a chance to tell what we know. Sort of like a town planning board."

He said he didn't expect to get everything he had asked for in the petition: "We probably won't get the whole nine yards, but the honorable discharge is the important thing. We'll be happy with *that*. But no reason to let the board know."

We agreed that of all the people I had interviewed it would be most important to ask Colonel Peckham, Colonel Wise, and Colonel Mayo to come to the hearing. Mayo lived just a few miles from the Pentagon; Peckham and Wise would have to travel from the West Coast.

Gerry wanted to make sure I had notes from all my interviews. I assured him I did, and he asked me to be sure to use the direct quotes when I made my presentation to the board. "We want to have the greatest impact we can," he said. Then he stopped before speaking Walter Mayo's name. "He will be the key to this. The prosecution's key witness in 1955. If Mayo will tell the board what he told you, Erna might get everything."

A week after this meeting with Gerry Williamson I received a letter from Colonel Peckham in California. He had suffered yet another heart attack and was going back into the hospital for more surgery. "I want to get to that hearing," he wrote, "but I don't know how this will all come out." He said he wasn't sure he would make it this time; neither was his physician. He had never felt weaker.

I remembered him lying on his bed, pressing a pillow to his chest while we talked in the San Jose hospital. I remembered his robe draped over the chair and the patch embroidered on it.

I called Congressman Emery's office to see if there was any

word on how long it would be before a date was set. Mike Danforth said there was no way of knowing: "Believe me, there isn't a thing anyone can do to influence the board at this point. We'll just have to wait. . . . If anything could be done, Emery and Cohen would do it. There isn't any precedent for this case, and the board doesn't even want one. It's a whopper of a case, and the Army has a lot of people to contact for opinions. They want to get their side ready."

On October 29 I telephoned the O'Connor Hospital in San Jose, just a few hours after Colonel Peckham's surgery was scheduled to be finished. I asked a nurse if she could tell me how he had made out.

"Who?" she asked.

"Peckham. Colonel Charles Peckham."

"Wait a minute. . . . I don't show anyone by that name."

"He's been in surgery."

"Not according to this chart."

"Please check again, maybe another chart."

While she was gone I looked over my desk to an old photograph of Ronald and Erna Alley, taken just after they were married. This was the only photograph I had showing them as young and hopeful people. I noticed this time that, just as Ronald's features were narrow and sharply defined, Erna's were rounded and soft. By the time I met them their faces had changed in opposite ways. Erna's was now thin and chiseled, his had been full when I met him that day. I thought again how difficult it had always been for me to picture him as a young man. When he was a prisoner of war he was seven years younger than his son and I were now. He had had such confidence as a young man. At the court-martial he told his Army lawyer that he felt it wouldn't have been fair to ask Peckham to speak on his behalf, because that would put him in the position of having to speak *against* the Army. After the court-martial in 1955 Colonel Peckham never saw Ronald Alley again. "I would have helped him," the colonel had told me when we first met.

I sat looking at the photograph, waiting to find out if Colonel Peckham had run out of time. Finally the nurse came back on the line. "I found him. He's in intensive care. He's resting comfortably. The operation is over."

In early November it seemed that Erna was beginning to lose ground. She was seeing a doctor regularly and taking medication.

Winter had reached Mount Desert Island, the stores were boarded up in town, and she spent long, empty days alone. When she telephoned me, she often lapsed into digressions about the court-martial in 1955; her voice would sound urgent at first, and then it would trail away and she would go on to another subject. The days of Ronald's trial had been the most difficult of her life, she told me. And now, waiting to return to Washington, the memory of those days came back. "I sit here all day," she said to me. "I just don't know what to do anymore."

Late in the day on December 18, 1981, the Army notified Gerry Williamson that the hearing would be held at the Pentagon on February 10. In early January the three of us met in Portland; Erna seemed composed. She was glad to finally know when she would be going to Washington. She said she was eager to have the chance to speak. She felt she would need several hours to recount everything: "I will need to tell the board all I know. I want to tell them about my telephone, the clicking and — "

Gerry Williamson interrupted. He put his hand out to slow her down. "We won't say anything about the telephone, okay? This is a discretionary act on the part of the board. We will point out things to show them how we feel the Army was wrong in what they did to Ronald, but we won't hammer away about bugged telephones or anything else that will leave a bad taste in their mouths. Remember, the board has something for us, something for Ronald. We have to make them want to *give* it to us."

It was unusual for Gerry to speak of the Army with such a conciliatory tone. He had always given the impression of being completely unintimidated by the Army's position. Deference and moderation had replaced the colorful diatribes I'd come to expect from him.

We spoke about the fact that Colonel Mayo had not replied to a request from Gerry that he appear at the hearing. We decided to wait until we got to Washington to deal with this. Both Colonel Wise and Colonel Peckham were planning to come, and perhaps it would be best to let them make an appeal to Mayo.

I was worried about two things. Believing that it was important to have the national media at the hearing, I had already contacted the television networks and the national-circulation news periodicals, and I had reason to believe many would send representatives to the hearing. Now I wondered if this was perhaps a bad idea. It might anger the Army board. Gerry wasn't worried about it.

My idea concerning the media was that they had missed this story in 1955, and this time, while we had the opportunity to tell the whole truth about the Alley case, the media ought to be present to record it.

After Erna had excused herself from the table I expressed another concern to Gerry: I wanted to know if he was apprehensive about the hearing, and if he thought the Army might be grandstanding. The hearing would give the impression that the Army was interested in the truth, though they might have firmly decided not to budge an inch.

"We'll have to go to Washington and see," Gerry said philosophically. "We don't have any choice now."

We were all relieved when, just a few days before leaving for Washington, a television station in Maine sent a reporter to Capitol Hill to interview Senator William Cohen. He appeared on the six o'clock news all over Maine, sitting in his Senate office in a white shirt and necktie, leaning back in a leather chair behind his desk. "It seems clear the major was made a scapegoat," he said with uncharacteristic bluntness. And then he moved closer to the camera and said that Major Alley deserved an honorable discharge.

Hearing this on television, Erna called me again and said how happy she was. "Gary will be coming with me," she said hopefully. "I will have Ronald on one side and Gary on the other." She wanted to believe that everything bad that could happen to her and her dead husband and her children had already happened, and that this trip to Washington was her best hope.

# CHAPTER 15

At dusk, the sunlight over Washington strayed and vanished and finally gave way to the gleaming prominence of the city's monuments that reach into the low sky. On the Capitol dome pinpricks of light pulsed against the sky like tiny pilots on a gas stove. Light fell past the columns of the Lincoln Memorial in tall, narrow bands that skated across the Potomac River. The Pentagon shimmered in the darkness like a star that had fallen to earth. The scene was striking and restful, and gave the feeling that nothing terribly wrong could be happening in America.

I was staying again with my friend John Bradford, who was now beginning his last year of residency. We talked about how he had been just beginning there when I'd come to Washington to stay with him and Marge, when I had begun my work on the Alley story. Much had changed since then. John tried to ease my concerns over the hearing. I couldn't stop thinking that I'd made a mistake by telling the media. "I think you did the right thing," John said. "You can't be sure what the Army will do; you couldn't have predicted their response anyway. But the real tragedy of this story will be averted now that the media will be there to *tell* the story. No matter how it comes out, the real tragedy would be if the story went untold."

At the Holiday Inn just off Interstate 395 in Arlington, Virginia, Gerry Williamson answered the telephone in his dauntless manner — "Pentagon, Williamson speaking."

"We got in an hour ago," he said. "Peckham and Wise are due in tomorrow. We're all set." Erna and Gary were settled in the room next to his.

In Washington on Monday morning it was very cold and windy, and there were reports that it might snow by late afternoon. Gary Alley had gotten up early. He stood outside the room, leaning on the iron railing, smoking a cigarette while his mother got ready. Then he walked her across the parking lot of the hotel to the dining room where I was waiting to meet them. He took the same big strides I had seen his father take walking to my office at the newspaper that Friday afternoon in 1978. Gary was thirty-two years old now. He was tall and broad-shouldered with blond hair and a blond mous-tache. He wore a suit and tie, and over it a brown leather jacket that fell just below his waist.

I stood up and walked toward them. "You look good, Erna," I said. "You look fine."

"Oh, I don't know," she said, and then, as if she had just remem-bered that Gary was with her, she turned to him. "Here's Gary."

We shook hands. I told him he reminded me of his father. "That's what everybody tells me," he said, lowering his eyes in a bashful way that was incongruous with his powerful build and deep voice. It was a voice like his father's.

"You've got your dad's accent, too."

"Yep. I got that all right," he said smiling.

He appeared so shy and unsure of himself; I thought it might be because he was on unfamiliar territory, so far from home. Perhaps he carried the physical strength of his father and behind that the insecurity of never having had time with him.

We were going to sit down at a table and wait for Gerry Williamson, who would be coming along for an interview with United Press International and then a local television station. Gary would go to Washington National Airport to pick up Colonel Peckham and his wife. Twice he started to leave while Erna and I were talking. But both times he came back. I could see he wanted to say something to me, and so I left the table and walked him to the lobby.

He told me he was concerned about his mother. "Ma's awful nervous. She's all wound up tight," he said. He had something else to say. "I'm not sure how to put this, but I want you to know that Ma appreciates all this, all you've done for her. And no matter what happens, I appreciate it, too."

I rejoined Erna, who was now talking with the reporter from UPI. When she told the story about her last minutes with her husband after the court-martial, before the stockade door was locked, I had to leave. It brought back too many memories of the past four years of this story. I saw Erna begin to cry and I had to walk away.

I tried to telephone Walter Mayo at his office on Wisconsin Avenue. He was not in, and at first the secretary told me he might be out of town for several days. She asked for a return telephone number in case he got in touch with her.

A few minutes later Gary Alley drove up with Colonel Peckham and his wife. What followed was a scene I had waited for and had imagined happening ever since the hearing had been set. The first time we met, Colonel Peckham told me there wasn't anything he wouldn't do to try and see that the truth about Ronald Alley was told. He worried then that he might not live long enough to be of any help. But here he was, stepping out of the car, his wife at his side. He introduced his wife as Addie, and smiled as she walked ahead and put her arms around Erna. "You've suffered so much," Mrs. Peckham whispered.

Colonel Peckham had the gravel back in his voice. "That boy of yours," he said to Erna. "Good God, he looks just like his old man! I can't get over it. Without the moustache, though — I'm not sure Ron would have approved of that."

"He's quite a boy," said Gerry Williamson.

"Well, he had quite an old man," said the colonel.

Though they were meeting for the first time, there was a feeling here of family members coming together for a reunion. Throughout the afternoon Gary listened intently as Colonel Peckham talked of the fighting in Korea and the conditions at Camp 5, and then Camp 2. "Your dad did what he could for his men," Peckham told him. "There are some men who owe their lives to him."

Gary took it all in, and nodded, and said very little.

Mrs. Peckham sat watching her husband, and occasionally she would look at her watch and then take a small embroidered cloth from her purse and arrange in the palm of her hand a half dozen or more pills. Then, when there was a pause in the conversation, she would go quietly over to her husband and give him his medication. Sometimes the colonel would pick up the dialogue just as she was reaching out to him, and then she would withdraw and stand off to the side and wait until he was finished. She was a handsome woman with sparkling eyes and red cheeks. Her husband had been through fifty-four operations since his return from Korea and when she sat next to Erna Alley she shared that look of long suffering. It left a weariness that no amount of makeup could conceal.

Occasionally Peckham would stop and look into Erna's face and then Gary's. He seemed to be overwhelmed by the scene around him. By the sight of a woman he had heard so much about, but had never before laid eyes on. By the sight of a young man who reminded him so much of his father, who himself was a young man the last time Peckham had seen him. "It's amazing," he said once, his voice low and steady. . . . "When I shut my eyes I'm right back there talking with his dad. I'm right back there."

Erna did the television interview in D.C., then returned for another interview at the hotel, this time with David Molpus of National Public Radio. During this interview she broke down several times. Whenever her voice would start to give way and her expression would become remote, Gary would fold his hands in front of himself and lower his head as if he were praying. He had learned to be near, to bear vigil during his mother's ordeals. Then he would get up and walk slowly over to her, and she would go on.

When I left the hotel that night there was still no word back from Colonel Mayo's office.

The first thing Tuesday morning, Gerry Williamson telephoned to say that Colonel Robert Wise had arrived late the night before.

---

205

I had almost missed Robert Wise when I traveled to the West Coast in the spring of 1981. He depends on the money he makes from shrimping each year to supplement his Army pension, and I had shown up in Seattle just as the season was starting. He told me the Army had been his life, and that as a young boy his father had told him that if he got the chance to join the Army he should be an infantryman, because that way he would do a lot of fighting and he would find out what kind of man he was. He took his father's advice to heart, and he saw a lot of combat in World War II and Korea. Now, at age sixty-three, he was still a very proud soldier — a tough little man, spare and wiry — but his face was gaunt and his brown eyes conveyed a heavy sadness.

I saw Colonel Wise standing next to Erna, holding her hand. "I'm going to talk about things tomorrow that I've never told anyone before, not even my wife," he said. "I want the Army to know what it's like to be a prisoner of war. What we all went through over there. What this woman's husband went through with the rest of us. I've had a long time to think about all this." He drew his shoulders back as if he were coming to attention — "I want to tell you right now, Mrs. Alley, that you can be proud of your husband. And I want your son to know he can be proud of his dad. I know what kind of man Ron Alley was. I know what kind of soldier he was. He was one of the best I ever met."

Wise made it plain that he was here on a mission: "This whole thing has got to be straightened out," he said sternly. And then he turned to face Gary. "I want you to know that it wasn't the Army that did this to your dad. Not the *real* Army; it was some men sitting behind desks here in Washington, who didn't know one damn thing about what it was like to be a soldier. Well, tomorrow they'll learn."

I left the Holiday Inn for an hour, drove up to Capitol Hill, and walked to the Dirksen Office Building to see if Senator Cohen had a few minutes. Sally Lounsbury, who had helped me many times over the last four years, told me she was going to the hearing in the morning. Then she took me in to see the senator.

I thanked him for everything he'd done and passed along Mrs. Alley's thanks. He was gracious. "I know she's waited a long time for this," he said.

He waited, knowing I probably hadn't come all the way over here to thank him. There was something else; I explained that I was worried the Army might try something at the last minute to keep the truth about Major Alley concealed. "If this is the 1955 court-martial all over again. . . ." I said.

"Have you got the media coming?" he asked.

I told him we did. He said good, that that would help.

I said I was concerned that the board might have already made its decision, and that the Alley case might again be used as an example to buttress some political point.

Senator Cohen raised a hand into the air. "I'll make some calls this afternoon," he said. "I'll call Secretary Marsh, and if I learn that anything like that is going on in this case I'll raise holy hell for you."

Back at the Holiday Inn I stepped into Colonel Wise's room as he was on the telephone. He had reached Colonel Mayo, Peckham told me.

"Walt, this is Bob Wise. . . . I've been here all day waiting for you to call me. What? . . . Yes, the Holiday Inn — somewhere. What? Yes, Charlie Peckham is here, too, and Don Snyder, Mrs. Alley, her son. . . . Well, damn it, Walt, get your butt over here. . . . I came from Tacoma, Washington. What? You're busy? Well, how busy *are* you, Walt? You can't be *that* busy. . . ."

Peckham spoke with Mayo next, and finally he agreed to come to the hotel to talk with them. They would talk alone with him; they wanted it that way.

In another room I spent some time with Erna. She was cold, she said, and she kept on her black overcoat with the collar turned up to her chin. She wore a plaid woolen skirt. She lit cigarettes and lost her place in her notes as she tried to go over her presentation. Loose-leaf pages fell from her lap to the floor. "I feel the weight on my shoulders," she said wearily. Some of her notes were written in German, some in English, and she stammered through them, writing things down with a black pen. "Have I already said that, Don?" she asked. I told her just to go on. When she finished, she folded the pages and held them in front of her and she began crying. "So this is what I've got," she said. "It's all I have."

Colonel Mayo met with Wise and Peckham and agreed to speak as a witness at the hearing in the morning. Gerry Williamson called the Army board to make sure we could present as many witnesses as we wanted. He was assured there would be no problem.

While there was still a trace of light in the sky, I left with Gary

Alley to drive the route he would take in the morning to the Pentagon. He wanted to go over it once more just to make sure.

Gary said he was only going to talk for a few minutes. "Like I said before, I'm just going to say what's in my heart. I never got to know my dad. There weren't many fishing trips. But I know he loved me. I know he wanted me to be proud of him.

"When I called home last night, I spoke to my boy. He had to tell me all about his basketball game; he was the high scorer. Oh, you ought to see him shoot. And I thought, one day I'll explain to him why I had to miss that game, and what I was doing down here in Washington."

Gary told me he was ready for the hearing. All his life he knew there had been something his dad was hoping for, something he couldn't reach. As we drove past the Pentagon and the mall river entrance where he would go in the morning, he turned his eyes back to the highway. "This is it," he said. "This is the chance my dad wanted. I think a part of me always prayed that someday I'd be down here doing this for him."

# CHAPTER 16

M ajor James Weiskoph, the Army board's public affairs officer, arrived at his office early on Wednesday morning. Outside, the low winter sun slanted across the brown flanks of the Pentagon and a rough wind swept through the empty parking lots.

Weiskoph, a small man, took quick, purposeful steps that belied the timid look on his face, the look of a man accustomed to taking orders. He went down a long corridor and turned into room 2E687, the Secretary of the Army's private hearing room. He was tense. It was just after seven-thirty, and already members of the press were milling around the corridors with their tape recorders and cameras. Ordinarily, hearings before the Army Board for the Correction of Military Records were closed to the media and held in a basement room. The board's executive secretary, John Matthews, had agreed to lift the press restrictions for this hearing. It was against his better judgment to do this, but word had been passed along from the Secretary of the Army himself that the press must be allowed in. Matthews made it clear that it would be up to Weiskoph to keep the press in line. He said he didn't want the hearing to turn into a media circus.

Weiskoph stood in the waiting room adjacent to room 2E687 and went over instructions with an Army sergeant on duty there. Then he opened a heavy oak door and walked into the hearing room to see that everything was in place. Inside, the furniture had been positioned to resemble a courtroom. Rows of straight-backed chairs were arranged symmetrically on both sides of a narrow center aisle that led to the front of the room, where members of the board would sit behind a long rectangular table. Just a few steps from this front table there were three more tables set in place, two on the right of the aisle for the stenographer and for Gerry Williamson, representing the petitioner; and the other to the left, where Matthews and the case examiner, Donald Lewy, would sit throughout the hearing. Just in front of Matthews and Lewy, witnesses would sit facing the board members. The carpeting and darkly paneled walls gave the room an atmosphere of intimacy.

Matthews, a towering, broad-shouldered man, watched as the press filed into the hearing room and artists for ABC and CBS took seats near the front tables. Out in the hallway a camera crew followed Erna Alley and Gary. Reporters fired questions at Colonel Peckham and Colonel Wise. An armed guard left his station at the entrance to the Pentagon and ran down the corridor in pursuit of Weiskoph. "What are these cameras doing here!"

"They're all right," said Weiskoph. "They're not going into the hearing room."

"I don't care about the *hearing room*," the guard protested. "Who gave them permission to be in this building?"

"It's okay," Weiskoph insisted.

"No, it's *not* okay. No cameras are allowed in here. You know that," the guard replied.

The media circus John Matthews was determined to prevent

had already begun. There was chaos outside the hearing room now, chaos caused by the sheer number of reporters. Matthews stood in the doorway to the hearing room and demanded reporters' credentials. He called over to Weiskoph: "If they're not on our list, they're not going in." He ordered two journalists to leave their cameras in the waiting room.

"This is expensive equipment," one man complained.

"I don't care," said Matthews.

Erna had a stunned expression as she entered the hearing room, with Colonel Peckham's wife at one side and Gary at the other. She took carefully measured steps as if she was uncertain of her balance. Her eyes wandered.

Donald Lewy, the man who had examined this case for the Army board, entered the room behind Erna. He pushed along a shopping cart filled with papers and documents. He was joined at the front table by Matthews, who spoke with him for only a minute, then came to the back of the room calling for Gerry Williamson.

Gerry went over and shook his hand. Matthews said he wanted a list of Mrs. Alley's witnesses. Gerry had no list, but told him who would be speaking. Matthews wanted to know the order in which they would speak. Gerry told him.

"This last person, Snyder, who's he?" asked Matthews.

"He's interviewed POWs who served with Ronald Alley," Gerry said. "He's going to present the notes from those interviews."

"It's hearsay, then," said Matthews.

Gerry didn't answer at first. "Well, yes. But we were told it would be fine, and permissible."

"Okay," said Matthews. He turned and walked back to the front of the room to confer with Lewy again. A few minutes passed before he came back to Gerry. "We're going to sequester the witnesses," Matthews said.

Gerry nodded, then asked if there was some mistake. "I wasn't told my witnesses would be sequestered," he said. Matthews shrugged his shoulders and continued toward the front of the room.

Gerry called Wise, Peckham, Gary, and me together. "There's been a surprise, and I don't want to worry Erna. But they're going to sequester the witnesses. That means you'll each have to wait outside until it's your turn to speak. They don't want any exchange of information between witnesses."

---

211

Gerry had been caught off guard, and he struggled to keep his composure. "Anything we say now will just aggravate things. We'll go along with them."

At exactly nine o'clock the five members of the Army board filed quickly through the waiting room into room 2E687, as if they were heading for a table reserved for them at a crowded restaurant. They wore civilian clothes, coats and ties. Some carried notebooks. They seemed oblivious to the reporters. They walked on mechanically, their eyes straight ahead. When they were inside the hearing room, Major Weiskoph closed the heavy door behind them, leaving Gary, Peckham, Wise, and me in the waiting room, where an Army sergeant sat silently behind a desk reading *Car and Driver* magazine.

Wise smoked his cigarettes pensively. Gary walked back and forth to the coffee machine and the men's room. Peckham paged through an old copy of *Army Times* that had been left on the table in front of us. "I'm sure glad they finally got rid of the Ike jacket," he said, looking over at Wise.

"Ike was the only one who looked good in it," said Wise.

An hour passed. Gary sighed heavily, stood up, and then sat back down again. "I should be in there with Ma," he said anxiously.

"It's all right, son," said Peckham.

Finally a photographer came out from the hearing room to smoke a cigarette.

"What's going on in there?" Wise asked.

"They're going pretty hard on her," he said. "She's having trouble getting through her notes."

Gary got to his feet again. Wise offered him a cigarette. "It's all right, son. Have a smoke. It's going to be a long day."

Colonel Mayo arrived soon. He hung up his overcoat and looked down twice at the pile of cameras sitting on the floor. "The press?" he asked incredulously, turning to Wise and Peckham. "No one said anything about the press being here."

"Couldn't keep them away," said Wise, offering his hand to shake. "Come on and sit down, Walt."

It was the first time since our meeting in 1981 that I'd seen Mayo. We shook hands. "I'm glad you could come," I said.

Mayo looked back at the cameras. "Yeah," he said.

Mayo sat down and asked Wise if he could have a cigarette. He had left his pack at the office.

"Sure," said Wise. He handed him a pack of cigarettes. "Walt, this is Ron's son," he said, turning toward Gary.

"Gary?" Mayo asked.

"That's right, sir. It's a pleasure to meet you."

"Doesn't he remind you of his dad?" asked Peckham.

"Yeah, yeah, he sure does."

It was impossible to know what it meant to either of them to meet for the first time; to have been brought together for just a few minutes on a day made necessary by events that had been set in motion twenty-seven years earlier, in a courtroom just a short ride from here. Walter Mayo had been full of contempt for Ronald Alley then. He had taken the witness stand, and his testimony had helped convict that man and send him to prison. And now he was suddenly face to face with the son of that man. In a few minutes Walter Mayo saw the man's widow. Erna had broken down in the hearing room, and the board had ordered a ten-minute recess. Holding a Kleenex to her eyes, Erna thanked Colonel Mayo for coming, and Mayo nodded to her and then asked Wise for another cigarette.

When the recess was over Gary was allowed into the room to try and help his mother. The door closed behind him, and that was all the time Colonel Mayo would spend with Ronald Alley's widow and son.

Walter Mayo must have known that he could have prevented all this, could have kept his silence. The silence would have been easier. Easier than sitting here waiting, looking across the room at the cameras he hoped would not turn on him, listening to Peckham and Wise and their war stories. "Did I ever tell you about the time . . . ?" Wise would start in. And Mayo would turn politely to him and try to listen, but very soon his eyes would glaze over and turn back again to the cameras.

It was a different story for Wise and Peckham. It was easier for them. They were here because they had always believed in Ronald Alley's innocence; they were men a lot like Ronald, men with a rock-hard sense of themselves. They had condemned men who had turned against Ronald, men like Walter Mayo. And so they had to be here, to straighten this whole thing out for a man who, like themselves, had made the United States Army the biggest thing in his life. All their lives they would hold onto the vision of themselves as soldiers, they would measure all other experiences against their

213

experiences in the Army. They had had their finest moments in the Army, their greatest accomplishments. Like Ronald Alley, they had never wished to put the Army behind them, because without the Army their identity was unclear. They were soldiers from end to end and they could not really imagine what life would have been like without the Army. But Walter Mayo could. He had put the Army far behind him and gone on to an expansive life. And that made all the difference.

Major Weiskoph opened the door again at 10:55 and called for Colonel Walter Mayo.

"Good luck," said Wise.

When he had left us, and the door had closed again, Colonel Peckham turned to me and said, "This is tough on Walt."

Thirty-five minutes later, Walter Mayo emerged from the hearing room. He looked disoriented. He seemed to be searching for the place where he had left his overcoat. The reporters swarmed chaotically after him, and the camera lights went on. "Why did you testify against Alley in 1955?" one reporter asked sharply.

"No comment," said Mayo.

Gerry Williamson hurried over to Peckham and Wise. "We almost had a donnybrook in there," he said, pushing his glasses up on the bridge of his nose. "This is a lot tougher than I ever thought it would be."

The board had been rough on Mayo; they had confronted him with his testimony from the 1955 court-martial record and several times they pushed him to explain whether he was at this hearing to speak *for* or *against* Alley. Finally he had told them he was here to speak for him, but he had said it reluctantly. He was on the fence.

David Molpus of National Public Radio pushed through the television camera crews. "Colonel Mayo, just one question," he said as Mayo got into his overcoat. "Do you think Ronald Alley was guilty?"

Mayo turned toward me and then, without looking back at Molpus, he said, "No."

Suddenly Matthews appeared at the door and hollered, "Get those cameras off, or we'll close this hearing!"

I walked over to Mayo. "I wasn't expecting this," he said.

"You told me a year ago that Alley was not a collaborator," I said. "Did you say that to the board?"

---

He paused and looked past me to Wise and Peckham. "I hope I helped. I couldn't refute my own testimony. I could only hope to put it in perspective."

"But did you tell the board?"

"I hope so," he said.

The door closed again. Gary Alley would stand in front of the board next. He spoke for only a few minutes, his voice shaking from time to time. He finished by telling the board that he had tried but had never been able to get close to his father because of what had happened to him. While he said this, Walter Mayo was on the way back to his office.

Throughout the afternoon the Army board listened as first Colonel Peckham and then Colonel Wise told what it had been like to be held prisoner in North Korea. They spoke without artifice or vanity. They were not sophisticated men; they owed nothing to ambition. They were just haunted, they said, by what had been done to a fellow soldier. They spoke plainly about this, never condemning the Army, because they loved the Army too much. They spoke, they said, not just for Ronald Alley, but for themselves: They wanted the Army to make this right for Ronald and for *them,* because they were soldiers and they wanted their faith in the Army vindicated. They asked the board for justice. They said Major Alley was a man they were honored to have served with.

By the time I was sworn in on the witness stand it was after four o'clock, and the five board members looked exhausted. I began to recount how I had met Ronald Alley, when suddenly the chairman of the board interrupted and asked Gerry Williamson what I was going to say that had any direct bearing on the case. Gerry tried to explain.

"But it's just hearsay?" the chairman asked.

"Hearsay," Matthews said from his chair.

I asked to be allowed to go on. The chairman consented. I hectically presented quotes from the meetings and telephone conversations. The chairman interrupted again, asking how I had obtained addresses of former witnesses. I said it was a source in the Congress. I tried to go on. Matthews interrupted this time as Lewy handed him sheets of paper from his shopping cart. The questions became hostile, and I turned, first toward Gerry Williamson and then toward Senator Cohen's aide, who was seated just behind him. She shook her head and then lowered her eyes.

Finally I asked for a recess. The board chairman granted it. In a separate room I yelled at Gerry that this was the 1955 court-martial all over again. He argued for moderation. "They know what you're going to say and they don't want it said, at least not in front of the press," he said.

"Then ask them to clear the room," I said.

"Listen. These guys want to go home. Let's just leave this alone. I'm as mad as you are, but let's let them have their way. You're only going to make it worse for Ronald."

The board would accept no further testimony. I had the feeling that it had all slipped away, that chance Erna and Gary had spoken about for months. What I regretted most was that I had not had the chance to make the Army see that there was a different side to the story of Major Alley, a side that would never be revealed by the documents the Army held in Donald Lewy's shopping cart. I had also wanted to read them a quote I had discovered in a corridor of the Pentagon while waiting to make my testimony. The quote was engraved on a plaque hung alongside an oil painting of General Douglas MacArthur. It quoted from a speech he had made to the United States Congress on April 19, 1951: "A great nation which voluntarily enters upon war and does not see it through to victory must eventually suffer all the consequences of defeat."

I wanted the board to see that this was what had happened to Ronald Alley, and in a sense to all the POWs in Korea. They were made to suffer the consequences of defeat. I wanted the board to see that trust and confidence in the military institution would be restored only when injustices were redressed, and that it was important for soldiers to know that the Army would stand behind them in El Salvador or anywhere else, even in defeat.

Into the evening we sat in room 144 at the Holiday Inn trying to figure out what had happened. I told Gerry that it would have been so simple for me to have gotten the quotes in writing, to have made my interviews conform to rules of evidence.

"We were told the rules of evidence wouldn't apply," he reminded me. "Besides, do you really think it would have made any difference?"

"I think the decision will go our way," said Colonel Peckham. "I think they heard what we were saying today." He turned to walk across the room, seemed momentarily to lose his balance, and reached for the wall to steady himself. "Addie wants me to rest for a while," he said. "I'm a little tired."

Gary Alley had been sitting on the bed alongside his mother. He looked up at Colonel Wise and then at Peckham.

"I just want to say something before you go, Colonel. I just want to tell you what this meant to me today. I . . . listening to you today, I feel I . . . it's like I finally know my father. I knew he . . . he must —" His voice left him. "I'm sorry," he said.

"It's okay," said Colonel Wise. "We're with you."

"I just want to say that now I'll be able to believe in my dad, and to believe —" He couldn't go any further. His shoulders began shaking, and he put his head down on his mother's lap and wept.

We held a news conference at the Holiday Inn on Thursday at noon. A Maine television station sent over a free-lance reporter and a cameraman. A staff writer from the *Washington Post* was there. No one else came. They had written their stories of the hearing; on television and radio and in the newspapers the stories told the grim details of the POW camps as they had been related by Wise and Peckham and Mayo. All the stories finally placed the case of Ronald Alley in its singular place in military history. All the stories made it seem that he would certainly be granted his honorable discharge now that so much time had passed.

But today the press had other stories to write and little time for this one. Erna told the reporter from the *Post* that she would go home to Maine to await the decision. "I hope the decision comes soon," she said. "I hope that this time the Army will do the right thing. It would be the most wonderful thing for Ronald."

\*     \*     \*     \*     \*

Colonel Wise stood alone in a crowd of travelers queuing up at the United Airlines ticket counter. He wore the blue suit he had worn at the hearing on Wednesday. The Purple Heart was still pinned to the lapel of his jacket. The last three days seemed almost unbelievable to him. He had traveled very far. Today he looked older than sixty-three; he looked very thin and drawn. I asked him if he was going to go shrimping again this year, and he said he and his son would be working on the boat just as soon as he got home. He was philosophical about what had happened here in Washington. "I look at Mrs. Alley and Gary and Colonel Peckham and I say to myself, Ronald Alley didn't die for nothing. . . . You know, I love people. Because I understand what they are trying to do. There's more compassion in a soldier's heart than most people understand. We are tough — soldiers have to be tough, tougher than we want to be sometimes. And we have to do awful things that we try to forget. But we know some things about love that you can't know if you haven't been a soldier. You just can't learn it any other way."

Very soon after we had shaken hands Colonel Wise picked up his suitcase and walked toward the gate where his plane was waiting. He was a small figure in the crowded, noisy lobby. And even as I tried to follow him with my eyes I lost sight of him.

Colonel Peckham and his wife were flying from Washington to their daughter's home outside Los Angeles. As they waited to leave we spoke briefly about what might happen. "If I have to come back to Washington, I will," Peckham said. "I'll do whatever it takes to get this done right."

I told him to take care of himself. "You deserve a little rest and relaxation now that you're out of the Army," I said.

"Oh no," he said. "I'm retired, but I'm still in the Army." Mrs. Peckham smiled at him and took his hand. "I'll always be in the Army."

# CHAPTER 17

I had been back in Maine for ten days when, on the morning of February 24, John Bradford telephoned me from Washington. "Your story is all over the *Washington Post,*" he said excitedly. "It's a great story by a reporter, wait a second. Her name is Sara Rimer. It starts on the front page."

It would be several days before I could get a *Post* in Maine, so I asked him to read me sections of the story.

The story was completely sympathetic to the petition for Ronald Alley's honorable discharge. Peckham, Wise, and Mayo were quoted at length, detailing the horror of imprisonment in Korea. I was most interested in the part concerning Colonel Mayo's testimony before the board. Rimer wrote:

---

Lt. Col. Walter Mayo, retired, a former POW who was a witness for the prosecution at Alley's court-martial, was questioned at last week's hearing. . . . Mayo, 57, of McLean, said: "I never saw him or knew of him to do anything detrimental to his fellow prisoners."

His description of Camp Five was as vivid as if he had been there yesterday, not 30 years ago. "The conditions were similar to a miniature holocaust. We were given two bowls of grain a day — cracked corn in the morning, a bowl of millet at night. We had no meat for six or seven months. Occasionally we got soybeans. We had no soap for at least nine months. We got lice. . . ."

Rimer quoted Gary Alley, writing:

Ronald Alley's son Gary, a broad-shouldered 32-year-old papermaker from Lee, Maine, who was six when his father went to Leavenworth, also addressed the board. "The other kids tormented me. They'd say, 'When are they going to let the jailbird out?' I was scared of a man I could hardly remember. Was my father a criminal? And if so, what horrible crime had he committed?"

. . . [For Gary Alley] the trip from Maine had been a milestone. "Mr. Peckham and Mr. Wise answered a lot of questions about my dad. I know he suffered a great deal. I know now he was innocent. I was probably the proudest person in that courtroom yesterday."

Rimer's story ended saying:

The board is expected to make its recommendation within the month to the secretary of the Army, who will make the final decision. Nearly three decades after the court-martial, after the conviction, after Fort Leavenworth, Ronald Alley's widow still has faith, as her husband did all of his life, in the United States Army. "I feel that they will do the right thing," she said. "I have a feeling in my heart that my late husband will be found not guilty. They will give him justice."

March began, and there was no decision, no word at all from Washington. Erna had begun calling me again and asking how much longer it would be. There was nothing I could tell her.

I tried to reach Senator Cohen that first week of March, but was told he was out of the country. In Congressman Emery's office, Mike Danforth said he had seen the *Post* story. He hesitated before telling me that his sources inside the Pentagon had related to him that the board was "hopping mad" about the *Post* story and all the publicity. The board was feeling pressured.

"That could work for you or against you," Danforth said. "The press makes what the Army did to Alley look reprehensible. If pushed into a corner, or if they feel pushed into a corner, the Army may take a hard line."

I said nothing of this to Erna and Gary. But it had been my greatest fear from the beginning, when I began to wonder if I'd made a mistake asking the press to attend the hearing. The story had been buried in obscurity for so many years, and if it had remained that way it certainly would have made things easier for the Army.

It seemed that there was nothing else to do one way or another, but wait. Then, on March 11, Sara Rimer telephoned me from her office at the *Post*. She had heard from a man named John Herzig, she said. He had read the story and called her claiming to have information that "could help Alley."

"This man says he worked in Army Intelligence," explained Rimer. "He says he worked in the Pentagon at the time the Army was putting together evidence against the POWs. He says the man who ran the investigations for the Army misrepresented the evidence in order to strengthen his cases against the POWs."

The man Herzig had named was Colonel Charles M. Trammell, Jr. That was the name with which I had begun my investigation three years earlier when I first went to Washington. I told Sara Rimer that I had stopped looking for him in 1979 when I'd been told he was probably deceased.

Rimer suggested I speak directly with Herzig. I telephoned him on March 12. He sounded very sincere and calm. He said he wanted to help Ronald Alley because he knew the investigation against him and other POWs had not been conducted fairly.

Herzig stated that he had been a captain in Army Intelligence in 1955, and for a period of six months he had been assigned to Colonel

Trammell's Pentagon office. "In 1955 I ended up doing research in Trammell's office," he said. "I knew the files he was putting together against the prisoners of war. I remember Alley's file; it was the biggest case."

Herzig told me his recollections were clear and accurate. He spoke precisely, saying he was absolutely certain the evidence had been "misrepresented."

He went on: "Trammell had a job to do. The Army had decided to *get* the Korean War POWs, and the Army made it clear that the prosecutions had better end in convictions."

Herzig said he had learned that statements made when the POWs were interrogated had been taken out of context by people working under Trammell's orders: "The accusations were plugged into reports wherever they could do the most damage to the POW."

Herzig went on to assert that he had notified Colonel Joseph Sterns of what he had learned of Trammell's actions. Sterns, like Herzig, was a former combat infantryman. As Deputy Director of Security Division in the Office of the Assistant Chief of Staff for Intelligence, Department of Army, Sterns was both Trammell's and Herzig's superior officer.

"Colonel Sterns saw what was happening. He saw it right off. Trammell was going around G-2 [Intelligence], doing things his own way. Sterns ordered an investigation to be opened on *Trammell*."

Herzig stated that he had heard this secret investigation had taken about a year, and that the findings had been disclosed to him by a counterintelligence agent who had worked on the investigation: "This report had been sent to the Adjutant General, who reviewed it and concluded that there *was* evidence of wrongdoing, but that it was 'not in the best interest of the Army' to pursue it. The investigation of Trammell just dropped out of sight, and the courts-martial went on." Herzig felt that the report had actually gone to the Judge Advocate General, the Army's chief lawyer.

I told Herzig I had to be certain he was telling the truth, and that if I came down to Washington he would have to go on the record and sign an affidavit that I could try to present to the Army board.

"I'll do whatever you think is best," he said calmly.

I said, "Well, if there was an investigation of Trammell —"

Herzig interrupted me: "Not *if*. There *was* an investigation of Trammell. It was conducted by the 902nd Counter Intelligence

Detachment under the direction of Colonel John Downey. It happened."

I said something to Herzig about how it was ironic that I had been looking for Trammell three years earlier after reading quotes attributed to him in Kinkead's book, *In Every War but One.* I recalled how he had come across as being a vigorous detractor of the POWs and how, in the book, he had appeared eager to applaud the Army's prosecution of the prisoners of war. I remembered how, at the beginning of my first trip to Washington in 1979, General Arthur Trudeau, the former Chief of Army Intelligence, and Senator Charles Potter had both tried to steer me to Trammell.

I explained this to Herzig and said, "It's a shame he's dead. I'd like to have had the chance to talk with him."

"Dead?" said Herzig. "That's bullshit. I saw him in a barbershop in Bethesda three months ago. I'll have a telephone number for him in a minute if you hang on."

I took down the telephone number and told Herzig I would catch the first flight to Washington in the morning.

I had a hard time sleeping that night. I had this fear that perhaps I was being set up by this story of Herzig's. After my experience in front of the Army board my worst suspicions of the Army had been confirmed; it seemed possible now that this story of Herzig's might be a trick. If I pursued it and persuaded the *Washington Post* to publish it, and then it turned out to be false, the credibility of all my research would be destroyed.

But, on the other hand, if I could somehow confirm Herzig's accusations, if I could show that some part of the investigation of Alley had been unfairly conducted, then all my research would fall into place. More important than that, in the face of this new evidence the Army board would have no choice but to vindicate Ronald Alley.

The Portland Jetport was buried under fog Friday. I spent the day talking with people in the offices of Senator Cohen and Congressman Emery. I explained that I was returning to Washington as soon as I could and that I was hoping to uncover new material that would be important to the Alley case. I asked only that, if the Army board was nearing a decision and if that decision appeared to be going against Ronald Alley, the Secretary of the Army intervene to buy some time. Sally Lounsbury promised to get a message through to Senator Cohen, who was a personal friend of the Secretary of the Army. And Mike Danforth said he would do the same in Emery's office. Danforth, however, offered a warning: "What happened to you, personally, at the hearing in February should never have happened. But I want you to know this board hates your guts. They really do. And if they learn that you're back in Washington trying to come up with more material that will make the Army look bad, well, it may affect their decision on Alley the wrong way. And you ought to be careful what you say to anyone about this."

Before I left Portland I asked Sara Rimer if the *Washington Post* would request, through the Freedom of Information Office of the Army, the files of the investigation that Herzig claimed had taken place in 1955. Bob Woodward and the *Post*'s Pentagon correspondent, George Wilson, were consulted. "They're going to help," Sara reported back to me. "They think this story is unbelievably important. We'll do whatever we can for you when you get down here."

I had to telephone Erna before leaving. I explained only that I had to return to Washington because there was someone who might be able to help her husband's case. "Why do they take so long to decide?" she asked me again.

I did not tell her the answer to that question, though it had been related to me by Sara Rimer; she had called the Army board and was told it might take another month to reach a decision. Major Weiskoph reminded her that she had "only heard one side of the story so far." He said the board had thirteen hundred pages of court-martial transcript to review.

Weiskoph's reminder to Sara was particularly disturbing, because it indicated that the board had dismissed my claim that the court-martial transcript told a story that had been unfairly shaded and written in 1955; the story of men pressured to testify against Alley, men told that if they didn't cooperate with the Army's case they too might become defendants. If the board was going to review the court-martial evidence just because it was a matter of record, and then weigh it against our testimony at the February hearing, we would not stand a chance. Unless John Herzig's story could be confirmed.

As soon as I arrived in Washington I telephoned Colonel Trammell, using the number Herzig had given me. He was alive all right. He told me he had read the story about Ronald Alley in the *Post,* but he said he really didn't remember much about the case. "You know, your memory gets hazy on details," he said.

I asked if we could get together to talk, and assured him I wouldn't take much of his time. "I guess I could chat with you. But I'm thinking about going out of town to start some traveling," he said. We agreed to meet first thing Monday morning, but he added, "In case I get sick or have to go away is there a number where I can reach you?" I gave him the number. I said nothing about Herzig.

Sunday afternoon I drove to Falls Church, Virginia, and met John Herzig for the first time. A fifty-nine-year-old man with pale eyes and a gentle, unassuming manner, he greeted me at the door of his condominium in a high-rise tower just off George Mason Drive. He wore faded jeans, a blue T-shirt, and bedroom slippers. He introduced his wife, Aiko, a soft-spoken American-born Japanese woman who had spent three years as a teenager in Manzanar, an American internment camp established in northern California during World War II.

We sat in the living room, and while I set up a tape recorder Herzig handed me a Certificate of Achievement awarded him in 1957 for his work in Army Intelligence. "I just want you to see I'm not an impostor," he said. The award had been signed by General Robert Schow, who had succeeded General Trudeau as Chief of Staff of Army Intelligence. The certificate commended Herzig for "his valuable contributions to the Department of Army Counter Intelligence Program, particularly those aspects of the program concerned with the return of American Prisoners of War in Korea." Herzig's intention was to show me the earnestness of his work in Army Intelligence, and by implication that he was knowledgeable and could be trusted.

We talked for nearly two hours. John Herzig was precise, emphatic, and seamless in his recollections. A lieutenant colonel who had retired from the Army in 1968, he said he cared about what had happened to Alley because he, too, had been a combat soldier and he knew what honor must have meant to Major Alley. Herzig had been a paratrooper platoon sergeant in World War II, and had spent thirty-four months in the South Pacific making combat jumps and amphibious landings behind enemy lines. He had been awarded a Purple Heart, the Bronze Star, and the Combat Infantryman's Badge, among other citations.

225

On a yellow, lined legal pad Herzig drew an elaborate diagram laying out the chain of command and the general and special staff network of the Army in 1955. He explained that Colonel Trammell, in his Office of Special Counsel, circumvented the normal chain of command and reported directly to the then Under Secretary of the Army, Wilbur M. Brucker. "Trammell had stretched the limits of truth, or outright misrepresented facts so that Brucker would lean on the POW cases," he said. Herzig was certain about this, and about the counterintelligence investigation of Trammell that followed. "I don't know if Trammell was actually approached about the investigation; I think there is a chance he didn't know it was being conducted.

"I knew people who worked on this investigation, people from Colonel Downey's 902nd Counter Intelligence Unit. I heard from them what I told you — that when the investigation of Trammell was completed, the word I got was that, upon review of the case by the Adjutant General, he decided it would not be in the best interest of the Army to go any further."

Herzig repeated that he had learned the findings of the investigation *did* reveal, however, that Trammell's office had been guilty of wrongdoing in its investigation of Alley and other POWs: "The investigators who did the work on Trammell were quite frustrated; their work was done for nothing. They had traveled all over, interviewing people who had worked with or for Trammell, and they had the goods."

At my request, Herzig gave me the names of four people he believed could confirm his story: Colonel Joseph Sterns, Deputy Director of Security Division and the officer who ordered the investigation of Trammell; Colonel John Downey, Commander of the 902nd Counter Intelligence Detachment, which conducted the investigation; Colonel John W. Price, an officer in Policy and Plans of Security Division, who had known about Trammell; and General Robert Schow, Chief of Army Intelligence, who sent the report on Trammell to either the Adjutant General or the Judge Advocate General.

On Monday morning I met Colonel Trammell at his home outside Georgetown. I found him friendly and cooperative, a white-haired elderly man dressed in a camel-colored sweater and a shirt and tie. He sat at his desk and was eager to show me the photograph of a sailboat, a Chesapeake-20, which he once raced.

During this meeting we spoke in general terms about the POW investigations and courts-martial. Trammell assured me that the investigation of Alley had been conducted properly: "I wouldn't have permitted any 'Get-Alley' spirit," he volunteered. "I don't know of any 'Get-Alley' sort of thing. The investigations at the level of my office were impartial."

Trammell went on: "I probably knew the evidence [on Alley] better than most anyone, and I stand on that evidence. It was gone over most carefully. It wasn't a whimsical thing. It was reviewed by many people."

Trammell said he had read the story in the *Washington Post* with the feeling that the board ought to grant Alley an honorable discharge. "I feel the evidence was there, but I feel that this board will see that after three decades Alley was treated unequally. I'm not saying there was an injustice, but there was an inequality."

I had decided not to confront Trammell, at this meeting, with Herzig's claims. If there had been an investigation on Trammell as Herzig swore there was, I might need Trammell's permission to review files of that investigation, and so it was important that I keep on friendly ground with him.

Throughout our conversation Trammell took notes, and at times our dialogue lapsed into total silence as we both wrote things down. A lawyer in Washington for many years, Trammell said he could appreciate my interest in getting at the truth. Then he said, "I'm all for justice too, but, well, to go back thirty years and dredge all that up again, well, it just seems to be going back a little too far for me."

By Tuesday evening, two names on Herzig's list had fallen through. Colonel Price told me he had no memory of any such investigation. He said his memory was "sketchy" and he wasn't even certain where Trammell had worked in the Pentagon.

I had traced General Robert Schow, the former Chief of Army Intelligence, to a retirement community in Florida. Eighty-five years old now, the general said he wished he could help, but he just couldn't remember anything. He didn't remember the name Trammell. "I'm just too old to remember much of anything," he said.

I telephoned Herzig that evening to tell him what had happened with these two names. He assured me there were other people who would remember. He said he was certain.

Someone in the Pentagon had forwarded a letter from me to a Colonel John Downey in Texas, but three days later he telephoned to say he wasn't the same John Downey; he had never worked in the Pentagon. The only other Colonel Downey in the Army's Retired Officers Association was listed as deceased. And so was the fourth name on Herzig's list — Colonel Joseph Sterns.

On Friday afternoon I went to see Bob Woodward at the *Post,* to ask for help. I told him that I believed Herzig's story, but that I was getting nowhere and hadn't been able to confirm any of it. I explained that Sara Rimer had requested files of the alleged investigation of Trammell through the Army's Freedom of Information Office, but I was convinced it could take weeks for an official response.

Woodward took me to a vacant desk on the fifth floor of the *Post* and told me to write down everything I knew about the investigation, everything Herzig had told me. I did this, and he then reviewed the information with me. He said, "Herzig's story rings true. I can raise a lot of hell in a hurry for you. I'm going to make a run for those files."

That same afternoon I went back over the tape recording I had made of my first meeting with Herzig, and studied the portion of the tape where he spoke about the investigation of Trammell: "First, every investigation has a file number assigned to it, okay? So someplace there's a number that relates to that investigation and to Trammell's name, and it starts with a C generally for some reason. I don't know why. I think it starts with a C. Then the next series of numbers indicates the unit designation at which level the investigation was opened. So, since it was a Department of the Army G-2-initiated investigation, it will then have a number that indicates the origin of it, and then a number based on the Central Records Facility designation of the next investigation in their records. That procedure is always followed. So someplace, since this was a formal investigation, there will be a number that says it was initiated at Department of the Army level and that it was on Charles M. Trammell, Jr. So that's the key as to how you get into that."

I had asked Herzig what it would mean, to him, if there was no record of the investigation. He replied: "Well, it would kind of assume a sort of Orwellian action on the part of the Army to erase the fact that there was an investigation conducted."

Herzig was unflinching. He was positive there had been an investigation. I went back to the *Post* to give these details to Bob Woodward.

Late that night I returned to John Bradford's house in Alexandria and found a message that John Herzig had called, and I was to return the call no matter how late. As I sat down at the telephone I was half-convinced that this would be the call where Herzig would back away from his story now that I had been in Washington a week without getting any closer to a confirmation.

When Herzig answered the telephone there was an edge to his voice that had not been there before. He was angry. "I thought about the whole thing," he began. "I asked myself why I wasn't facing the Army with this, rather than going through you. So I called the board. Three times they refused to listen to me. They kept saying it wasn't relevant to the board's considerations of the Alley case. They shut me off. I was angry as hell. I had a witness in the office who heard the whole thing; he couldn't believe it either. I told the board I had new information on the Alley case, and they just refused to let me talk. They wouldn't listen."

Monday morning I took a written statement from Herzig to Senator Cohen. I explained everything that had happened and I told him I was convinced now that the Army board wasn't interested in hearing the whole truth about Alley's case.

Senator Cohen listened and then leaned over his desk and said: "When I heard that the board didn't let you speak at the hearing I was disappointed. I called Jack Marsh [Secretary of the Army]; I tried to get to you and tell you, but never did. I told Marsh I was going to raise hell at the Pentagon if this wasn't handled properly."

Cohen asked me to put down the details on paper, explaining the Herzig claims. He promised to get a letter off "right away" to the Secretary of the Army.

There was at least one person in Washington, D.C., who believed that no amount of evidence on my part would persuade the Army to grant Alley an honorable discharge. Dr. Albert Biderman, a scientist at the Bureau of Social Science Research and the author of *March to Calumny,* a book critical of the Army's treatment of the Korean War POWs, told me it was hopeless. Biderman had read the

*Washington Post* story, and he remembered the Alley case from 1955. He told me we wouldn't get a favorable decision out of the Army because the POW affair had direct contacts to Ronald Reagan and his present administration.

According to Biderman, after the Korean War Reagan did a series of television broadcasts sponsored by General Electric, which in substance supported the right-wing claim that the Army needed to toughen up in order to combat Communism. These broadcasts, claimed Biderman, were part of the "right-wing propaganda" aimed at showing how the POW conduct in Korea was a harbinger of trouble for the United States, unless the Army became more aggressive in the indoctrination of its troops.

Biderman believed that the same mentality that had prevailed in the 1950s had been revived by the administration of Ronald Reagan; he thought this augured poorly for Alley's case.

After two weeks in Washington I called Colonel Trammell and confronted him with John Herzig's story. I enumerated all of Herzig's claims and told Trammell that Herzig had gone to the Army board attempting to tell them that Major Alley had been unfairly treated. I said, "Herzig has told me his side of the Alley story. I want to give you a chance in my book to tell your side of things."

Trammell answered right away: "Well, you have to understand and keep in mind that this evidence we gathered was not actually introduced into court. Our investigations weren't conducted for the purpose of establishing collaboration. That was just one of the tasks. Our investigations were on a much larger scale. It's possible that enmities were involved, but these were eventually narrowed down."

I asked Trammell if he remembered the name Herzig.

"There was a brief period when I was extremely busy when I was allowed to bring people in for temporary duty for special purposes. I believe Herzig was one of them. How do you spell his name?" he asked.

I spelled it for him, then told him Herzig's accusation that the 902nd Counter Intelligence Detachment had investigated his Office of Special Counsel.

There was a brief silence. Then Trammell said he didn't "recall that one way or another." He went on to say: "If all of this is true, why wasn't he [Herzig] testifying to it in the Alley trial? You have to remember this was a big operation, and there might have been some enmities, but there was nobody coming forward then. It just doesn't speak well of him [Herzig], waiting all those years."

I asked Trammell if he knew of any cases where evidence against the POWs had been intentionally misrepresented. He replied: "It was a large operation, there was a wide scale. It would have been pretty hard for there to have been a conspiracy. There weren't just two or three people involved. There was a big-scale operation. It wasn't created to dig out information about anybody, but to learn about the POW camps, about treatment and what went on, and to construct a story of what went on in the camps. Only part of this was the question of collaboration."

I said, "Yes, but what you discovered about collaboration was vitally important to the decision to actually court-martial Alley. Right?"

His reply: "Yes, but . . . it went like this. If you were to say when you came back that John Smith did this, it was recorded. But that evidence didn't go to court-martial directly."

According to Trammell, this evidence, if it was serious enough, was presented, and before anything could be done it had to go up through a chain of command to the Under Secretary of the Army.

I said, "The importance of the information obtained in your part of the investigation is obvious though, Colonel."

"Yes," he said. "But there was a careful review channel that said whether or not there was enough evidence to *permit* a trial. And then the prosecutor had to see that there was enough evidence to go ahead. There was a separate charge procedure."

"Herzig claims that you were personally involved in improprieties, Colonel."

"I don't think it's fair to say that I or a small staff was out to get somebody."

"Herzig says you wanted to get evidence that would result in convictions of Alley and the others in order to enhance your own career."

Trammell denied this. He told me again that while the Alley case was an inequity, it was not an injustice. He said, "I stand on the evidence." Then, responding to Herzig's accusations, he replied, "I think it's too bad that these people didn't have the convictions at the time to say something. Maybe some toes were stepped on or something. Maybe that's why he's come forward now."

---

When I mentioned Trammell's comments to Herzig, he told me that he had risked his career by revealing what he had learned about Trammell's questionable actions to their joint superior officer, Colonel Sterns, particularly given Trammell's apparent influence with the Under Secretary of the Army. However, he was certain that Sterns was an officer of great integrity who would follow the right course of action.

Herzig had known nothing about my encounter with the Army board until he read the *Washington Post* article. Then he contacted me as soon as possible to offer his assistance to me and to the Alley family. It was clear to me that Herzig wanted to see justice done, but also to see that the Army was not acting, again, on contrived information and bad advice.

*   *   *   *   *

By Monday, March 30, Senator Cohen and Congressman Emery had not been able to come up with any files on the investigation that Herzig swore took place in 1955. And the Department of the Army had sent a letter to the *Washington Post* that said a thorough search had been conducted and, "as a result of this search we have concluded this command has no records concerning this subject, or any indication that such an investigation was ever conducted."

The letter was signed by Thomas F. Conley, Chief, Freedom of Information/Privacy Office, Department of the Army, US Army Intelligence and Security Command, Fort George G. Meade, Maryland. The office assured the *Washington Post* that if their command had no records then there were no records anywhere, and John Herzig's story was just not true. I spoke with Sara Rimer and Bob Woodward, thanking them for their help.

Driving from the *Post*'s offices back to Alexandria, I decided to go back to the Pentagon once more. From a pay phone in the concourse I called a man named Vincent Mizner. Someone had given me his name months ago, telling me that he was a researcher in the office of the Assistant Chief of Staff, Intelligence, Department of the Army. He was described as the best researcher working in the Pentagon. When I got him on the telephone, I explained about the Alley case, John Herzig's story, and the Army's official reply. I told him I needed help, and he seemed challenged by the chance to do some digging. He promised he would do "some real checking." Then he said, "Everybody around here is talking about the Alley case. The board is right underneath me, in a room downstairs."

Twenty-four hours later I spoke again with Vincent Mizner. "Well, I've been doing a hell of a lot of research," he said. "I worked all day after you called. And I can tell you your source, Herzig, is right."

I asked him if he was sure.

"There was an investigation all right. It did take a period of a year, just like you said."

"You found proof of it, then?"

"I used all my sources here. I verified it through institutional memory, through the people who were involved in the investigation. It happened all right. You can rest assured that such an investigation took place. I have the proof right here on my desk."

Mizner thought there was an outside chance the file containing the report on the investigation might be at the Carlisle Military Barracks in Carlisle, Pennsylvania, part of the US Army Military History Institute. I telephoned out there right away and spoke with a researcher. I explained to him what I was after, and he used a computer to come up with the retired files of the 902nd Counter Intelligence Detachment. He said he found record of a file marked "Special Projects — 1955." He believed this was exactly what I wanted, and he asked me to hold the line while he went to retrieve it from the vault.

When he came back on the phone he said, "I'm afraid I've got disappointing news. I just checked the file; it's been picked clean."

"Can you go back and check once more?"

"There's nothing there. It's no use," he said. "I'm sure this is the right file, but it's empty."

I told Senator Cohen what had happened, and he agreed to speak again with the Secretary of the Army. I telephoned Colonel Herzig. "There's nothing else I can do here," I told him. "I'm going back to Maine, to wait."

"I'm going to try to come up with more names," he said. "Before it's too late for Alley."

# CHAPTER 18

Ι t was early April when I again telephoned Vincent Mizner at the
Pentagon. He had promised to keep looking for additional evidence of the secret counterintelligence investigation, but this
time when we spoke he was taciturn and vague. He said he
wasn't allowed to say anything: "This is an official matter now,
so I can't reveal the actions that we're contemplating." I asked what
this meant, and he said that word had come down to him from his
superiors that anything he might find now was to be reported only to
official Army personnel. "They will report to Senator Cohen,"
Mizner said.

I telephoned Senator Cohen's office right away, and Sally

Lounsbury assured me there had been no word from the Secretary of the Army since I'd left Washington. All she knew was that Vincent Mizner had been ordered to look for the report of the investigation.

Congressman Emery's aide, Mike Danforth, had been in touch with Vincent Mizner. "This fellow says, yes, there was an investigation of Colonel Trammell's office, and now he's got the Secretary of the Army telling him to go find the results — and fast." Danforth said he had learned that Mizner had come across 120 crates in the Pentagon that might contain new information relevant to the investigation.

"He didn't say anything to me about that," I told Danforth.

"Well, he has to be very careful what he tells anyone at this point," Danforth said.

Ten days later, against the advice of Danforth, I telephoned Vincent Mizner again. He was even more evasive, saying anything he told me might get him into trouble for "stepping on the toes of Mr. Plant" of the Army board.

I said, "What's that supposed to mean, Vincent? You told me that the investigation of Trammell's office did take place."

Mizner answered quickly: "Look, all I had then was a verbal confirmation of the thing. From institutional memory. Everyone knows we're talking about something that happened thirty years ago. A man can't be expected to be right on something that happened so long ago. It's just a man saying, 'Yeah, I think I knew something about that.' It's only hearsay."

Mizner had backed down completely from the position he had held when I was in Washington in March. He came across as being frustrated. He said that he had wanted to go on looking for more files but had been prevented. He said: "There's records systems I can't get to. They wouldn't appropriate the funds for me to go out and do the search myself, so it could take a while."

When I asked Mizner who was looking for the files, he said: "I can't say what is happening, what action we're taking. I'm not allowed to tell you anything."

It was May, and there was still no word. I wrote a letter to the Secretary of the Army urging him to be sure the Army board considered all the information pertinent to the Alley case, and telling him that I personally believed Colonel John Herzig's claims. It was May 24 when I received a reply to this letter, not from the Secretary of the

Army but from Francis Plant. His reply was brief. He said I could be assured that the Alley case would be given a thorough review.

Two days after Memorial Day, at one o'clock in the afternoon, Mike Danforth called me again. "Things are happening fast," he said. "I don't want this conversation to get beyond the two of us."

He related that he had spoken several times that morning with the Congressional Liaison Officer at the Pentagon. "I started a small fire down there. I had some harsh words with him, and I found out that your information about Colonel Herzig's accusations caused quite a stir. I'm sure people have been running and jumping at the Pentagon, and I'm worried that we may be getting the runaround, too. I asked the officer when we were going to have the results of the Army's official investigation into Herzig's claims, and he told me we might not get anything on paper. When I asked why not, he backed off. He was vague. But I have a feeling whatever they turned up is top secret. I've never encountered such a thing. I told the Liaison Officer I was going to call him every half hour from now until I got an answer."

At 5:15 that afternoon Danforth called back. "I've been told that tomorrow is the day. Tomorrow Cohen and Emery will hear something definitive. It'll be coming straight from the Secretary of the Army."

I asked if he had talked with Sally Lounsbury in Cohen's office, and he said he had. "She knows what I know," he said.

It was just after four o'clock on Wednesday afternoon when Danforth called again, this time with a familiar message: "I guess we're going to have to just keep waiting," he said. "There's all sorts of intrigue in Washington about this, but so far no answer. I've been told the Army is wrestling with a real hog. I think something turned up that makes the Army look awfully bad, and they're trying like hell to figure out what to do about it."

Later that same afternoon in Washington, D.C., an emissary of the Secretary of the Army went by car from the Pentagon to Capitol Hill to hand-deliver a letter to Senator William Cohen. Thursday morning, Sally Lounsbury conveyed to me the contents of that letter: "I'm afraid I have bad news for you," she said.

It was a long letter from the Secretary of the Army, describing in detail an extensive search through Army records to produce evidence concerning Colonel Herzig's charges. The letter concluded that there was no evidence anywhere. "I'm sure the senator is disappointed," Sally said.

Mike Danforth was also disappointed, and discouraged. He speculated that the intrigue of the last two days had probably come about because the Congressional Liaison Officer had been kept in the dark. "On the Herzig twist," said Danforth, "I'm afraid it's all done. It's a dead end. Now we can only hope we haven't given the Army board more motive to kick you in the face."

*That* had to be considered. That, and the questions that would remain unanswered: Why did Vincent Mizner first confirm the investigation, and then back away from this confirmation? Maybe he *had* been overly optimistic, and the evidence he had said was there just vaporized. Or maybe he had been pressured to accept another conclusion. Why did it take so long for the Secretary of the Army to respond to Senator Cohen? Initially, Sally Lounsbury had been told that the Secretary's formal reply concerning the secret investigation would be given to Senator Cohen during the first week of May. Sally had originally expected the letter to arrive on May 3; she had told me that day: "There isn't any letter yet. I'm very curious to see it, especially since they won't discuss it over the phone. Maybe I'll have it by this afternoon." Why had it taken until June 3 for the reply to be delivered? Maybe the Secretary's investigation had just taken longer than originally anticipated. Or maybe his investigation had produced evidence that the Army needed time to deal with.

The last request I made of Senator Cohen and Congressman Emery was that I be notified of the Army's decision before Erna was, so that I could go to Bar Harbor and be with her if the final word was bad.

# CHAPTER 19

Just after nine o'clock on the morning of July 13, 1982, the telephone call finally came from Congressman David Emery's office. "I'm afraid I have bad news for you," were Mike Danforth's first words. "It's very bad. It's going to break your heart."

I listened as he read the Army's official statement. By a vote of three to two, the Army Board for the Correction of Military Records had denied the petition of Erna Alley. After more than five months of deliberations, the Army ruled that the 1955 court-martial had been "manifestly correct."

"They played this just the right way," said Danforth. "They waited for the publicity to die down, and then they closed the book.

If they hadn't, they would have had a line of petitioners to deal with at the Pentagon door. It's over this way."

I wanted Congressman Emery to ask the Pentagon not to release any statements until I was in Bar Harbor with Erna Alley. "I'll need four hours to get there," I said. Danforth told me he would do his best.

I telephoned Gerry Williamson with the same request. And then I called Gary. "I had this feeling in my stomach that you would call today," he said. Gary wanted me to get to Bar Harbor first: "If it's all right, would you be the one to tell Ma?"

Erna was out on the front porch of her home in Salisbury Cove. It was a hot, sunny afternoon. I parked my car in the driveway, and as I walked toward her, I glanced up at the sign that said there was NO VACANCY at Erna's German Motel. Then I looked into her eyes. "I knew you would be coming today," Erna said. "I kept one room for you." She knew why I was here standing in front of her and saying nothing. We held each other, and she didn't cry.

When Gary arrived we telephoned Colonel Peckham and Colonel Wise. Then we went along to Major Alley's grave. Erna asked her son if he would drive the long way, so we could go past the cottage in Oak Point, the place that was so special to her because of the plans she and Ronald had made to retire there. This summer the cottage had to be rented to tourists; there was a honeymoon couple renting the place this week. They appeared, very startled, on the porch, and when Erna stepped out of the car she asked, "Do you have any trash for me to take?"

"What?" the young man asked.

"I thought you might have trash for me to pick up."

The man shook his head, looking at Gary and then at me for some explanation.

"Come on, Ma," Gary said.

The grass at the cemetery had just been cut, but it was brown from a rainless July and it carried no sweet scent. There was the faintest smell of ocean hanging over the hills. The man from the Legion hall had remembered to put up a small flag at Major Alley's grave.

I stood off to one side and watched as Gary pulled away blades of grass that had grown around the headstone.

---

"At least I know now," he said. "Now I know what you stood for, and what you were always trying to make me see."

Erna moved close to him. "What would have hurt Ronald the most," she said, "was that they thought he was a Communist. He hated Communism. Hated it." She looked at me. "Ronald was no Communist."

She lowered her head then. "We did the best we could," she said. "I know you'll understand."

And that was all. I wanted to believe they were both free now. That we were all free.

# EPILOGUE

Eight years have passed since I first met Ronald Alley and his family. As I write these last pages, it is early spring 1986. I am not without regret. At the time of the Pentagon hearing in February 1982, I worked extremely hard to elicit media attention; I believed this would help persuade the Army that Ronald Alley's honorable discharge must be granted. I believe now that this was a mistake, and that it backed the Army into a corner and increased their antagonism against Major Alley.

Within a week of the Army's decision, Joseph P. Murphy, one member on the Army Board for the Correction of Military Records who voted to exonerate Major Alley, spoke to a Maine reporter about the board's reaction to the media. Murphy said, "Some members of the board believed that Mrs. Alley was doing this to get an ending for the book. That and all the media attention are, theoretically, not supposed to influence you. But I think it all had an effect."

Murphy also said that studying the Alley case gave him a feeling Major Alley had been singled out as a scapegoat. "A stricter set of standards was applied to Alley than was applied to anyone else in the war," Murphy said. He also explained that the board's three-to-two decision against Alley hung on the vote of one board member, who seemed during the five months following the hearing to be in favor of the honorable discharge appeal, and then, just at the end, voted against it.

To this day there is no doubt in my mind that Major Alley was neither a collaborator nor a traitor to his country. He deserves his honorable discharge.

I have wanted to believe that when this book was finished, Erna Alley's fight would be finished and that she would be free to go on to a new life. I see now that this is not possible. The struggle is not over for her. She will never stop fighting until her husband is vindicated. I wish I could have done more for her. I have never met a braver or more honest person, and I hope that in some way this book will benefit her as time goes on, and that in the end she will prevail.

It is also my hope that somehow this book and others like it will force the Army to change its ways. I am speaking of the Army in Washington, D.C., the Army Major Alley learned was never to be trusted. That Army must be held accountable for each and every instance in which it betrayed its soldiers. Anything less cheapens the enormous sacrifice so many soldiers have made in devoting their lives to its cause.

# PERMISSIONS

T he author and publisher would like to thank the following for their kind permission to reproduce material in this volume:

UPI/Bettman Newsphotos for photos 1, 5, 8, and 10; Diana Abrell at *The Bar Harbor Times* for photo 2; Erna Alley for photos 3, 4, 7, 16, 21, 23, and the small photo 26; *The Bar Harbor Times* for photo 6; Colonel John Herzig for photo 9; Dean Abramson for photos 11, 18, 22, 25, and the large photo 26; Mrs. Charles Peckham for photo 12; Turner Entertainment Company for photo 13, ©1954 Loew's Incorporated Ren. 1982 Metro-Goldwyn-Mayer Film Co.; NBC for photo 14, courtesy of The National Broadcasting Company, Incorporated; Don Snyder for photo 15 (photographer unknown); *The Washington Post* for photo 17 by Lucian Perkins; Colonel George Rasula for photo 19; *Bangor Daily News* for photo 20; and Alan Porter for photo 24.

"Alley's Work for Reds Told." Copyright 1955. Reprinted by permission of © *The Washington Post* and the Associated Press. "Alley Called Red Monitor." Copyright 1955. Reprinted by permission of *The Baltimore Sun*. "Alley Called Red Writer." Copyright 1955. Reprinted by permission of © *The Washington Post*. " 'Advised,' Alley Trial Witness Says." Copyright 1955. Reprinted by permission of © *The Washington Post*. "Ex-POW Says Alley Was Tortured." Copyright 1955. Reprinted by permission of © *The Washington Post*. "Alley's Wife Takes Stand." Copyright 1955. Reprinted by permission of © *The Washington Post* and the Associated Press. Article about Erna Alley which appeared in *The Boston Globe* in 1958. Copyright 1958. Reprinted courtesy of *The Boston Globe*. Editorial, *The Bar Harbor Times*, December 29, 1955. Copyright 1955. Reprinted by permission of *The Bar Harbor Times*. "A Line Must Be Drawn." Copyright 1955 Time, Inc. All rights reserved. Reprinted by permission from TIME. "No Bands Playing." August 15, 1955. Copyright 1955. Reprinted by permission of *Newsweek*. "For the Brainwashed: Pity or Punishment?" by Anthony Leviero, August 14, 1955, *The New York Times Magazine*. © 1955 by The New York Times Company. Reprinted by permission. "The Colonel's Korean 'Turncoats' " by John Greenway, November 10, 1962, *The Nation*. Copyright 1962 by The Nation Company/The Nation Magazine. Reprinted by permission. *In Every War but One*, by Eugene Kinkead. Copyright 1959. Reprinted by permission of W.W. Norton & Company, Inc. "U.S. Reopens Case On Collaborator: Widow Wins Hearing in Effort to Clear Major Imprisoned in North Korea in 50's," October 4, 1981, *The New York Times*. © 1981 by the New York Times Company. Reprinted by permission. " 'Collaborator' Devoted to the Army," by Sara Rimer, copyright 1982. Reprinted by permission of © *The Washington Post*.

# INDEX

# J

Jakes, Ernie, 121
Johnson, George, 19
Joint Intelligence Processing
Teams, 81, 83

# K

Kanggye, North Korea,
168–172, 174
Kelly (prosecuting attorney,
Alley court-martial), 157
Kennedy, John F., 53
Kinkead, Eugene, 80–82. *See
also In Every War but One*
Korean War, 76
beginning of, 36
Chinese involvement in.
*See* Chinese involvement
in Korea
POW camps. *See* POW
camps
Ronald Alley combat in,
38–44. *See also* Chosin
Reservoir, North Korea

# L

Laulies, Erna. *See* Alley, Erna
Leavenworth Prison. *See* Fort
Leavenworth
Lewy, Donald, 210, 211, 215
Logan, Colonel William T., 51–
53, 70, 91, 92, 106
Lounsbury, Sally, 163, 206, 223,
234–235, 236–237

# M

MacArthur, General Douglas,
119, 182
*March to Calumny,* 80, 229
Marsh, Jack, 229
Matthews, John, 198, 210,
214, 215
Mauch, Eric, letter about
Ronald Alley, 100–102
Mayer, Colonel William E., 80
Mayo, Walter, 155, 156, 157,
158–163, 198, 200, 204, 207,
212–215, 217, 220
McCarthy, Senator Joe, 83, 91,
114, 154, 159
Army-McCarthy hearings,
90, 91, 98
Mining Camp, 121
Mizner, Vincent, 232–233,
234–235
Molpus, David, 205, 214
Murphy, Joseph P., 241–242

# N

Nardella, Ralph, 155
*Nation, The,* 80
*New York Times,* 45, 79,
195–196
*New Yorker* magazine, 80
*Newsweek,* 78
Nixon, Richard, 105
"No Bands Playing," 78

# O

Operation Big Switch, 47

# P